THE ANALYTIC IMAGINARY

THE
ANALYTIC
IMAGINARY

Marguerite La Caze

Cornell University Press ITHACA AND LONDON

First published 2002 by Cornell University Press

Printed in the United States of America

Library of Congress Cataloging-in-Publication Data

La Caze, Marguerite.
 The analytic imaginary / Marguerite La Caze.
  p. cm.
 Includes bibliographical references and index.
 ISBN 0-8014-3935-3 (alk. paper)
  1. Analysis (Philosophy) 2. Thought experiments. 3. Figures of
speech. 4. Metaphor. I. Title.
 B808.5 .L33 2002
 146′.4—dc21   2001003199

Cornell University Press strives to use environmentally responsible
suppliers and materials to the fullest extent possible in the publishing
of its books. Such materials include vegetable-based, low-VOC inks
and acid-free papers that are recycled, totally chlorine-free, or partly
composed of nonwood fibers. Books that bear the logo of the FSC
(Forest Stewardship Council) use paper taken from forests that have
been inspected and certified as meeting the highest standards for
environmental and social responsibility. For further information, visit
our website at www.cornellpress.cornell.edu.

Cloth printing   10 9 8 7 6 5 4 3 2 1

To Damian

Contents

Acknowledgments

First, I wish to thank Marion Tapper for suggesting that I read Michèle Le Dœuff's *The Philosophical Imaginary* and for all her support over the years, Kimon Lycos for talking to me about aesthetics, André Gallois and Roger Lamb for discussing personal identity, and Terri Field for her helpful comments. I am indebted to Michelle Boulous Walker and Tuan Nuyen for written comments and discussion of an earlier version of this book. Genevieve Lloyd and Dorothea Olkowski have also provided useful written comments for which I am very grateful. Thanks to Michael Levine for all his support for my work and to Max Deutscher for all his comments, enthusiasm and continual encouragement. I am especially grateful to Damian Cox for his confidence in me, his insightful suggestions, and the way he is always ready to discuss philosophy.

Thanks are also due to members of the Philosophy Department at the University of Queensland, the Philosophy Department at the University of Western Australia, and the School of Philosophy at the University of Tasmania for their support. I am pleased to thank Lorraine Code and an anonymous reader at Cornell University Press, who gave me wonderful feedback and suggestions. I would also like to thank Catherine Rice and Asia Bonacci at Cornell University Press, whose consultation and efficiency is deeply appreciated. An earlier version of some of the material in this book appeared as "Analytic Imaginary" in *Michèle Le Dœuff: Operative Philosophy and Imaginary Practice,* edited by Max Deutscher (Amherst: Humanity Books, 2000).

MARGUERITE LA CAZE

Tasmania

THE ANALYTIC IMAGINARY

Introduction

Imaginary and Images

A philosophical imaginary refers to both the capacity to imagine and the stock of images philosophers use. There is a stock of images in analytic philosophy that govern the way reasoning can be conducted, and an imaginary which is surprisingly coherent across a range of debates and views: I call this the analytic imaginary. The nature of this imaginary will emerge from my investigation of the way influential images are used in important areas of contemporary analytic philosophy. Analytic philosophy is the dominant philosophical tradition in English-speaking and Scandinavian countries and is often characterized by the use of analysis of language and concepts to solve philosophical problems. It is generally thought that analytic philosophers rarely use images, if at all. Contrary to that common perception, a wealth of images are used in analytic philosophy, including the areas of ethics, personal identity, political philosophy, epistemology, and aesthetics to be discussed in this book. However, analytic philosophers are seldom reflective about the nature of the images they use and do not recognize that they play a deeply significant philosophical role. Images are extremely important to the expression of philosophical thought, to the way debates are structured, and assumptions are shared; they can also work to persuade and to provide support for a particular view and to exclude alternative views and methods. Metaphors play a role of this kind, as do analogies, thought experiments, myths, and models.

"Image" is an important term for this book. I am using it in a very broad sense as an umbrella or cluster concept to cover notions from different disciplines, because it best captures the range of cases I discuss. These notions include figures of speech discussed in theories of rhetoric, such as "metaphor" and "analogy," terms that have precise meanings in analytic philosophy, such as "thought experiment," and terms that have a number of different sources and meanings, such as "myths" and "models." Myths and models, for example, are used in religion and science, as well as in philosophy. Thus, my use of "image" cuts across the traditional categories of rhetoric, poetics, and studies of argument and figurative language, making the approach in this book distinctive. While each of these is a useful category, none of them are broad enough to cover the range of images I examine here.[1] Image is also the best term because it highlights the image-making capacity of the imaginary.

I examine examples of five types of "images" in this book: analogies, thought experiments, myths, metaphors, and models. It is clear from this list that I focus on a few specific types of figurative use of language, rather than on the full range of tropes and stylistic devices that would include irony, hyperbole, litotes, neologisms, punning, and many others. The choice of images is governed by the nature of analytic philosophy, to which irony, hyperbole, litotes, and so on, are much less central. The analogies, thought experiments, myths, metaphors, and models I discuss are distinguished by their importance in central contemporary debates and the extent of their influence in analytic philosophy.

Analytic Philosophy, Rhetoric and Images

Although most philosophers feel confident in identifying analytic authors and texts, giving a definition of analytic philosophy is a much more elusive task. For one thing, several movements within analytic philosophy can be distinguished, including logical positivism, ordinary language philosophy, and American pragmatism.[2] Although contemporary analytic philosophers are not a homogenous or easily circumscribed group, they are linked by shared interests and methods. As John Heil puts it, "Today it is difficult to find much unanimity in the ranks of analytic philosophers. There is, perhaps, an implicit respect for argument and clarity, an evolving though informal agreement as to what problems are and are not tractable, and a con-

1. For example, Group μ, *A General Rhetoric*, trans. Paul B. Burrell and Edgar M. Slotkin (Baltimore: John Hopkins University Press, 1981), give an extremely detailed theory and taxonomy of rhetoric, which, nevertheless, does not cover a number of the images discussed in this book. Also, it is focused on these figures in general, rather than in philosophy.

2. See Robert R. Ammerman, ed., *Classics of Analytic Philosophy* (Indianapolis: Hackett, 1990), pp. 1–12, for a brief history of analytic philosophy.

viction that philosophy is in some sense continuous with science."[3] This description identifies analytic philosophers as sharing a method broadly conceived, a set of issues, and a view about the relationship between philosophy and science.

Another characterization of analytic philosophy is given by Thomas Mautner, who writes pithily: "Critics accuse the analytical movement of aridity and irrelevance; sympathizers see merit in its respect for rationality and its suspicion of rhetorical posturing and false profundity."[4] As this quotation suggests, in its slighting reference to "rhetorical posturing" in opposition to rationality, analytic philosophy is not generally known for its use or appreciation of images. Rather, it has a reputation for eschewing and denying the philosophical significance of images, associating them with pretentiousness and an improper use of rhetoric, unless they are seen to have a connection to a scientific approach.

A depreciation of images is not unusual in the history of philosophy, even by those who are unusually gifted in the use of images. Plato's images, which include those of the cave and the sun in the *Republic*, and the chariot of the soul in the *Phaedrus*, are unforgettable. He does not talk specifically about images, but discusses poetry and rhetoric, which involve imagery. In the *Republic*, Plato notoriously claims that there is "from of old a quarrel between philosophy and poetry."[5] He criticizes poetry because of its power to reinforce the wrong kind of emotions—the "childish loves of the multitudes," which should be subordinated to reason.[6] His concern is that poetry and stories will lead people away from the truth. Plato also worried about the effect of stories and images on children, claiming that "the young are not able to distinguish what is and what is not allegory."[7] Some stories are allowable in the ideal state, if they present accurate views of gods and heroes.

The *Gorgias* contains Plato's most damning condemnation of rhetoric. He argues that rhetoric is a part of flattery, and not the highest part, and stands in the same relation to justice as cookery does to medicine.[8] On this account, the rhetorician aims at pleasure, rather than the good, appealing to our lower desires—to be flattered and indulged. In the dialogue, Plato has Socrates argue that rhetoric is not an art at all; rather it is just a "routine and a knack," a "semblance of a part of politics," in other words, a shadow of justice, and is

3. John Heil, *The Cambridge Dictionary of Philosophy*, ed. Robert Audi (Cambridge: Cambridge University Press, 1995), p. 23.

4. Thomas Mautner, ed., *A Dictionary of Philosophy* (Oxford: Blackwell, 1996), p. 15.

5. Plato, *The Collected Dialogues*, ed. Edith Hamilton and Huntington Cairns (Princeton: Bollingen, 1999), *Republic*, p. 832; 607b.

6. *Republic*, p. 833; 608a.

7. *Republic*, p. 625; 378d.

8. *Gorgias*, p. 267; 465c.

aimed at producing beliefs rather than knowledge.[9] Toward the beginning of the *Gorgias*, rhetoric thus appears as something that not only has potential for abuse, but is of no value at all, is inferior to sophistry, and is "ignoble."

However, later in the dialogue, Plato has Socrates distinguish between two kinds of rhetoric, one that is simply flattery and one that is noble and is aimed at improving the souls of the audience by saying what is best.[10] Furthermore, at the very end of the dialogue, he says that "rhetoric and every other activity should ever so be employed, to attain justice."[11] This point gives rhetoric a place, provided it is focused on the good and is addressed to free people, rather than appealing to mobs that include women and children. The *Gorgias* also connects poetry and rhetoric, taking rhetoric to be poetry without music, rhythm and meter.[12]

In the *Phaedrus*, Plato discusses the subject of rhetoric as the art of persuasion, and considers structure, style, tone, and expression in a more sympathetic vein.[13] Nevertheless, "those admirable artifices . . . the brachylogies [short speeches] and imageries and all the rest of them,"[14] are only preliminaries to the true art of rhetoric, which requires the training of the philosopher. Plato has Socrates say that rhetoric is only proper when it is based on knowledge and an understanding of the kind of rhetoric which is appropriate to the listener. Thus, one cannot conclude that Plato is against the use of images in general, but rather that he believes they are often misused, particularly by the Sophists, who "could make trifles seem important and important points trifles by the force of their language."[15] His views do not amount to a rejection of images, but they suggest that a stance of suspicion towards them is the most appropriate one to take. Plato also sets up an opposition between philosophy and images in which philosophy is superior and images are ultimately dispensable. These views continue to influence philosophers. Images are connected with appeal to the popular and less reasonable elements of humanity.

While the disparagement of images is common in philosophy, the form that sees images as interfering with the kind of clarity necessary for good philosophical writing, hinted at by Mautner, has important precedents in seventeenth century British empiricism.[16] A surprising number of the im-

---

9. *Gorgias*, pp. 266, 238; 463b, 463e, 454e.
10. *Gorgias*, p. 286; 503a.
11. *Gorgias*, p. 307; 527c.
12. *Gorgias*, p. 285; 502c.
13. *Phaedrus*, pp. 512–515; 266e–269c.
14. *Phaedrus*, p. 516; 269a.
15. *Phaedrus*, p. 512; 267a–b.
16. Arguably, this attitude is also foreshadowed by the English advocates of the "plain style," such as John Dryden. See Edward P. J. Corbett, *Classical Rhetoric for the Modern Student* (New York: Oxford University Press, 1971), pp. 617–618.

ages and ideas discussed in this book are related to images used by Thomas
Hobbes and John Locke. Yet these two philosophers are also central sources
of dismissive views of images in philosophy. Hobbes and Locke are quite extreme in their views about the usefulness of imagery—they claim that *all* figurative uses of language should be eschewed in philosophy. For example, in
the *Leviathan*, Hobbes considers people abuse speech "when they use words
metaphorically; that is, in other sense than what they are ordained for; and
thereby deceive others."[17] He argues that "the use of Metaphors, Tropes, and
other Rhetoricall figures, instead of words proper" is a cause of absurd conclusions and "in reckoning, and seeking of truth, such speeches are not to
be admitted."[18] Hobbes's view of figurative language, rhetoric and images is
that they are deceitful and contrary to truth.

Locke also holds that all figurative uses of language in philosophy are misleading because they involve deceit. They mislead, according to Locke, because they affect us emotionally: "all the artificial and figurative application
of Words Eloquence hath invented, are for nothing else but to insinuate
wrong *Ideas*, move the Passions, and thereby mislead the Judgment; and so
indeed are perfect cheat."[19] However, like other philosophers who hold this
view, the very phrases he uses to denounce figurative language are themselves rich with images. Interestingly, Locke's formulations make explicit the
connections between the use of imagery, and an emotional, feminine eloquence which he believes is too popular. His claim is that " 'Tis evident how
much Men love to deceive and be deceived, since Rhetorick, that powerful
instrument of Error and Deceit, has its established Professors, is publicly
taught, and has always been had in great Reputation . . . *Eloquence*, like the
fair Sex, has too prevailing Beauties in it to suffer itself ever to be spoken
against."[20] Locke is implicitly connecting imagery and women with deceit-
fulness in this passage. The point seems to be that if something or someone
is attractive, then we should suppose that they will take no criticism, and thus
will probably lead us into error. His claim that rhetoric is too popular came
at a time when rhetoric was actually losing its hitherto central place in education.[21] Given that Hobbes and Locke are so strongly against figurative language, it is even more fascinating that their own tropes and stories mark the
inauguration of an industry of thought experiments and myths which continues in analytic philosophy today. In Hobbes's *Leviathan* we find the body
as a metaphor for the state, and in Locke's work there is the famous image

17. Thomas Hobbes, *Leviathan* (London: Aldine Press, 1953), p. 13.
18. Ibid., p. 21.
19. John Locke, *An Essay Concerning Human Understanding* (Oxford: Oxford University Press,
1979), p. 508.
20. Ibid.
21. See Corbett.

of the mind as *tabula rasa*.[22] In chapters 3 and 4 we shall see the successors of Locke's stories of the talking parrot, and the cobbler and the prince, and Hobbes's myth of the ship of Theseus and of the state of nature.

It is not only the empiricists who held the view that images lead to error. The rationalists, including Descartes, had a similar opinion concerning imagery.[23] We again find that Descartes's work is rich in imagery. For example, he uses the metaphor of foundations in the *Meditations*, the tree of knowledge in the *Principles of Philosophy*, and the image of the shelter of morality in *Discourse on the Method*. I will discuss these images in chapter 1, and the influence of rationalist philosophy on contemporary analytic philosophy in epistemology and the use of a foundational image in aesthetics, in later chapters.

Some contemporary analytic philosophers take the view that metaphors, for example, are mere rhetorical devices or simply useful to introduce a topic. Such a view is generally connected to the idea that images are relatively easy to paraphrase or break down into literal truths. Aristotle is often used in support of this view, because he argued that there is little difference between a metaphor and a simile.[24] Such a view is known as the comparison or substitution view. Philosophers who hold it tend to claim that images are at most useful as persuasive tools in philosophy. The empiricists are often blamed for contemporary rejections of imagery, because their view of images was adopted by the logical positivists and it still has quite a strong influence on recent analytic philosophy. The logical positivists, however, took things further than the earlier empiricists "to the extreme position that they [metaphors] can make no truth claims at all."[25]

There are a number of serious problems associated with the foregoing accounts of the role of images in philosophy. The most obvious problem is the mistaken idea that images can be entirely removed from philosophy. Another is the assumption that any ambiguity in language is deceptive, and

22. Locke, p. 104.

23. René Descartes, "Discourse," in *The Philosophical Writings of Descartes*, trans. John Cottingham, Robert Stoothoff, and Dugald Murdoch, vol. 1 (Cambridge: Cambridge University Press, 1985), p. 114: "Those with the strongest reasoning and the most skill at ordering their thoughts so as to make them clear and intelligible are always the most persuasive, even if they speak only low Breton and have never learned rhetoric."

24. For example, this is Paul Henle's view on metaphor in "Metaphor," in *Language, Thought, and Culture*, ed. P. Henle (Ann Arbor: University of Michigan, 1958), as well as that of Nelson Goodman in *Languages of Art: An Approach to a Theory of Symbols* (Indianapolis: Hackett, 1976), pp.68–95, and more recently, Roger White, *The Structure of Metaphor: The Way the Language of Metaphor Works (Philosophical Theory)* (Oxford: Blackwell, 1996). See Aristotle's *Rhetoric*, in *The Complete Works of Aristotle*, ed. Jonathan Barnes, vol. 2 (Princeton: Princeton University Press, 1984), p. 2243; 1046b20–25.

25. For a discussion of this point see Mark Johnson, ed., *Philosophical Perspectives on Metaphor* (Minneapolis: University of Minnesota Press, 1981), p. 35.

therefore undesirable for philosophical work, a position that assumes language can and should be purified of ambiguity. A third is the claim that when language affects the emotions, it is unsuitable for philosophical reasoning. A fourth is the notion that images only work to persuade, rather than to do any philosophical work. In my view, all these claims are misguided, and it will become clear that the refusal to take images seriously has serious consequences. While philosophers who subscribe to these beliefs will continue to use images, they will remain unaware of the implications of using them.

The first issue is fairly easily dealt with. A cursory glance at the history of philosophy shows that even philosophers considered to be quite dry writers, such as Kant, use many and varied images. This is also true in analytic philosophy, in that even the works of the most arid and technical writers are rich in images in the form of thought experiments, metaphors, and so on. From a broader perspective, imagery is an inescapable part of language and therefore of philosophy. It might be felt that it is desirable at least to try to remove images from philosophy, if they are so deceptive. However, ambiguity is prevalent in language and is not *essentially* deceptive. As Chaim Perelman notes in *The Realm of Rhetoric*, "In natural languages, ambiguity— the possibility of multiple interpretation—would be the rule."[26] Though, of course, ambiguity can be deceptive, it can also be the source of new ideas and associations; images are often used for this reason in philosophy. One could say that preserving ambiguity is more appropriate than denying its existence, but the point I am making is that there is a creative dimension to imagery that relies on this ambiguity. Context places some limitations on the range of likely interpretations, while the richness of the image opens up possibilities. The openness of images is consonant with the unfinished nature of philosophy. Wittgenstein's analogy of language as a game has been extremely provocative, as philosophers have tried to delineate its implications for our understanding of language.[27] Its lack of precision is related to its potential for opening up new possibilities. I am not claiming that images are immune from criticism. Rather, I am suggesting that the basis for the possible critique of images is not that *all* images are deceptive, but rather that a particular image is inappropriate, or, as is my primary concern in this book, that images can act in an exclusionary way. This approach involves taking images in philosophy to be playing a very serious and important role.

26. Chaim Perelman, *The Realm of Rhetoric*, trans. William Kluback (Notre Dame: University of Notre Dame Press, 1982), p. 44. Martin Warner also notes that we can "drop stitches, friends and hints" without that being a sign of equivocation, in "Rhetoric and Philosophy," *Philosophy and Literature* 19 (1995): 109.

27. See Ludwig Wittgenstein, *Philosophical Investigations*, trans. G. E. M. Anscombe (Oxford: Basil Blackwell, 1983), p. 39.

Traditionally, philosophers have maintained that images have no place in philosophy because of their connection with the emotions, the idea being that philosophical reasoning is mislead by emotion.[28] For example, Plato believes that imagery appeals to our baser passions, and Locke argues that images lead our judgment astray by "moving" our passions. One could respond to this view by claiming that images do not move passions; yet, that is hardly plausible, partly because philosophy itself moves passions. It is not surprising that images also move us, perhaps more than non-imagaic language, because of the richness of the associations they evoke. The question then becomes whether exciting our emotions in general is an undesirable aspect of philosophy, on the grounds that it will disrupt the processes of reasoning. In recent times, feminist philosophers and others working on emotions have shown that emotion has an important part to play in reasoning. For example, Alison Jaggar argues that emotion and reason are mutually constitutive and necessary to each other, Miranda Fricker argues that reason and emotion ought to be aligned rather than opposed, and Robert Solomon argues that emotions are rational.[29] If it is accepted that emotions act in conjunction with reason, this point suggests that images are also important to reasoning, or at least that their association with emotion does not imply that they cannot be important in philosophy. I will develop this view of the relevance of emotions to reasoning throughout the book by looking at particular images and showing how important the emotional effect of these images are to ideas and arguments.

Finally, the view that images work *only* to persuade is, in my view, too limited, because this still assumes that ideal language and philosophy would be purified of images and their appeal to emotion and audience. Jeff Mason, in his book on philosophical rhetoric, argues that rhetoric in philosophy is not incompatible with the search for truth, but he considers images primarily as a function of the attempt to persuade and convince others of one's views.[30] It might be thought that taking images to function at least in part rhetorically or persuasively is to make a rather damning criticism of their use. However, philosophers always use images, and a problem lies in any attempt to repudiate or deny them, not in the use of images. Revealing the rhetorical

---

28. One exception to this view is David Hume, who so famously said, "Reason is, and ought only to be the slave of the passions." *A Treatise of Human Nature*, ed. L. A. Selby-Bigge (Oxford: Clarendon, 1978), p. 415.

29. Alison Jaggar, "Love and Knowledge: Emotion in Feminist Epistemology," *Inquiry* 32 (1989): 151–176; Miranda Fricker, "Reason and Emotion," *Radical Philosophy* 57 (Spring 1991): 14–19, and Robert Solomon, *The Passions: Emotions and the Meaning of Life* (Indianapolis: Hackett, 1993).

30. See Jeff Mason, *Philosophical Rhetoric: The Function of Indirection in Philosophical Writing* (London: Routledge, 1989).

side of philosophy should not lead to the removal of its images, but to a greater sensitivity to their force and care about the kind of images we use. However, to refer to the use of imagery as rhetorical can be somewhat misleading, because of the common perception that if an image is used rhetorically, then it is used *only* for persuasive purposes. Attention to the rhetorical aspect of philosophy is quite different to a philosophical theory of rhetoric or particular figures, such as the theories of metaphor found in the work of Donald Davidson and Roger White.[31] In this book, in so far as rhetoric is important, it is in terms of the first project—in relation to the rhetorical aspect of philosophy, rather than in terms of a philosophy of rhetoric.

My own view is that although the rhetorical, or persuasive, aspect of images is extremely important, they also work, as I will demonstrate, in other ways. Furthermore, a concentration on contemporary analytic philosophy requires attention to the specific type of images most in use, an attention not to be found in most books on philosophical rhetoric.[32] Mason argues that the "plain style" of the philosophical logicians is itself a form of rhetoric or mode of persuasion, even though it is not as obviously so as the "hot tropical style" of a Nietzsche or Kierkegaard.[33] While I agree with this view, my concern here is not with style, as such; Mason acknowledges that even the driest of texts uses images such as metaphor and analogies. There are many famous images in analytic philosophy, including Otto Neurath's ship of language, W. V. O. Quine's fabric of knowledge or belief (and web of belief metaphors), Hilary Putnam's twin earth thought experiment and his analogy between brains and computers, Frank Jackson's "Mary" thought experiment, John Searle's Chinese room, the ever-popular brain-in-the-vat, Donald Davidson's swampman, and David Chalmers's zombie.[34] Images such as these are the stock-in-trade of the analytic philosopher. In this book, I trace some of the most significant images of contemporary analytic philosophy

31. See Donald Davidson, "What Metaphors Mean," *Critical Inquiry* 5, no. 1 (1978): 31–47, and White.

32. P. Christopher Smith, *The Hermeneutics of Original Argument: Demonstration, Dialectic, Rhetoric* (Evanston: Northwestern University Press, 1998), for example, focuses on the work of Plato, Aristotle, and Heidegger.

33. Mason, pp. 128–129.

34. See Otto Neurath, "Protocol Sentences," in *Logical Positivism*, ed. A. J. Ayer (New York: Macmillan, 1959), pp. 199–208; W. V. O. Quine, *From a Logical Point of View: Logico-Philosophical Essays* (Cambridge: Harvard University Press, 1953); W. V. O. Quine and J. S. Ullian, *The Web of Belief* (New York: Random House, 1970); Hilary Putnam, *Representation and Reality* (Cambridge: MIT Press, 1988); Hilary Putnam, *Mind, Language and Reality: Philosophical Papers*, vol. 2 (Cambridge: Cambridge University Press, 1975); Frank Jackson, "Epiphenomenal Qualia," *Philosophical Quarterly* 32 (1982): 127–136; John Searle, *Minds, Brains and Science* (London: Penguin, 1984); Donald Davidson, "Knowing One's Own Mind," *Proceedings and Addresses of the American Philosophy Association* 60, no. 3 (1987): 441–458; and David Chalmers, *The Conscious Mind* (Cambridge: MIT Press, 1997).

through debates to show how they are altered and modified in that context and how they characterize the analytic imaginary.

There are some notable exceptions to the negative attitudes to the use of images in philosophy, even within analytic philosophy.[35] However, my argument in this book is not *dependent* on the particular philosophers under discussion being explicitly either for or against the use of images in philosophy, although it is important that they do not see them as significant in the way that I do. Rather, I am concerned with thinking critically about the way philosophers use images, a thinking that draws out latent implications instead of criticizing explicit views on images. More importantly, I will show that the way analytic philosophers use images belies their own claims to neutrality and objectivity.

Levels of Embeddedness

A central issue concerning the role of images in philosophy is the extent to which images are needed to express or put forward philosophical views. I argue that images are essential to philosophical work and are not removable in the sense that they can always be spelled out in literal or non-imagaic language.[36] However, there is a further controversy over whether all images are equally necessary, and even whether certain particular images are necessary. For example, Genevieve Lloyd argues in "Maleness, Metaphor, and the 'Crisis' of Reason" and in *Being in Time* that some metaphors are constitutive of thought, embedded in the thought, or fundamental in a way that other images are not.[37] Two examples she uses of metaphors which can be removed more or less without detriment to the argument are Francis Bacon's metaphors of nature and Kant's ship of reason. Bacon describes nature as either whore or chaste bride to be wooed, and Kant's ship of reason is something that must be prevented from sailing out of the sight of experience. Bacon's example is interesting because a number of feminist philosophers have done work on these metaphors, arguing that they are essential features

35. For example, I. A. Richards argues that metaphors have considerable cognitive value in *Philosophy and Rhetoric* (New York: Oxford University Press, 1936). See also Max Black, *Perplexities* (Ithaca: Cornell University Press, 1990); George Lakoff and Mark Johnson, *Metaphors We Live By* (Chicago: University of Chicago Press, 1980); and, *Philosophy in the Flesh: The Embodied Mind and Its Challenge to Western Thought* (New York: Basic Books, 1999).

36. Michèle Le Dœuff holds this view, and I will discuss her work in chapter 1.

37. Genevieve Lloyd, "Maleness, Metaphor, and the 'Crisis' of Reason," in *A Mind of One's Own*, ed. Louise M. Antony and Charlotte Witt (Boulder: Westview Press, 1993), and Genevieve Lloyd, *Being in Time: Selves and Narrators in Philosophy and Literature* (London: Routledge, 1993).

of his thought.[38] In apparent contradiction to this point, Lloyd argues that even without the metaphors, Bacon is able to express his views.[39] In the case of Kant, she claims that he manages to express the same ideas "less elegantly . . . in some of the more tortuous sentences of the *Critique of Pure Reason*."[40] In other words, Kant does not need the image to say what he wishes to say.

It is possible to reconcile these two views. Part of the apparent disagreement about the status of images centers around notions of expressibility. It might appear that Lloyd's view that thoughts can be expressed less elegantly without images contradicts the view that images are essential to philosophical argument. It may be thought that if it is accepted that ideas can sometimes be expressed without a particular image, then images have been reduced yet again to the status of mere rhetoric. This is not the case. I propose to incorporate and extend Lloyd's insights, and the insight that images are essential to philosophy, by introducing three levels of what I will call "embeddedness." One is the level of expressibility—one needs the image to express the thought. The second level involves the provision of a framework that gives substance to the thought expressed. The third is the level of persuasion and concerns the way in which the image makes the thought convincing.[41] I call these levels expressibility, enframement, and persuasiveness. Images can work on any or all of these levels, and all the images discussed in this book work on more than one level.

With regard to the first level of embeddedness, which is the "deepest," Lloyd argues that sexual symbolism is often embedded in conceptions of reason, in "for example, the conceptualization of reason as an attainment, as a transcending of the feminine."[42] For example, Lloyd quotes Hegel in *The Philosophy of Right*, who claims that "Women are educated—who knows how?— as it were by breathing in ideas, by living rather than acquiring knowledge. The status of manhood, on the other hand, is attained only by the stress of

38. For example, Michèle Le Dœuff, "Ants and Women, or Philosophy without Borders," in *Contemporary French Thought*, ed. A. Phillips Griffiths (New York: Cambridge University Press, 1987), and in the interview with Raoul Mortley in his book, *French Philosophers in Conversation* (London: Routledge, 1991); Sandra Harding, *Whose Science? Whose Knowledge? Thinking from Women's Lives* (Ithaca: Cornell University Press, 1991); Evelyn Fox Keller, *Reflections on Gender and Science* (New Haven: Yale University Press, 1991); and Carolyn Merchant, *The Death of Nature: Women, Ecology, and the Scientific Revolution* (San Francisco: Harper, 1980).

39. Lloyd, "Maleness, Metaphor, and the 'Crisis' of Reason," p. 82. Her view develops a discussion in *The Man of Reason* in which she argues that Bacon's metaphors "give a male content to what it is to be a good knower." Lloyd, *The Man of Reason: "Male" and "Female" in Western Philosophy* (London: Methuen, 1984), p. 17.

40. Lloyd, p. 169.

41. It might be suggested that there is a fourth level in which the image is merely decorative. There may be such cases, but they are of no relevance to this book because my primary interest is in the philosophical uses of images.

42. Lloyd, "Maleness, Metaphor," p. 82.

thought and much technical exertion."[43] Other examples of metaphors at the first level are spatial and temporal metaphors, metaphors of movement and rest, and metaphors of the senses. Lakoff and Johnson, for example, consider orientational metaphors to be of the kind that "organizes a whole system of concepts with respect to one another."[44] One specific case they discuss is the structuring of perceived positive qualities in terms of upward metaphors, and perceived negative qualities in terms of downward ones. They give the following characterization: "Rational is up; emotional is down. The discussion fell to the emotional level, but I raised it up to the rational plane. We put our feelings aside and had a high-level intellectual discussion of the matter. He couldn't rise above his emotions."[45] Altering such images requires a rethinking of the entire field of endeavor, and perhaps an examination of our cultural understanding of the concepts in question. In epistemology, it is difficult to write a sentence about knowing without using visual and spatial metaphors, like seeing the point, accommodating points of view, perspectives, and so on. In chapter 5, I examine problems with visual and spatial metaphors in epistemology, a central use of metaphor in the history of philosophy, to which analytic philosophy gives a distinctive interpretation.

Images that work at the second level of embeddedness, enframement, are central to the analytic imaginary. These images guarantee the continuance of the framework, methodology, and objects of discussion. Without them these certainties must change. A particularly good example of enframement is the role social contract myths play in liberal political philosophy. I discuss this role in chapter 4. The third level, persuasiveness, often works in conjunction with the other two. Useful, striking images will always facilitate persuasion, and the images discussed in this book are not exceptions.

These distinctions should not be taken as signs of a renunciation of the view that images are essential to philosophy, or of disagreement with Lakoff and Johnson's view that metaphors are essential to language and thought. My point is that certain particular images may not be essential to certain particular thoughts. For example, although we so often use visual metaphors when talking about knowledge, this does not mean that epistemology *must* be completely dominated by visual metaphors. Or to take Bacon's metaphors, although they may constitute an integral part of *his* theory and *his* thought, this does not mean that one's conception of science must involve thinking of nature as a woman. Another important aspect of metaphor noted by Lakoff and Johnson is that although metaphors structure experi-

---

43. Lloyd, *The Man of Reason,* p. 38. G. W. F Hegel, *The Philosophy of Right,* trans. T. M. Knox (Oxford: Oxford University Press, 1952), pp. 263–264.

44. Lakoff and Johnson, p. 14.

45. Ibid., p. 17.

ence, they can also exclude features of experience. For example, talking about arguments in metaphors relating to war, such as attacking and defending, or winning and losing, excludes the co-operative aspects of argumentation. Images can be complicit in defining philosophy as a narrow domain, in making rationality appear to be something that is either wholly present or entirely absent, or in making rationality appear as something that we have measurable quantities of. In the case of the analytic imaginary, images work to define the nature of debates, and what is considered as appropriate contributions to them. This leads me to the two central concerns of this book: the role of images in the analytic imaginary, and the way in which they work to exclude women and feminist philosophy. Images are both philosophically central and gendered in important ways, and a greater awareness of the analytic imaginary and how images work entails a greater understanding of the way in which they are gendered and exclusionary.

Functions of Images

One important concern that I address in this book is how to clarify the diverse functions or roles of images in analytic philosophy. The images I discuss are an integral part of the views and arguments put forward by analytic philosophers, and are representative of the kinds of images used in analytic philosophy. The features that stand out are generally relevant to the field of analytic philosophy. They are conscious, deliberate images, generally designed to fulfill a particular purpose, rather than unwitting upsurges from the unconscious. However, although they are conscious or deliberate images, they can still contain presuppositions and have implications of which their authors and readers are unaware. I will critically examine these aspects of the images in order to better understand the imaginary of analytic philosophy. It is still overwhelmingly true that analytic philosophers see metaphysics and epistemology as the central areas of philosophy, and even as the only questions that are truly philosophical. What this often means is that even when other areas are ventured into, it is still the metaphysical and epistemological questions in relation to those areas that are being addressed. Aesthetics, in particular, is often approached in this way, and therefore it is particularly useful to examine images used in analytic aesthetics, as I do in the final chapter. The attempt to transfer methods of argument from one field to another, often in inappropriate ways—such as, from mathematics and science to ethics and aesthetics—is endemic in analytic philosophy.[46]

46. Stephen Toulmin notes this point in *The Uses of Argument* (Cambridge: Cambridge University Press, 1958). His project is very different from mine because he focuses on forms of argument, rather than images.

Images can start off debate, open philosophy up to new ideas, and connect a text to previous philosophical work. In this book, I will demonstrate that images can also have other roles, or a number of different roles at once. For example, the very contemporary images in the abortion and personal identity debates discussed in the following chapters involve scientistic and futuristic fantasies, yet sometimes these futuristic fantasies reach back to past philosophy in their content. Scientism in philosophy is described as "the view that philosophical problems require none but scientific techniques for answering them."[47] The images discussed here represent innovation in the sense of a shift of thought or progress in the debate, but a shift which has imposed limits on a range of further possibilities within the analytic imaginary.

In order to better understand the diverse functioning of images in analytic philosophy, I focus on the different ways in which the five types of chosen images work. Their level of embeddedness or constitutiveness will vary. Furthermore, the purpose of specific images will vary greatly. For example, some images are designed to explain phenomena, such as the models in aesthetics, and some to justify a position, for example, the analogies used in the abortion debate. Nevertheless, there is a web of links between the images, both in the roles that they play, and in the features of the analytic imaginary which emerge from my examination of these roles. Several of the images are traced through the work of a number of philosophers. Seeing how the image is used and transformed clarifies the way debates are structured and limited, a further aspect of the workings of the analytic imaginary.

One of the fascinating aspects of the analytic imaginary is the way certain particular types of images are used in specific areas. Thus the way I have found five different images from five different areas is an accurate reflection of the images which are typically used in those areas: analogies in ethics, thought experiments in personal identity, myths in political philosophy, metaphors in epistemology, and models in aesthetics. The connections between types of images and areas run deep and merits close attention, both across other fields in philosophy and historically. These five central examples provide a significant basis for thinking about these connections. Part of my project in trying to understand the analytic imaginary is to suggest how analytic philosophy could become more open-ended. Before that can be shown, we must understand in what sense it is closed and excluding.

47. "Scientism," in *A Dictionary of Philosophy*, ed. A. R. Lacey, 3d ed. (London: Routledge, 1996). See also "Scientism" in *The Oxford Companion to Philosophy*, ed. Ted Henderich (Oxford: Oxford University Press, 1995) and Tom Sorell, *Scientism: Philosophy and the Infatuation with Science* (London: Routledge, 1991).

The Images' Role in Exclusion

My other central concern is to show how particular images can work to exclude different sets of ideas, including feminist ones. In discussing issues of the exclusion and denigration of women, it is important to keep in mind the distinction between contingent remarks about women and theories which fundamentally exclude women. Elizabeth Porter, in *Women and Moral Identity*, describes the distinction as one between sexism and genderism. Sexism "refers to acts of discrimination against women or unwarranted differential treatment of them," whereas genderism "assumes a privileged status for gender-specific characteristics—perhaps even unwittingly—without being justified in doing so."[48] To give a thorough critique of the male bias in reason, we need to know which philosophical theories are gender biased, and an examination of the images used in philosophy can assist us to do this. These images can be as revealing of gender bias when women are excluded or not referred to, as when "woman" is used as a metaphor or when women are explicitly discussed. Much of the work concerned with revealing this kind of gender bias has focused on influential texts in the history of philosophy.[49] There has been some criticism of the methods of analytic philosophy, including its tendency to abstract from context; however, this discussion has not focused on the imagery of analytic philosophy.[50]

The kinds of exclusion which we need to understand range from the actual exclusion of women from the academy to the way theories denigrate women's interests, issues, and aspects of human experience associated with women, such as emotion.[51] I have already suggested how emotion can be understood as important to good reasoning. Because of a perceived connection between women and emotion, images can be an important site for investigating these links— in the attitudes toward emotion expressed in the

48. Elizabeth J. Porter, *Women and Moral Identity* (Sydney: Allen and Unwin, 1991), p. 90.

49. For example, Genevieve Lloyd's landmark text, *The Man of Reason* (London: Methuen, 1984).

50. See Ann Garry, "A Minimally Decent Philosophical Method? Analytic Philosophy and Feminism," *Hypatia* 10, no.3 (1995): 7–30.

51. For example, see Geraldine Finn, "On the Oppression of Women in Philosophy—Or, Whatever Happened to Objectivity?" in *Feminism in Canada: From Pressure to Politics* (Montreal: Black Rose Books, 1982), pp. 145–173; Paula Ruth Boddington, "The Issue of Women's Philosophy," and Joanna Hodge, "Subject, Body and the Exclusion of Women from Philosophy," both in *Feminist Perspectives in Philosophy*, ed. Morwenna Griffiths and Margaret Whitford (Bloomington: Indiana University Press, 1988), pp. 205–223; Susan Sherwin, "Philosophical Methodology and Feminist Methodology: Are They Compatible?" in *Feminist Perspectives: Philosophical Essays on Method and Morals*, ed. Lorraine Code, Sheila Mullett, and Christine Overall (Toronto: University of Toronto Press, 1988), pp. 13–28; and Candice Vogler, "Philosophical Feminism, Feminist Philosophy," *Philosophical Topics* 23, no. 2 (1995): 295–319.

images, for example. One of the features of the analytic imaginary is an avoidance of emotion, which is interesting in the light of the suspicion of the emotional power of images.

My approach to the particular question of the exclusion of women from philosophy will be different from others' approaches in that I show how women's experiences *and* feminist philosophy have been marginalized in specific debates in contemporary analytic philosophy. Images can work to close off certain questions. Subscribing to the image can make certain ways of doing philosophy unacceptable and certain questions unaskable or invisible. Each chapter includes a discussion of the kind of reconceptions excluded by the images that have been used, reconceptions which could serve to open up the debates and transform the analytic imaginary. These "reconceptions" are not intended to *replace* existing images and ways of thinking, but to enrich the analytic imaginary. Just as imagination can be more or less fertile, an imaginary can be more or less impoverished and benefit from greater openness, plurality and variety—in addition to precision and rigor. An understanding of the workings of images can help to answer some of the questions posed by feminists about philosophical rationality, particularly those concerning the relation between certain images and methods and an ideal of rationality that excludes women and feminist philosophy. It is important to extend the range of our understanding by looking at contemporary philosophy and thinking about how feminist philosophy can contribute to a rationality that is not male or masculine. Many feminist philosophers have been able to employ traditional theories, frameworks, and images subversively for feminist purposes. Alternatively, if theories and images are not used critically, the image can subvert feminist intentions by incorporating a number of implicit assumptions which exclude women. Therefore, care needs to be taken when using images and in attempting to create new ones. In the chapter on the myth of the social contract and the chapter on visual and spatial metaphors in epistemology, I show how feminist philosophers who have used or responded to these particular images have taken on some of the untenable aspects of the original projects.

Images themselves tend to be categorized in a gendered way: that is, there are masculine images and feminine images. The feminine are the flowery, eloquent, persuasive, beautiful images, which Locke finds so deceptive. The masculine are considered logical, scientific, designed to test hypotheses, and to explain and provoke, like the thought experiments, analogies, and models I discuss in this book. The differences between masculine and feminine images involve the type of image, the form it takes, and the intended purpose of the image. Images that are masculine in this sense have more legitimacy in analytic philosophy.

Outline

Before I discuss, in much more detail in chapter 1, views on the role of imagery in philosophy, let me clarify the structure of this book. First, I explain Michèle Le Dœuff's concept of the philosophical imaginary and describe her methodology as it is worked through particular readings of Kant's, Descartes's, and Sartre's images, showing how her ideas are useful to my project, even if my project is quite distinct from hers. In order to understand the nature of the analytic imaginary, we need to look at particular images in analytic philosophy so that we can understand their diverse functioning and pay attention to the specific context in which analytic philosophy is practiced.

In each of the following chapters I analyze the functioning of images in contemporary analytic philosophy through the three different levels of embeddedness I have outlined: expressibility, enframement, and persuasiveness. These influential images work through these different levels simultaneously and are integral to the philosophical debate at hand. In chapter 2, I discuss the use of arguments by way of considering analogy in the abortion debate, and with a particular focus on Judith Jarvis Thomson's very striking "famous violinist" analogy. This analogy has influenced the abortion debate in important ways, for example, by keeping it focused around issues of rights and excluding discussion of the experience of abortion. There the pervasive characteristics of the analytic imaginary begin to emerge: that it is possible and desirable to imagine ourselves in other's places, and that we can use that imagining as a basis for theorizing.

In chapter 3 we encounter thought experiments in personal identity, such as brain swaps, tele-transportation, cloning, and fission, which determine and limit notions of the self within the analytic imaginary. These thought experiments bring the world of science fiction into philosophy, polarize questions both about the nature of personal identity and the nature of the methodology we should use to think about these questions, and introduce the theme of self-generation.

In chapter 4 I explore the myth of the social contract and its particular application in John Rawls's theory of justice; included is discussion of "the veil of ignorance" and "the original position." In Rawls, myths disguise social inequalities and make it difficult to theorize group oppression.

Chapter 5 is an examination of visual and spatial metaphors in Thomas Nagel's epistemology, particularly the metaphor of the "view from nowhere," and the effects of such predominant metaphors within the analytic imaginary. These metaphors both reinforce splits between the knower and the known and set up an impossible and undesirable goal of objectivity.

In chapter 6 I examine the workings of an explanatory model in aesthetics put forward by Kendall Walton that concerns children's games of make-believe. I demonstrate how, in trying to interpret all art forms through the use of a single model, Walton's imaginary, and others like it, place serious limitations on the possibilities of understanding art. Finally, I show how the themes of avoidance and denial of important aspects of human experience and the tendency toward scientism characterize the analytic imaginary.

The images of analytic philosophy work simultaneously to persuade, express, support views, and constrain debate by excluding differing approaches and ideas. Running throughout the analytic imaginary is a surprisingly coherent fantasy about the individual's ability to understand and put oneself in the place of others. My project in this book is to provide an analysis of and reflection on the nature of the analytic imaginary and to suggest how it could be enriched.

To begin to understand the analytic imaginary, we need to explore the relation between the use of particular images and a philosophical imaginary. Since a very constructive way to understand this relation is through Michèle Le Dœuff's reading of key images from the history of philosophy, I will examine her work in the first chapter.

1

Philosophical Images

Michèle Le Dœuff's characterization of the philosophical imaginary and her readings of images from the history of philosophy provide a useful basis for understanding the analytic imaginary.[1] Her use of the term "the philosophical imaginary" needs some explaining, however, as does her view of the role of images in philosophy. The flexibility of her method will become apparent as I examine her readings of several important images in the history of philosophy: images used by Kant, Descartes, and Sartre. Finally, I shall show how her methodology is relevant to understanding the central images of contemporary analytic philosophy and thus the analytic imaginary.

The Philosophical Imaginary

There are good reasons for discussing Le Dœuff's work in order to comprehend the analytic imaginary. First, her work suggests how we can understand philosophical imaginaries by analyzing the images philosophers use. Second, her concentration on foundationalism, theories which presuppose or argue that knowledge must be based on a foundation of certainty, is particularly valuable because of the prevalence of foundational theories and im-

1. Michèle Le Dœuff (1948–) publishes work on the history of philosophy and science, on the nature of the philosophical imaginary, the work of Simone de Beauvoir, and contemporary feminist issues. She has also translated works by Shakespeare and Francis Bacon into French. Her best-known works in English are *The Philosophical Imaginary*, trans. Colin Gordon (London: Athlone Press, 1989), and *Hipparchia's Choice: An Essay Concerning Women, Philosophy, etc.*, trans. Trista Selous (Oxford: Blackwell, 1989), both of which I discuss here.

ages in analytic philosophy. Thirdly, her critique of the epistemological and metaphysical concerns of past philosophers is useful for understanding contemporary preoccupations with the same questions. Other philosophers discuss the idea of imagination and the imaginary, and produce important insights, yet none think through the idea of a specific philosophical imaginary in the way Le Dœuff does.

The *imagination* often refers to a capacity or faculty of being able to form and reproduce images and ideas. This sense of the imagination is important for the philosophical imaginary, because it is partly constituted by these images. Another important view of imagination is that it plays a synthetic role in perception. For example, Kant argues that imagination is a faculty uniting thought and perception in a single act, so that ordinary seeing is an act of imagination. He distinguishes between this "productive" role of imagination, where concepts are applied to experience, and the "reproductive" role, where one groups a perception with an earlier one.[2] Paul Ricoeur also distinguishes between the productive and the reproductive imagination, although in a different way: between the creative side of imagination or the capacity to produce things that are non-existent, and the capacity to reproduce things that are absent.[3]

In everyday speech, the imaginary is also sometimes linked with illusion and distinguished from reality (in the sense of "I must be imagining things"), though this is really better understood as mistaken perception. We can imagine things that may or may not be real. There is also the sense in which we may praise someone for being imaginative, and this is connected with the idea of a philosophical imaginary, because philosophers are in part trying to invent something new when they make up their images. The connection between imagination and fantasy is of some relevance, because fantasy is an exercise of imagination, but one that we consider less illuminating or more removed from the subject than something truly imaginative.

Le Dœuff is primarily concerned with the creative side of imagination and with breaking down the sharp contrast between the imaginary and the real, or rather the contrast between the products of the imagination and the products of reason. She posits this by saying that philosophers often "think in images." The conception of the philosophical imaginary outlined by Le Dœuff encompasses both a particular capacity to imagine and a stock of imagery which is governed by the needs and gaps of philosophy.[4] Thus her notion of the imaginary incorporates both the faculty of the imagination and its prod-

---

2. Immanuel Kant, *The Critique of Pure Reason*, trans. Norman Kemp Smith (London: Macmillan, 1958), pp. 142–143; A118/B152.

3. Paul Ricoeur, "Imagination in Discourse and Action," in *Rethinking Imagination: Culture and Creativity*, ed. Gillian Robinson and John Rundell (Routledge: London, 1994), p. 120.

4. Le Dœuff's concept of the imaginary can be contrasted with that of Jacques Lacan, which concerns one's identification with an image of oneself. See Lacan, *Ecrits: A Selection*, trans. Alan Sheridan (New York: Norton, 1977).

ucts, the images. The needs and gaps in philosophy will vary, so the philosophical imaginary will not remain homogenous. The imagery of philosophy is integrated with its theoretical problems, but it also has a specific "affective resonance" or emotional coloring of a certain kind. Images reveal the subjectivity of the philosophers, because they appeal to that subjectivity. She says that this affectivity is peculiar to philosophy; it is the desire and emotion of the "learned subjectivity," the social minority that the student of philosophy becomes part of by learning its images.

Le Dœuff's *The Philosophical Imaginary* collects essays, linked together by a preface, in which she advances readings of particular images that concern their history in philosophy and the philosophical imaginary. Among the best examples of the affective aspect of the philosophical imaginary are the scholarly utopias Le Dœuff discusses in the collection and in a separately published paper.[5] She hypothesizes that utopias are a theme in the collective imagination of scholars, and she compares the utopian visions of Thomas More in *Utopia*, Francis Bacon in *New Atlantis*, and Tomasso Campanella in *City of the Sun*. Le Dœuff argues that "the major concern of a utopia is to focus thought on the conditions of possibility for optimal and maximal public (or state-controlled) education."[6] The utopian authors, despite differences on a number of issues like the question of private property, share in common the goals of a lingua franca that is also the language of education wherein nations overcome differences and the population is kept in check. For them, the perfect society is one where everything is run for the benefit of education and the increase of knowledge, and scholars are given the highest status and greatest range of social benefits. These dreams of a perfect society illustrate well the way these authors' imaginations are dominated by their lives as intellectuals and scholars. So the philosophical imaginary can be understood as a type of scholarly imaginary where the importance of philosophy and philosophers is rather exaggerated. The philosophical imaginary emerges in these cases as the projection of "the collective consciousness of a new caste of secular, learned men, attached to the new notion of the state which appears in the Renaissance."[7]

According to Le Dœuff, the specificity of the philosophical imaginary does not mean that it has no relation to everyday life and historical circumstance. She describes the imaginary as "*of* one's theoretic situation—the emblem of its truth" and "thought in the service of desire."[8] Her view is that usually groups, such as philosophers, adopt an image because it answers a meaningful question for them. Each time an image is "borrowed," it is transformed

5. See "Daydream in Utopia," in *The Philosophical Imaginary*, and "Utopias: Scholarly," *Social Research* 49, no. 2 (1984): 441–466.
6. "Utopias: Scholarly," p. 446.
7. Ibid., p. 457.
8. *The Philosophical Imaginary*, p. 14.

"by the act of borrowing itself."[9] Probably what she is implying here is that in a new context an image takes on a new meaning, as well as being an answer to a new question; I would add that images are transformed by the uses the borrower puts them to. Le Dœuff's method illustrates how we can perceive the specificity of an image, for example, by tracing its origin in literature and examining how philosophy reworks it. She reminds us that imagery reflects temporal variation, and circulates "*between* different groups, fields, practices and knowledges."[10] It follows that there will be different philosophical imaginaries, of which the analytic imaginary is an important variation.

Le Dœuff makes the related point that the images of philosophy must be transformed to be accepted as popular myth.[11] Utopias are a good example, because the idea of a utopia and utopian views did not become part of popular culture until they were associated with the French revolution.[12] Utopian views that do not find a ready audience and that need an accompanying explanation she calls atopias. This way of understanding the passage of images comes from her method of erudition, which traces the movement of images between popular myth and philosophy, and illustrates her thesis that there is a dynamic relation between images and theoretical work. She argues that there is a continual feedback or dialectic between concepts and images, without attempting to break down the distinction altogether.[13] This is a very useful way to think about images, because it maintains a link between the so-called literal and the imagaic, while making it possible to focus on particular ways of using images.[14] An awareness of the particular images used by a philosophical community is the key to understanding its imagi-

9. Ibid., p. 4.

10. Ibid.

11. She cites Plato's fable of Atlantis. Ibid., p. 18.

12. Le Dœuff, "Utopias: Scholarly," p. 444.

13. *The Philosophical Imaginary*, p. 19. A number of philosophers have noted some similarities between Le Dœuff's work and that of Jacques Derrida in "White Mythology: Metaphor in the Text of Philosophy," in *Margins of Philosophy*, trans. Alan Bass (Chicago: Chicago University Press, 1982), pp. 207–271. While they clearly share an interest in the functioning of metaphor in philosophical texts, Derrida is more concerned with metaphors in the context of theories of metaphor and understanding the way abstraction veils metaphors, whereas Le Dœuff has an interest in the workings of a range of images, often extended ones, in relation to philosophers' projects.

14. The relationship between images and concepts is rarely discussed in philosophy. However, many philosophers have discussed the relationship between concept and metaphor, which is often confused with other tropes. There are two views about the relation between concept and metaphor in philosophy. One, common in the history of philosophy, as we have seen, is that the concept is opposed to metaphor and should be kept pure of contamination by it. At the other extreme is the early Nietzschean idea that we must dissolve the concept/metaphor distinction. Friedrich Nietzsche, "On Truth and Falsity in Their Ultramoral Sense," in *Early Greek Philosophy and Other Essays*, trans. Maximilian A. Mügge (New York: Russell and Russell, 1964), p. 180. Le Dœuff's position is between these two extremes.

nary, an idea which will become clearer through my examination of Le Dœuff's views concerning philosophical images and her method of analyzing particular images.

Le Dœuff has been taken to task for not being sufficiently systematic in her approach to the philosophical imaginary. For example, Meaghan Morris finds Le Dœuff's refusal to offer a theory of the imaginary or to give a definition of an image, in a collection of essays on the philosophical imaginary, "surprising."[15] However, Morris admits in the paragraphs that follow that this refusal allows Le Dœuff greater flexibility in what she chooses to discuss as well as in her methodology, because it allows movement between pictorial, rhetorical, and psychoanalytic themes. Nevertheless, the criticism might produce a nagging doubt for some readers concerning whether a refusal to define terms and systematically regulate them is a sign of a failure, or inability to systematically discuss important theoretical questions. In my view, discussions of philosophical imaginaries need not involve a *theory* of the imaginary as such. If images, imagery, and the imaginary are defined and precise instructions as to how to read imagery given, a tightly controlled regime of questions is set up. Projects for understanding philosophical imaginaries would be weakened by succumbing to the expectation of a unifying theory of the image and the imaginary. Each reading of an image would have to follow much the same structure. Only a closed philosophy would set up such a theoretical structure in which each image would become simply an illustration of the theory. Le Dœuff's notion of an open-ended philosophy, rather than one that only tolerates certain kinds of philosophical work, or is closed in the sense of being a "boy's club," also provides a useful way of thinking about the relation between feminism and philosophy, which is another important question that Morris raises.

Morris asks how Le Dœuff's work can be seen as feminist when she does not write in a feminine style and she does not raise explicitly feminist issues in all of her essays.[16] In *The Philosophical Imaginary,* only two of the essays— "Long Hair, Short Ideas" and "Pierre Roussel's Chiasmas"—deal with obviously feminist issues. Yet such a varied approach is consonant with the project of open-ended philosophy. If it is important not to foreclose on questions before they are posed, one should not be constrained to write in a particular way or to always pursue the same themes. The idea of open-ended philosophy allows different approaches in different contexts, encourages exchanges with other disciplines, and does not dictate a set of views. As Elizabeth Grosz puts it when she describes this aspect of Le Dœuff's project:

15. Meaghan Morris, "Operative Reasoning: Reading Michèle Le Dœuff," in *The Pirate's Fiancée* (London: Verso, 1988), p. 79.

16. Ibid., pp. 74–76.

"This is a profoundly feminist gesture insofar as only such a notion of philosophy will enable it to accept whatever contributions feminism may offer without pre-empting what either may find useful in the other."[17] Thus, it is possible to write in a way relevant to feminist concerns without always writing on women philosophers, or recognizably feminist topics. Le Dœuff believes that these approaches, as well as research on the history of philosophy, are valuable. For her, feminist philosophy "tends to take the form of exploratory thinking rather than assuming the role of an agency of control or 'fountainhead' of insight or principles that secondary and derived forms of thought may make use of."[18] As such, she thinks it is an excellent example of the type of open-ended philosophy she recommends we pursue. This approach can be contrasted to the way philosophers have often developed their thought.

Le Dœuff's View of Images

Le Dœuff observes that throughout the history of philosophy, when philosophers define philosophical discourse, they refer to "the rational, the concept, the argued, the logical, the abstract."[19] Furthermore, they define philosophy specifically in opposition to stories, descriptions, literature, and myth. Nevertheless, as we have already seen, one finds many metaphors, word-pictures, stories, and examples in philosophical works. Le Dœuff describes a number of strategies that philosophers have used to explain away these phenomena. One recourse has been to say that the images are merely decorative, that they can be ignored without detriment to the argument.[20] Other strategies are more complex: Le Dœuff argues that the "shameful side of philosophy" (the imagery in philosophy) is projected on to an Other, and that the occurrence of images in philosophy can be sent either upstream or downstream. The downstream variant (the didactic/pedagogic) is where the use of imagery is seen as an adaptation of philosophy for students. The imagery is supposed to speak directly and clearly to the student who does not yet understand concepts or know philosophy.

The upstream hypothesis is that images are the result of "the resurgence of a primitive soul,"[21] the child or the irrational in the philosopher coming

17. Elizabeth Grosz, *Sexual Subversions: Three French Feminists* (Sydney: Allen and Unwin, 1989), p. 228.
18. Le Dœuff, "Modern Life," *New Left Review* 199 (1993): 135.
19. *The Philosophical Imaginary*, p. 1. Le Dœuff mentions Hegel, in particular, as a proponent of this position.
20. Peter Ramus (1515–1572) is the best known exponent of this position. See Warner for a discussion of Ramist views of rhetoric.
21. Ibid., p. 6.

to the surface. The paradigms of this projected Other are the child, nursery stories, the "people," old wives' tales, and folklore. For example, Louis Coutu-rat claims that the irrational will always "enchant what there is of the common people in us,"[22] and it should be repudiated, as does Plato, Hegel, Emile Brehier, and Condillac. Her criticism of *both* the upstream and downstream explanations of the role of images is that they deny the image the status of a proper element in philosophical work, and assume an idea of the Other, of "the people which lives off legends,"[23] completely distinct from the learned, the philosophers, who define themselves in opposition to those common people.

Le Dœuff argues against the prevailing views of imagery in philosophy and provides a "critique of the allegedly complete rationality of theoretical work."[24] In contrast, she believes that the images used in philosophy are necessary for the development of projects, so a history of philosophy that ignores these images is incomplete. By examining her methodology, I will show the importance of analyzing specific imagery to grasping the philosophical imaginary.

Le Dœuff's Methodology

Le Dœuff begins her studies with a hypothesis concerning the functioning of imagery in philosophical texts, which she divides into the narrow version, where the imagery is related to a difficulty, and the broad version, where the imagery is related to a contradiction.

(1) The narrow version is that the interpretation of imagery in philosophical texts is necessarily united with the search for points of tension in a work: "imagery is inseparable from the difficulties, the sensitive points of an intellectual venture."[25]

(2) The broad version involves the idea that the "meaning conveyed by images works both for and against the system that deploys them." The images work for the system, because they are able to supply something that is needed for the system to work that it is unable to provide itself. Imagery may smooth over problems, close gaps, and/or cover a contradiction. However, images also work against the system, for what Le Dœuff says is almost the same reason—"their meaning is incompatible with the system's possibilities."[26] Images are able to do this because they are ambiguous enough to

22. Ibid., p. 7.
23. Ibid., p. 6.
24. Ibid., p. 2.
25. Ibid., p. 3.
26. Ibid.

convey two different or even opposing ideas. She claims that her most important work on the philosophical imaginary goes on somewhere between the narrow and broad versions of her hypothesis—between finding a difficulty and finding a contradiction. This hypothesis is a useful starting point, and I will show that recognizing a tension or difficulty in the text helps us to understand all of the images of analytic philosophy discussed in this book.

In *The Philosophical Imaginary*, the readings which Le Dœuff gives of the different images vary considerably, according to the intended use of the image. While her readings of Kant and Descartes focus on foundational metaphors, her essay on More concerns a literary description of an island, and her essay on women's relation to philosophy, "Long Hair, Short Ideas," discusses the history of philosophy and a number of imaginary portraits of "woman," for example, woman as dark continent, or emblem of disorder.

Le Dœuff notes that an understanding of the fundamental symbolic meaning of an image is a crucial starting-point for any analysis of the role images play in philosophy, as in her discussion of Descartes's imagery, and that of More's island utopia. For example, it can be noted that a house may signify shelter or that a crescent shape is like a stage. From here it is important to relate the meaning to the thought in the work, so that one can understand the difficulty or tension that the image is covering up. Le Dœuff argues that, given that images are so useful in the text, and so much a part of it, we can hypothesize that they are in fact "made to measure." Close readings of particular images are the most important elements of her understanding of a specifically philosophical imaginary.

Le Dœuff outlines a method for reading images that she describes as "a concluding appraisal designed to help outline a program for further work."[27] As my aim in this book is to extend these techniques of reading to a very different field, it is appropriate to treat this method as a series of suggestions rather than a fixed template. Le Dœuff concedes that the order outlined is not a necessary one, and that understanding of the images lies at the intersection of the different paths of investigation. She notes that the approach must be "a combination of a traditionally textual approach and a sociological one."[28] For her, there are four stages or complementary ways of looking at the image: noting the way images are derived, finding the instances of the image, tracing its source, and structural analysis. Le Dœuff's reading of a striking passage from Immanuel Kant's *Critique of Pure Reason,* in which he describes an imaginary island of truth, will enable me to draw out a number

27. Ibid., p. 7.
28. Ibid., p. 4.

of important points that can help us to understand the workings of images in analytic philosophy. This is the passage from Kant:

> We have now not merely explored the territory of pure understanding, and carefully surveyed every part of it, but have also measured its extent, and assigned to everything its rightful place. This domain is an island, enclosed by nature itself within unalterable limits. It is the land of truth—enchanting name!—surrounded by a wide and stormy ocean, the native home of illusion, where many a fog bank and many a swiftly melting iceberg give the deceptive appearance of farther shores, deluding the adventurous seafarer with empty hopes, and engaging him in enterprises which he can never abandon and yet is unable to carry to completion. Before we venture on this sea, to explore it in all directions and to obtain assurance whether there be any ground for such hopes, it will be well to begin by casting a glance upon the map of the land which we are about to leave, and to enquire, first, whether we cannot in any case be satisfied with what it contains—are not, indeed, under compulsion to be satisfied, inasmuch as there may be no other territory upon which we can settle; and secondly, by what title we possess even this domain, and can consider ourselves as secured against all opposing claims. Although we have already given a sufficient answer to these questions in the course of the Analytic, a summary statement of its solutions may nevertheless help to strengthen our conviction, by focusing the various considerations in their bearing on the questions now before us.[29]

The stages of Le Dœuff's reading are as follows:

(1) The first stage is to note the "mark of denial carried by thought in images."[30] The precise way the image is presented by the philosopher reveals the intended function of the image. Among others, one possible function is the explanation of ideas to the novice philosopher. Le Dœuff observes that in the passage Kant claims that he will only be repeating what has already been established, but in fact he goes on to say something new—to give the justification of his project. This circumscribed land of truth is the understanding achieved by Kant's own work in the Transcendental Analytic. It is secured within limits, safe, and free from deluding fogs and life-threatening icebergs. According to Le Dœuff, this complex metaphorical passage provides a rationale for his critique of philosophy and his provision of a basis for the sciences through his own philosophy. One of the purposes of this image is to introduce into the text Kant's understanding of his project. Le Dœuff says that there is a second mark of (unintentional) denial in Kant's reference to enchantment or seduction in describing the island ("the land

29. Kant, p. 257; A236/B295.
30. Le Dœuff, p. 8.

of truth—enchanting name!"). As Le Dœuff dryly points out, "to announce a seduction is also to denounce it—and enjoy dispensation to let the seduction work, 'even so'."[31] Kant wants his readers to be seduced by the land of pure understanding, although he also suggests that we may be under a compulsion to be satisfied with it.

(2) The second stage is to investigate whether the image is an isolated feature in the text, or whether the same image is used in similar and different ways in other parts of the philosopher's work. In Kant's case, Le Dœuff finds that there are many islands in his work, and also that there is a "system of opposition between islands in the South which must be abandoned and islands in the North which must not be left."[32] For example, the land of truth can be contrasted with the island of the South Seas of "Speculative Beginning of Human History" where life would be whiled away in indolence or play, a life that Kant insists "man" could never be satisfied with.[33] This stage involves finding the distinctive traits of the image in a text by comparing the roles it plays in various places.

(3) The third stage is the "stage of erudition." Le Dœuff points out that it is necessary to trace the source of the image, which may be found in an earlier philosophical work, or some other text, such as the Bible.[34] This places the image in a historical context and makes our understanding of the image's meaning clearer. In this case she finds the precedent for Kant's island of truth in Francis Bacon's work, where he says, "'Indeed, if political conditions and projects had not put an end to these mental trips, these mariners would have touched on many another shore of error. For the island of truth is surrounded by a mighty ocean in which many an intelligence will drown in storms of illusion'."[35] This stage prepares the ground for the fourth stage.

(4) Le Dœuff describes this stage—of structural analysis—as first the discovery of the "sensitive or problematical point the image bears on,"[36] and second as the reinsertion of the original question that the image evades. She sees the quote from Bacon's *The Great Instauration*,[37] which Kant adds to the second edition of the *Critique of Pure Reason,* as pointing to that question. In relation to Kant's island, she argues that Kant can no longer claim, as Bacon could, that the sciences need the assistance of philosophy to establish a base, because the sciences are well under way, and this is the tension or difficulty

---

31. Ibid., p. 8.
32. Ibid., p. 9.
33. Kant, *Perpetual Peace and Other Essays,* trans. Ted Humphrey (Indianapolis: Hackett, 1983), p. 59.
34. See Le Dœuff, p. 94.
35. Quoted in ibid., p. 9.
36. Ibid., p. 10.
37. Bacon, *The Philosophical Works of Francis Bacon,* ed. John Robertson (London: Routledge, 1905), p. 247.

for him. Nevertheless, Kant wants "to establish the conviction that we should fix our dwelling in the land of understanding, and prevent the understanding, which has at last applied itself to its proper, empirical employment, from wandering off elsewhere,"[38] and the metaphor works to form this conviction by implying that without critical philosophy we will be lost in the cold sea of illusion.

An extremely important point about the functioning of imagery comes out of her analysis. Le Dœuff sees Kant's claims as to what might befall the understanding as rather arbitrary, and concludes that: "images are the means by which every philosophy can engage in straight-forward dogmatization, and decree a 'that's the way it is' without fear of counter-argument, since it is understood that a good reader will by-pass such 'illustrations'—a convention which enables the image to do its work all the more effectively."[39] This claim addresses the rhetorical force of images. The idea is that there is something about the use of images that invites or seduces the acceptance of the reader, because intelligent people are expected to avoid examining them. In accepting the image, we also accept the argument. For example, who would respond to Kant's image of the island of truth by saying, "No, I want to be on the wide, cold and stormy sea, confused by the fog of illusion"—thereby implying that they are not interested in understanding and careless about their own destruction? Le Dœuff says that the images' "most primary promise is to make an end of problems of frustration and fear,"[40] although perhaps it is also offering the ascetic pleasures of renunciation.

An implication of Le Dœuff's reading is that in order to criticize the argument fully, we need to provide a critique of, or alternative to, the image. In this case, she points out that with Kant's imaginary we avoid the fogs only by "renouncing the dream of discovery, the call of new lands, and hope."[41] This reading may be a little strong, given that Kant says "*Before* we venture on this sea" [emphasis added] we should look around the island. Nevertheless, he does not make further exploration appealing, so creating an image or metaphor around the idea of discovery and the enrichment that can be gained by venturing across the seas would then be a good way to respond. New images can play a constructive role in developing new ideas.[42]

This analysis also reveals what is specifically philosophical about the image. Although there are many images of islands in everyday life, surely only a phi-

38. Le Dœuff, p. 11.
39. Ibid., p. 12.
40. Ibid., p. 13.
41. For this reason, Le Dœuff refers to the island as the "island of castration." Ibid., p. 12.
42. For a good example of Le Dœuff's recognition of the creative role of imagery, see her chapter on Galileo's shift to making the dimension of time pivotal in scientific understanding, "Galileo or the Supreme Affinity of Time and Movement." Ibid., pp. 29–44.

losopher would talk about an island of truth, and only Kant would use the island image to convey what he has achieved in the Transcendental Analytic. Le Dœuff also sees the image as appealing to a group of scholars already marked by the discipline of education. The image is an emblem of this aspect of the imaginary, and recognizing the specificity of the image is an essential part of understanding it. Images are united with the tensions, difficulties, and contradictions in the philosophers' work, and they can also work persuasively and dogmatically, seducing the reader to accept the philosopher's view without question, because good readers are supposed not to pay much attention to images.[43] By using images in this way, the philosopher can both distract attention *and* elicit agreement. Kant himself claims that examples and illustrations "are necessary only from a *popular* point of view; and this work can never be made suitable for popular consumption. Such assistance is not required by genuine students of the science."[44] It should be noted that the images of analytic philosophy challenge the view that all images are intended to be passed over by the reader, although their significance is still downplayed.

Cartesian Metaphors

Le Dœuff's analysis of Kant points to one of her primary concerns: foundational images and their self-justifying nature. Among the important examples of foundational images that Le Dœuff discusses are Descartes's metaphors of knowledge as a tree with roots and branches, and of morality as a lodging place. She examines the connection between these images and what has seemed to be a fairly trivial, commonplace claim that Descartes formulated a provisional morality in the *Discourse on the Method*, something temporary and destined to be replaced. Yet this is a "mistake," because what Descartes actually says about his morality is that it is a morality *"par provision,"* a juridical term meaning "what a judgment awards in advance to a party," a first installment, capable of completion, that will not be taken away.[45]

Le Dœuff asks the question of how we can make sense of this commonplace "mistake." Descartes says his moral code consists of "three or four" maxims. They are: to obey the laws and customs of my country; to be firm and resolute in my actions; and to try to master myself rather than fortune, and to change my desires rather than the world, and to "devote my whole

---

43. Ibid., p. 12.

44. Kant, *Critique of Pure Reason*, p. 13; A xviii.

45. Le Dœuff, p. 62. Though it also could be overridden, in a sense, according to Anthony David's explanation which is that the final judgment could go against the party. See his paper, "Le Dœuff and Irigaray on Descartes," *Philosophy Today* 41 (1997): 368.

life to cultivating my reason, and advancing as far as I could in the knowledge of the truth."[46] The nature of Descartes's maxims could be one explanation of commentators' and translators' tendency to think of them as provisional. Le Dœuff notes that commentators have complained that Descartes
does not mention any duties worthy of the name.[47] She says that there are
two possible readings of Descartes's work. One is blinkered and meticulous,
showing what is wrong with the "provisional morality" interpretation. Accepting morality as "*par provision*," we can say that Descartes is content to live
by his maxims and that they enable him to spend his life gaining further
knowledge, as he wishes. One can add that morals are not certain in the way
that metaphysics are, but their certainty is sufficient for conduct.[48]

The second reading, which Le Dœuff prefers, is global: it takes Descartes's
metaphors into account and shows that he is not an entirely innocent party
to the interpretive mistake. Her reading here connects the interpretation of
his work with a debate in France around 1880 focusing on the need to teach
morality to schoolchildren. At the time, the pedagogues argued that there
is a common morality suitable for such teaching and therefore philosophical understandings of morality are irrelevant. Philosophers' response to this
challenge was to rule Descartes's morality invalid. This approach necessitated
calling his maxims provisional in order to reinstate the idea that philosophy
must legislate over morals, thereby implying that Descartes's morality is
non-philosophical. Le Dœuff argues that the historians of philosophy could
not accept that a philosopher had put morality in the extra-philosophical
domain, as the teachers had done.[49] Their view, apparently, was that
Descartes's morality was insufficiently philosophical, so it would have to be
replaced by a different one in order to be considered philosophical. One can
say that ideology influences these philosophers' re-reading of Descartes: they
are trying to assert their authority over the domain of morality.

Le Dœuff hypothesizes that: "there is a historical link of both contagion
and opposition between the politico-pedagogues' philosophy and the in-
vestment (in the mode of miscomprehension) by the historians of philosophy of a hitherto neglected aspect of Descartes's philosophy."[50] Nevertheless, there are ways in which Descartes contributes to the confusion. First, he
indulges in a series of evasions: he calls his morals imperfect in *The Principles* (1644) (though this could be compatible with their being a first install-

46. Prior to setting out his moral code, he says that trying to reform public institutions is
akin to knocking down a whole city and starting again from scratch. Descartes, *Philosophical Writings*, vol. 1, p. 117.
47. Le Dœuff, p. 78.
48. Ibid., p. 68.
49. Ibid., p. 79.
50. Ibid.

ment); he claims that he never wrote on morals (1646); that regulating the behavior of others is the business of sovereigns and their officers, not philosophers (1647); and that he needs public aid with the expense (1644).[51] Le Dœuff observes wryly: "So there was once a philosopher who refused to deal exactly with morals, for lack of public funding."[52] She accounts for these evasions by expressing the view that "Descartes can say nothing on morals because his system excludes any possibility of an ethics in the traditional sense of the term."[53] How one views this issue partly depends on how one takes "traditional sense of the term." If one means by this a set of principles or categorical imperatives, it is clear that Descartes does not attempt to put forward such a system. Le Dœuff argues that ethics cannot be established on a basis of certainty, so the reason Descartes cannot formulate an ethics is his insistence that all knowledge has to be based on certainty.[54] Her view will become clearer if we look at her discussion of Descartes's metaphors, which she believes allow for, even encourage, the interpretation of his morality as provisional.

Le Dœuff notes that Descartes's house and tree metaphors are borrowed and commonplace and asks, "How can a metaphoric mode undergo transformation while on the road, even in the course of a single text, and what does this transformation indicate? Next, from what language is it borrowed?"[55] She says that the two metaphors, the house and the tree, are interchangeable, as Descartes uses to the same effect, for example, the images of knocking down and uprooting, building and cultivating(the source for both is the Gospel according to Matthew, chapter 7.) Here is the passage where Descartes's house is projected: "Now, before starting to rebuild your house, it is not enough simply to pull it down, to make provision for materials and architects (or else train yourself in architecture), and to have carefully drawn up the plans; you must also provide yourself with some place where you can live comfortably while building is in progress."[56] In Descartes's hands, the dwelling becomes a provisional lodging. It is not a matter of its having weak or solid foundations, or being built on rock or sand, as it is in the Bible.[57] This transformation makes ethics seem compatible with episte-

---

51. Ibid., pp. 88–90. Le Dœuff says that suggesting to Elizabeth of Bohemia that they read Seneca together, when she wishes to discuss morals, is also an evasion.

52. Ibid., p. 90.

53. Ibid., p. 91.

54. Vance G. Morgan argues that Descartes is able to avoid this problem through his distinction between two types of certainty, metaphysical and moral. Morgan, *Foundations of Cartesian Ethics* (Atlantic Highlands: Humanities Press, 1994), pp. 27–30.

55. Le Dœuff, p. 92.

56. Descartes, vol. 1, p. 122. Descartes compares the benefit of what comes last of all (morals) with the fruit of a tree, which gives the most benefit. Descartes, p. 186.

57. Descartes does write, however, in the *Discourse* that "I compared the moral writings of the ancient pagans to very proud and magnificent palaces built only on sand and mud." Descartes, p. 114.

mology. Since ethics does not have to rely on certainty or a solid foundation, but rather on its degree of comfort, it is possible to consider it separately from epistemology. The tree, in the preface to *Principles of Philosophy*, is described like this: "the whole of philosophy is like a tree. The roots are metaphysics, the trunk is physics, and the branches emerging from the trunk are all the other sciences, which may be reduced to three principal ones, namely medicine, mechanics and morals. By 'morals' I understand the highest and most perfect moral system, which presupposes a complete knowledge of the other sciences and is the ultimate level of wisdom."[58] The tree promises a morality out of the totality of knowledge. Yet this tree, where morality is both a branch and the result of the branches, cannot be drawn, and morality is supposed to be both a fundamental branch of knowledge and an outgrowth of other knowledge.[59]

Le Dœuff's argument is that Descartes's use of the house and tree metaphors, with their biblical sources, is an act of redemption and nostalgia, intended to restore the ancient idea of philosophy as wisdom. Furthermore, she argues, the question of morality introduces disorder into the metaphors and the text. Le Dœuff concludes that a text is not wholly innocent of the blunders which commentators make about it. Moreover, our re-readings transform the text for our own purposes. She notes that Descartes's comments on morality in the *Discourse* are relatively neglected, partly due to the perception of them as provisional, which is promoted by the image of the shelter. This reading shows how important it is to take the images of philosophy seriously as part of understanding and interpreting philosophical work.

In these analyses of Kant's and Descartes's images, Le Dœuff concerns herself primarily with foundational metaphors. Foundational metaphors encapsulate the fundamental presuppositions of philosophers' projects in spite of the fact that they are also common metaphors found in everyday speech and literature, and thus are very likely to be read as mere pedagogic devices. Le Dœuff's interest in these kind of fundamental images is related to her idea that philosophy creates its own myths around basic metaphors as part of a self-founding or self-justifying enterprise, and that these kind of images are about philosophy itself. In her view, no discourse can be self-founding. Analyses of foundational metaphors enable us to critically assess the fundamental projects of the philosophers, their texts, and their philosophical milieu. Nevertheless, Le Dœuff also shows that other kinds of images do important philosophical work.

58. Ibid., p. 186.
59. Vance G. Morgan accounts for the problem of morality being dependent on complete knowledge of the sciences by noting the organic nature of the tree, so that morals grow with the growth of science. Morgan, pp. 24–25. However, he does not consider the problem of how morals can be both a branch and the fruit.

Images in Existentialism

Other aspects of Le Dœuff's style of analysis emerge in her book, *Hipparchia's Choice,* which is written in the form of four notebooks ranging over a series of topics. In contrast to foundational metaphors like Kant's island of truth, she discusses some isolated images and examples in Jean-Paul Sartre's work, which she relates to Sartre's overall project, and a general theme concerning his attitude towards women. Le Dœuff argues that Sartre is asserting his authority as a philosopher over women and other men, which he couches in terms of virile metaphors. Her view is that Sartre uses women as a paradigm example of the Other in order to cover up the weak points in his system with respect to his theory of knowledge and metaphysics.

Sartre uses the commonplace metaphors of knowledge as seeing, but makes them peculiarly his own by connecting them with aggressive sexual metaphors. His assumption is that knowledge is a type of appropriative vision, best understood in terms of sexual appropriation. He says that "What is seen is possessed; to see is to *deflower*"[60] and that "Knowledge is at one and the same time a *penetration* and a *superficial* caress"[61] and argues that the scientist "is the hunter who surprises a white nudity and who violates it by looking at it."[62] For Le Dœuff, the view implied by these metaphors could hardly have been upheld as serious epistemology even in 1943, given that knowledge needs to be understood as a process, yet what is remarkable is that it was passed over without comment for many years. She believes that this understanding of the subject of knowledge as raping the object of knowledge, represented as a white woman, is connected with Sartre's use of sliminess and holes as representations of an eternal feminine.

Another excruciating example of Sartre's metaphors is: "The obscenity of the feminine sex is that of everything which 'gapes open'. It is an *appeal to being,* as all holes are. In herself woman appeals to a strange flesh which is to transform her into a fullness of being through penetration and dissolution."[63] In Le Dœuff's view, it is not enough to regard these images as the incredible outpourings of Sartre's idiosyncratic fantasies. We also need to understand the way they function in his metaphysics. These images of the eternal feminine help to set up an ontological hierarchy between women as the "In-itself" (the non-conscious aspect of Being) which the male "For-itself" (consciousness) must overcome.

60. Jean-Paul Sartre, *Being and Nothingness,* trans. Hazel E. Barnes (New York: Pocket Books, 1956), p. 738.
61. Ibid., p. 740.
62. Ibid., p. 738.
63. Ibid., p. 782.

Le Dœuff connects these images with female characters who appear as examples in Sartre's phenomenological analyses when the topic is sexuality. One of the female figures in *Being and Nothingness* is the "frigid" woman, a figure who is taken from case studies by the psychiatrist Stekel, and used to justify the concept of bad faith, the intellectual mistake of denying our own freedom and responsibility. According to Sartre's reading of Stekel, the frigid woman is in bad faith or lying to herself because, her husband reports, she shows objective signs of pleasure during sex. In one sense the example shores up Sartre's system by exemplifying bad faith, and enabling Sartre to contrast the bad faith of the frigid woman with the authenticity of those who recognize and affirm what is really going on (the husband, Stekel, Sartre). However, the details of the example, especially the reference to objective signs of pleasure, undermine Sartre's primary thesis that it is the individual who chooses how to understand their experience. For Sartre (usually), even a headache is something we can choose to accept or reject. Furthermore, Le Dœuff argues, the very notion of an *objective* sign is an anomaly, because a sign, being a pointer to something else, needs to be interpreted. The discrepancy between Sartre's description of the "frigid" woman and his overall position on experience and objectivity serves to back up Le Dœuff's view that philosophers abandon their usual philosophical standards whenever the topic is women.[64] This abandonment of standards can be seen in these examples, as well as the way in which they support aspects of Sartre's system.

Le Dœuff argues that it is "the mediation of imaginary elements which makes it possible to formulate pairs of opposites such as 'bad faith/authenticity' or to carry out operations such as 'the integration of the In-itself by the For-itself'" [the incorporation of the object by the knower].[65] Thus the particular products of Sartre's imaginary are related to the philosophical concepts in his work. Le Dœuff believes that Sartre displays a good example of what she calls a "macho" imaginary, characterized by the megalomania of the male philosopher. The philosophical imaginary is not necessarily always "macho," but it is a feature that occurs all too frequently, and is always connected with an attempt to assert philosophical dominance and the maintenance of a closed system.

This analysis of Sartre's existentialism should be seen beside Le Dœuff's challenge to what for a long time almost constituted the orthodoxy about Beauvoir: that she simply took Sartre's views and applied them to women. In her paper, "Simone de Beauvoir and Existentialism," and in *Hipparchia's*

64. *Hipparchia's Choice*, p. 70.
65. Ibid., p. 88.

Choice, Le Dœuff discusses the relation between Beauvoir's thought and Sartre's. She notes that in *The Second Sex* there appears to be "a curious mixture" between the provision of "a *detailed* and *precise* consciousness of women's oppression" and the use of a "whole conceptual apparatus that is now a trifle obsolete"—existentialism.[66] Contrary to those who claim that Beauvoir naively adopted existentialism,[67] Le Dœuff argues that she subverts the framework of existentialism and transforms it into a point of view, rather than a metaphysic or system, by undermining some of its major tenets. On the one hand, existentialism is a useful tool for Beauvoir to expose the oppression of women as strange, unnatural, and unjustified. It can perform this function because one of the fundamental theses of existentialism is that there is no human essence, only existence, and thus there can be no justification for oppression based on biology, psychoanalysis, or any other such theory. Le Dœuff argues that, on the other hand, Beauvoir makes three fundamental transformations of existentialist thought as expressed by Sartre. The first is that she overcomes the limitations of the concepts of woman as object and the Other. The second is that she makes it possible to theorize oppression by taking into account women's concrete situation, which could not consistently be done within Sartre's system. Beauvoir's third achievement, most relevant in this context, is that she eliminates the Sartrean images of the female body as "holes and slime."

As Le Dœuff notes, the view presented in *The Second Sex* has been a stimulus for feminists around the world, as it has helped to show the nature of women's oppression, something that a theory which is a mere application of the concepts of *Being and Nothingness* to women would be incapable of doing. It is interesting to note that Beauvoir also uses Stekel's work on frigid women, in *The Second Sex,* but to very different effect from Sartre, because she is interested in women's experience of sexuality.[68] The stark contrast between the two different authors' use of the same material is, Le Dœuff argues

66. Le Dœuff, "Simone de Beauvoir and Existentialism," *Feminist Studies* 6, no. 20 (1980): 277.

67. See, for example, Jean Grimshaw, who refers to Sartre as Beauvoir's "philosophical mentor" in Feminist Philosophers (Brighton: Wheatsheaf Books, 1986), p. 118; Charlene Haddock Seigfried, "Gender Specific Values," *Philosophical Forum* 15 (1984): 434; and Judith Okeley, *Simone de Beauvoir: A Re-reading* (London: Virago, 1986), p. 77. In more recent years, there have been a range of more nuanced readings of the direction of influence and on Beauvoir's work, such as Margaret A. Simons, *Beauvoir and The Second Sex: Feminism, Race, and the Origins of Existentialism* (Lanham: Rowman and Littlefield, 1999); Debra B. Berghoffen, *The Philosophy of Simone de Beauvoir: Gendered Phenomenologies, Erotic Generosities* (Albany: State University of New York Press, 1997); Karen Vintges, *Philosophy as Passion: The Thinking of Simone de Beauvoir* (Bloomington: Indiana University Press, 1996); and Toril Moi, *Simone de Beauvoir: The Making of an Intellectual Woman* (Oxford: Blackwell, 1996).

68. Beauvoir, *The Second Sex,* trans. H. M. Parshley (Harmondsworth: Penguin, 1983), pp. 412–414.

in *Hipparchia's Choice,* a function of their different projects.[69] These readings of Beauvoir's and Sartre's work show that Le Dœuff's analysis extends beyond the commonplace and foundational metaphors of her readings of Kant and Descartes. A mode of reading images needs to be also versatile enough to suggest how we could understand images other than metaphors and extended metaphors, and also images which are more idiosyncratic than classical. Le Dœuff's work goes some way towards providing this necessity.

Philosophy

The critical nature of these analyses of images, combined with Le Dœuff's view that images tend to cover gaps and contradictions, raises a number of questions about the place of images in philosophy and the nature of philosophy itself. As I argued in the Introduction to this book, images are a necessary aspect of language and philosophy, yet we still need to understand the complexities of their role. It is clear that Le Dœuff is not arguing that we should eliminate images from philosophy (even if she thought that this were possible) since they are an important part of philosophical reasoning. In *Hipparchia's Choice,* she says that if all the images and little stories were removed from philosophy, you would not have a pure form of philosophy, but a hollow one. All such a philosophy could say would be, "Look, I am." Furthermore, *no* thought can do without images—such considerations apply not just to philosophy, but to any form of thinking.[70] What she is critical of in Kant, Descartes, Sartre, and others is that they use metaphors to provide a sly self-justification for their philosophical project. For Le Dœuff no discourse can be self-founding, and an approach to the issues about the value of images needs to involve a fresh conception of philosophy.

Le Dœuff's view of philosophy is that it has traditionally been concerned with its borders or limits, its difference from other disciplines, and its specificity. Such a philosophy claims its hegemony over other disciplines: "hegemony is the absolute right of a power to formulate its own difference in comparison with its various others, its own superiority to them, without being challenged."[71] This is philosophy as queen of the sciences, rather

69. Le Dœuff, *Hipparchia's Choice,* pp. 88–92. See also my paper "Simone de Beauvoir and Female Bodies," *Australian Feminist Studies* 20 (1994): 91–106, for a discussion of other ways in which Beauvoir overcomes the misogyny of Sartrean existentialism.

70. Le Dœuff, *Hipparchia's Choice,* p. 169.

71. Le Dœuff, "Ants and Women," p. 52.

than underlaborer.[72] She calls this type of philosophy, exemplified in the work of Kant, Descartes, and Sartre, closed philosophy. Closed philosophy is based on certainty, aims at providing a complete system, determines in advance what form the answers to questions will take, and often uses foundational images. Thus, images are complicit in the practices of closed philosophy.

Le Dœuff says that it is not a coincidence that she formulated her ideas on the philosophical imaginary more clearly through her work on women and/in philosophy, but warns that "The icon of the feminine in philosophical texts is not a universal notion."[73] However, she thinks that the images of women in philosophy have a specificity beyond what they share with the opinions and attitudes of everyday life. For example, she points out that while philosophers have tended to use images of women as emblems of disorder, by contrast, men outside the academy see women as spoil-sports. This view reflects her perspective on the philosophical imaginary in general—that although it is related to the imaginary of everyday life, it has the characteristics of a learned minority.

A perennial problem with images in philosophy is their pernicious use to exclude or denigrate groups such as women, children, non-European ethnic groups, and members of the working class. As we saw above, Le Dœuff demonstrates that Sartre's metaphors and images of women in *Being and Nothingness* both show his misogyny and are used to maintain a closed system. For her, dogmatism is often linked to anti-feminism. Rationality only seems whole when it is associated with an exclusion of those thought incapable of reason or when it is rejected. As noted earlier, she believes that male philosophers' reasoning lacks rigor when it comes to talking about women. One example occurs in Rousseau's *Lettre à d'Alembert sur les spectacles* where in the footnotes he advocates tolerance towards the ideas of others and openness in one's manner of reasoning, but in the text argues that women should be excluded from the clubs where intellectual matters are discussed.[74] Le Dœuff thinks that male philosophers often reiterate the comforting myth that women and other groups cannot philosophize because this makes philosophy seem more impressive in the sense that it is the practice of an elite, exclusive group. "Male rationality" conceives rationality as having an essence in which women do not partake.

As in Sartre's case, it is not men as such who perpetuate the illusion of total rationality, but the machismo or masculinism that arises from a position of power. Such misogyny can often reveal a weakness in the philosophi-

72. John Locke says, "'tis Ambition enough to be employed as an Under-Labourer in clearing Ground a little, and removing some of the Rubbish, that lies in the way to Knowledge." *An Essay Concerning Human Understanding* (Oxford: Oxford University Press, 1979), p. 10.

73. Le Dœuff, *The Philosophical Imaginary*, p. 3.

74. Le Dœuff, "Women, Reason, etc.," *differences: A Journal of Feminist Cultural Studies* 2, no. 3 (1990): 9–12.

cal system itself. One way this can be exposed is by examining images of women in philosophy. Le Dœuff says: "Nobody can object to the presence of myth and fantasy figures as such in philosophy. But I strongly object to the use of 'woman' as a construct of the imagination." [75] She objects because what is said is regularly an insult and is often accepted by readers without question. Traditional philosophy often uses "woman" as a metaphor for disorder and darkness. Yet, as Le Dœuff's work shows, examining other kinds of images can also help us to understand the processes of exclusion. Even Kant's system of opposition between Northern and Southern islands reflects a certain Eurocentric view that true philosophy can only be found and carried out on cold Northern islands.

So how can we respond to the problem of the way images can sometimes exclude important ideas and experiences? Le Dœuff argues that instead of attempting to devise a closed and complete metaphysical system, philosophers should practice "open-ended" philosophy, a philosophy that incorporates work that is being done in other disciplines and does not foreclose a question before it has been posed.[76] An open-ended philosophy may not need foundational metaphors to cover contradictions, as it would not have *fundamental* contradictions of the kind Le Dœuff exposes, and it would not be attempting to provide a new system. She suggests a new metaphor of philosophy—a Brechtian dramaturgy, a play that always has an act missing, so is "left wide open to history."[77] Philosophy has to accept its intrinsic incompleteness, and acknowledge the importance of other disciplines in what should be a collective enterprise. Scrutinizing philosophy can knock it off its pedestal. Her practice of philosophy follows this prescription, in that her use of the essay form enables her to discuss the philosophical imaginary and the relation of women to philosophy without presupposing a grand metaphysical system. Allied to this acceptance of the lack at the heart of philosophy is Le Dœuff's reconception of rationality as a dynamics or process which is on-going and fluid, not a capacity which we either do or do not have, or a measurable quantity. What is needed is the rational effort, within a limited range, to understand, explain things, and make them clearer.[78] The idea of an open-ended philosophy is particularly influential on my approach to understanding the analytic imaginary. By discussing how Le Dœuff's methodology works in relation to specific images, I have shown its flexibility, which

75. Le Dœuff, interview with Raoul Mortley in *French Philosophers in Conversation* (London: Routledge, 1991), pp. 86–87.

76. Le Dœuff, *Hipparchia's Choice*, pp. 166–169.

77. Le Dœuff, "Women and Philosophy," in *French Feminist Thought: A Reader*, ed. Toril Moi (Cambridge: Blackwell, 1987), p. 199.

78. Another way in which Le Dœuff exhibits her openness to the thought of others is in engaging critically with the work of her peers, a practice relatively rare among well-known contemporary French thinkers. Moreover, she shows an awareness of work carried out in cognate disciplines and in science, which is reflected in the range of her analyses.

means that it can be fruitfully adapted to different fields. Furthermore, her characterization of the philosophical imaginary gives us a useful guide to which the analytic imaginary can be compared and contrasted.

The Distinctiveness of the Analytic Imaginary

The discussion of the philosophical imaginary so far raises questions concerning the nature of the analytic imaginary as compared with other philosophical imaginaries. The first question is whether Le Dœuff's method is relevant to a range of images, even beyond those types she explicitly discusses. If we look at the expressions she uses to refer to the content of the philosophical imaginary, we find a range of general terms such as images, little stories, fables, the poetic, thinking in images, and reverie, as well as specific tropes, such as metaphors, myths, analogies, and examples. Le Dœuff observes that the attempt to exclude thought in images always fails and gives as an example of the prevalence of images the fact that "Socrates talks about laden asses, blacksmiths, cobblers, tanners."[79] The first point we must note about this collection of philosophical images is how dissimilar they are, so that the analysis which might apply to one type of image will not necessarily apply to another. We should also be clear about the difference between using an example to make a particular point about, say, blacksmiths, and using such an example in a metaphorical or analogical way to make a point about a philosophical problem or issue. Socrates is famous for using analogies between crafts or arts and people's actions in order to show, for example, that we should act morally. But R. G. Collingwood in *Principles of Art*[80] uses similar examples simply to make a distinction between art and craft. These two ways of using images or examples are quite distinct and need different analyses. Le Dœuff's very different readings of different images demonstrate that the variety of images to be found in philosophy constitute a conceptual resource for analysis and understanding.

There are a number of important points that emerge from my reading of Le Dœuff's work that are relevant to understanding the images of contemporary analytic philosophy. One is that images function to distract attention and elicit agreement from the reader, and we will see that this feature of her readings is relevant to the range of images I discuss. In other words, they work on the level of persuasion. Another is the notion that images work to cover difficult areas in a philosophical enterprise. The images of analytic philosophy which are to be examined all show this feature to a greater or lesser ex-

79. *The Philosophical Imaginary*, p. 6.
80. R. G. Collingwood, *Principles of Art* (London: Oxford University Press, 1938).

tent. The kind of difficulty will depend on the particular project at hand and may not involve a contradiction as such. The philosophical work of the images involves their hiding assumptions which might be unacceptable or untenable, thus concealing a difficulty or tension. In that sense, the image functions to enhance the persuasiveness of the work if a close reading to reveal these assumptions is not undertaken. The image, being the site where problematic assumptions can be discovered and explored, can also work against the author once they are analyzed. Images also work to constrain debate and to exclude certain experiences and alternative views. This enables the continuation of an already established philosophic approach and set of questions which together are taken to define the limits of the "properly philosophical" domain. These points relate to the level of enframement. Morris points out that Le Dœuff exposes a number of functions of images, such as forms of innovation in her study of Galileo, nostalgia in the images of the tree and building in Descartes, and legitimation in the essays on Roussel and on images of the feminine.[81] These functions are clearly relevant to the analytic imaginary.

Nevertheless, there are also a number of ways in which the images of analytic philosophy differ from those examined by Le Dœuff. For one thing, these images are not designed to be overlooked by the reader. All are deliberate, or what I call avowed images, meaning that the philosophers concerned allow that they have *some* role to play in their work. Yet in each case, the image plays a more varied and contestable role than is avowed by the philosopher concerned. The image or imaginary anecdote is displayed rather than hidden by the analytical philosopher. Nonetheless, the image can have functions that are not avowed. For example, the use of fantastic thought experiments or counterfactuals as a method of uncovering allegedly necessary conceptual truths serves to distract attention from the precise way in which a story is both told and left untold. Although Le Dœuff argues that images are essential to philosophical thought, she does not discuss the way images vary in relation to the level of expressibility, which is very important to understanding the analytic imaginary.

Some of the images I examine are classically inspired, like the philosophical images Le Dœuff discusses, but others are strikingly eccentric and novel. Not all are foundational in the sense of encapsulating the fundamental presuppositions of the philosopher's projects. My project broadens the scope of inquiry to incorporate other types of images, beyond the analysis of the foundational images of "grand-scale" or systematic philosophy that provide a metaphysical and epistemological structure. Contemporary analytic philosophers do not write works on such a grand scale as Kant or Descartes or even Sartre—often the lack of system-building and the "piece-

81. Morris, p. 85.

meal" nature of analytic work is taken to characterize the field of analytic philosophy. However, the work is a rich and varied source of important analogies, thought experiments, myths, metaphors and models. These kind of images do not function in precisely the same way as foundational images. They are more likely to cover untenable assumptions or tensions rather than a contradiction.

The localized nature of the field of study as well as the way debates are conducted in analytic philosophy means I will trace images forward through specific responses to particular texts rather than backward to their sources outside philosophy. While Le Dœuff does some tracing forward in her essay on Roussel, she is taking a wider historical sweep and showing how the general form of the image appears in various discourses. My tracing will be more limited because of the concentration on a relatively brief historical phenomenon. Alternatively, some understanding of the philosophical antecedents of analytical approaches to questions and theories is necessary. The British empiricists are particularly important to the development of analytic philosophy in this respect, although Kant and Descartes are also influential.

The differing historical context within which analytic philosophy has emerged affects the type of images used and the nature of the analytic imaginary. Like philosophy in general, analytic philosophy both reflects historical changes and transforms its products, such as technology, to suit itself. The increasing professionalization of philosophy leads to the borrowing of images from other professions such as law and science, rather than from a classical education. Furthermore, analytic philosophy's relation to science is not generally one of asserting dominance over science but of feeling that science is paramount and philosophy its ally. An imaginary characterized by this view is less likely to be attempting to legitimate a more dominant role, in the way Le Dœuff detected in Kant. Another strand of analytic philosophy (what has come to be known as ordinary language philosophy) claims that philosophy is merely the articulator of common sense, and only differs from common sense in its level of sophistication. Such an imaginary will clearly differ from that of a philosophy which sees itself in a more creative, active role.

Le Dœuff says that we should combine a traditional textual approach to the reading of images with a sociological one. Her way of proceeding is to read in a way that is adequate to the task at hand, whatever that task happens to be. For example, in her reading of Descartes's images, she connects the interpretation of his work with debates in France about the nature of education. The international nature of analytic philosophy makes this kind of analysis more difficult, though certainly not impossible. My aim in this book is to consider how the images work within the philosophical debates themselves, across national boundaries. Indeed, it may be the very abstract nature of the images, which will become obvious, that makes such internationalization seem possible. Of course, it is only certain Anglophone readers who are part of this internationalization.

One other sociological aspect worthy of note is the issue of pedagogy and the pedagogic role of philosophical images. While I believe that Le Dœuff is right to say that images are not primarily pedagogical, the use of particular kinds of images in specific ways can have a very significant effect on a student's introduction to philosophy. Images introduce and promote ideas considered central and exclude others. By examining textbook examples of analytic imagery, I show how they can at times contribute to the process of marginalization and exclusion of women's experiences and aspects of feminist philosophy, as well as of alternative approaches to the topic. This process often begins when students are introduced to philosophical topics through its images and arises in an obvious way in philosophers' use of thought experiments in personal identity.

A rich understanding of the analytic imaginary can only emerge through the consideration of a variety of examples of images. Even the term "the analytic imaginary" is an extremely broad one. Through the careful examination of different uses of images in different areas of contemporary analytic philosophy, I show how particular images work in specific cases, rather than give a theory of the imaginary applied to analytic philosophy. I use Le Dœuff's suggestions if they are appropriate to a particular image—following the spirit and open-ended style of her work can allow the articulation of some new and interesting observations about the analytic imaginary. This context-sensitive approach will make more subtle and complex Le Dœuff's characterization of the philosophical imaginary as a scholarly imaginary of a learned minority. Readings of the images of analytic philosophy should be open, contextual readings that respond to each particular image and the way it is used philosophically. This way of proceeding can also help to answer questions concerning the exclusion of women and feminist work from contemporary analytic philosophy and how it can be overcome.

2

Analogizing Abortion

Analytic philosophers' use of images extends beyond the tacit appeal to metaphors. In this chapter, I will examine the workings of Judith Jarvis Thomson's "famous violinist" analogy, used in an obvious and forceful way in the abortion debate. Analogies have been used throughout the history of philosophy to further philosophical arguments and to explain important concepts. The analogy considered here is of a particular kind: argument by analogy. Whereas an analogy can be used to explain something unfamiliar in terms of some more familiar thing, an argument by analogy makes an inference from certain similarities between two things to the probability of there being further similarities, in order to provide support for a conclusion. Analogy, as used in philosophical argument, is defined by William L. Reese as "a relation of similarity between two or more things allowing the drawing of a probable or necessary conclusion depending on the kind of relation in question. In general, finding similarities in some respects we reason by analogy that there will be similarities in other respects. If the cases are not sufficiently similar to support the reasoning we have a *false analogy*."[1] The analogue must be similar to the original case in all relevant or important respects in order for the conclusion to be reasonably drawn. Analogies of this kind are very important in ethics, because they can be used to show that if an ethical principle is accepted in one case, then it should be accepted in a relevantly similar case. These kind of analogies have come to prominence

---

1. William L. Reese, *Dictionary of Philosophy and Religion: Eastern and Western Thought* (Atlantic Highlands: Humanities Press, 1980), p. 13.

recently in philosophical debates about abortion. Undoubtedly the most well-known and influential is the "famous violinist" analogy used by Judith Jarvis Thomson in her 1971 article, "A Defense of Abortion."[2] An interesting feature of the analogy is that, as an image, it does not refer back to philosophical precedents; rather, it starts a chain of reworkings within analytic philosophy. Use of this analogy in Thomson's article led to a spate of replies, both sympathetic and antagonistic, which discussed or referred to the analogy. Therefore, I trace the analogy *forward* through the literature, rather than searching for its antecedents, and examine its role in Thomson's argument and the ensuing debate.

The characteristics of the role of philosophical images that emerged from my discussion of philosophical imaginaries in chapter 1 will guide, though not determine, my reading. Each image tends to have specific kinds of roles, both because of the nature of the image itself, and because of the context in which it is used. Thomson's analogy works on several levels. The analogy works forcefully on the level of persuasion, and it also provides a framework within which the debate is constrained. The analogy promotes a discussion couched in terms of self-defense and killing, individual rights, and overriding principles. It introduces a number of assumptions about how we should understand the relation between the fetus and the pregnant woman, about being pregnant, about the body, and about abortion in general. Construing the debate through the analogy leads to a blindness about the distinctiveness of abortion as a moral issue, and obscures a number of tensions concerning issues central to abortion, including conceptions of the self, responsibility, emotions, and the relevance of abortion to women. Furthermore, the features of the analogy itself often lead to a focus on irrelevant details. Importantly, the analogy also reveals a pervasive feature of the analytic imaginary. The use of this analogy, as well as a number of related analogies, excludes ways of reconceptualizing abortion which will be presented in the final section.

The Analogy

The use of this image is as conspicuous as it is covert in the examples discussed by Michèle Le Dœuff. The image is sensational and certainly not designed to be passed over casually, as its presence is forcefully signaled. It is at

---

2. Judith Jarvis Thomson, "A Defense of Abortion," *Philosophy and Public Affairs* 1, no. 1 (1971): 47–66. Thomson also uses a number of other analogies that I will refer to briefly. However, because the violinist analogy is by far the most important, I will concentrate on it.

the center of what can impress the reader as a novel and striking tale, and perhaps it is the novelty of the tale that has given the argument such currency. Thomson imagines a fantastic scenario in the form of an analogy in order to support a particular conclusion about abortion. Her analogy is designed to capture the morally relevant features of a situation where a woman is pregnant and is contemplating abortion. The analogy works as part of an argument by analogy, as in the definition above.[3] Thomson wants to discuss one traditional argument against abortion, based on the premise that the fetus is a person or human being and has a right to life. The theorists who begin with this premise draw from it an intermediate conclusion: that this right to life outweighs the right of the woman to decide what happens to her body.[4] The conclusion which they believe follows from this is that abortions are morally impermissible. Usually, those philosophers who are pro-choice dispute the initial premise of the argument. Thomson's strategy is different in that she proposes to accept the premise that the fetus is a person, but then to demonstrate that the conclusion does not follow. She is trying to show that the fetus's right to life does not lead to the intermediate conclusion that this right outweighs the woman's right. The analogy, which is intended to show that abortions are morally permissible in at least some circumstances, goes like this:

> You wake up in the morning and find yourself back to back with an unconscious violinist. A famous unconscious violinist. He has been found to have a fatal kidney ailment, and the Society of Music Lovers has canvassed all the available medical records and found that you alone have the right blood type to help. They have therefore kidnapped you, and last night the violinist's circulatory system was plugged into yours, so that your kidneys can be used to extract poisons from his blood as well as your own.[5]

The violinist is dependent on you, because if you were unplugged, he would die. The hospital director says it is morally wrong to unplug yourself from him and argues that the violinist's right to life outweighs your right to

3. Thomson's story of the violinist could also be considered a thought experiment or a counter-example, but I think that we can best understand its philosophical role by treating it as part of an argument by analogy. However, it also works as a counterexample, and I will discuss this aspect of its role further on in the chapter.

4. For example, Baruch Brody believes that the fetus's rights outweigh the woman's in every case; except where the fetus is going to die anyway, taking the fetus's life is the only way to save the woman, and killing the woman will not save the fetus. See Baruch Brody, "Thomson on Abortion," *Philosophy and Public Affairs* 1, no. 3 (1972): 339. John Finnis also thinks that fetuses have full human rights from the moment of conception. See Finnis, "The Rights and Wrongs of Abortion: A Reply to Judith Thomson," *Philosophy and Public Affairs* 2, no. 2 (1973): 145.

5. Thomson, p. 49.

decide what happens in and to your body. At first it is only for nine months, but then you are told that you cannot ever be unplugged from the violinist. Now Thomson says: "I imagine you would regard this as outrageous, which suggests that something really is wrong with that plausible-sounding argument I mentioned a moment ago" (the traditional argument against abortion).[6]

After adding that the hospital director informs you that you will die within the month if you remain attached to the violinist, she draws the strong conclusion that: "If anything in the world is true, it is that you do not commit murder, you do not do what is impermissible, if you reach around to your back and unplug yourself from that violinist to save your life."[7] Thomson claims to have established that abortion is permissible in certain cases. This is a typical way in which analytic philosophers attempt to argue the case. Indeed, it is fascinating to note just how many analytic discussions of abortion use arguments by analogy which depend upon the persuasive force of a central image or figure they contain.

We need to examine the analogy closely to understand what it can tell us about the analytic imaginary. An important feature of the analogy is Thomson's use of the second person in the analogy. Her direct address to the reader in the analogy is clearly meant to suggest that it is a situation that *anyone* could find themselves in. It invites the reader to identify with the "you" in the analogy, although an obvious characteristic of pregnancy is that it is unique to women. The philosophical role of the analogy is structured by this address to the reader. It opens the way to ignoring women's experiences of pregnancy, and searching instead for abstract rights and principles, creating a path to the abstract and universalizing nature of the entire debate within the domain of analytic philosophy. All the other elements of the analogy—the violinist, his kidnapping, and so on—have ramifications for the way abortion is understood within the debate. The analogy as a whole covers a number of tensions in such an analysis, distracting attention from these difficulties, and forcing agreement with Thomson's views in particular and liberal views in general.

Compelling Agreement

The analogy works powerfully on the persuasive level—this "violinist" is famous in analytic philosophy. One of the first things to observe about Thomson's approach to the analogy is that she assumes it to reveal certain truths

6. Ibid.
7. Ibid., p. 52.

about abortion that may not otherwise be obvious. She argues that once we recognize the truth in the violinist example, we are compelled to accept the analogous conclusion in the case of abortion: as she says "if anything in the world is true," it is true that abortion is not murder if it is done in order to save your life. The idea is that most readers will think it is morally permissible for "you" to unplug yourself from the violinist. If the violinist analogy is accepted as being similar to abortion in the relevant respects, it follows that one should think that abortion is morally permissible. Thus, it is quite clear how the analogy functions to compel agreement from the reader, an effect which Thomson relies on heavily. Of course, it can only function in this way if we feel definitely that we must be able to unplug ourselves from the violinist. Judging from the responses, most philosophers have found the argument by analogy compelling. However, they have often disagreed with the conclusion, so have found it necessary to declare the analogy false.

Thomson's article is extremely influential.[8] The fact that almost every analytic philosopher who has written on abortion discusses or refers (after its inception) to the violinist analogy gives an excellent gauge of its force. Philosophers who respond to Thomson's article differ widely in their views on the moral status of abortion. However, they share more assumptions about how we should understand abortion than the premise that the fetus is a person. They use the analogy, making major or minor adjustments to it in order to make it a genuine analogy, and to support their conclusions. By tracing the history of these responses we can see how the analogy structures the debate and begin to understand the analytic imaginary.

Self-Defense and Killing

As the analogy shows, Thomson sees abortion as a type of self-defense, at least when a woman's life is in danger. The analogy is constructed to make the unplugging seem to be self-defense against the claims of the violinist. In cases where a woman's life is not in danger, she construes abortion as a type of property right, because she believes that women own their bodies. This concept of property will be discussed in the next section.

A number of philosophers argue against the contention that abortion is self-defense. John Finnis, in his paper, "The Rights and Wrongs of Abortion:

---

8. Some of the philosophers who have discussed Thomson's violinist analogy in their work on abortion include: Baruch Brody, Nancy Davis, John Finnis, R. M. Hare, F. M. Kamm, Rosalind Hursthouse, Catriona Mackenzie, Hugh V. McLachlan, Jeff McMahon, Steven L. Ross, Michael Tooley, and Mary Anne Warren. I will discuss the most important articles in the course of this chapter.

A Reply to Judith Thomson" wants to answer two questions: "whether or not unplugging from the violinist is . . . direct killing" and "whether or not abortion is . . . just like unplugging the captive philosopher from the moribund musician."[9] Finnis's way of describing the problem implies that abortion must be understood in one of two ways: either as self-defense, or as direct killing. Direct killing is where the killing is an end in itself or a means to an end. Yet Thomson, in using the analogy to argue for abortion as self-defense, also implies that the major moral issue in abortion is what type of killing it is. Finnis's strategy is to modify the analogy and use it for his own ends in an important way. It is interesting to note that he has already transformed the analogy to the extent that he treats the violinist as being hooked up to *Thomson* (the "captive philosopher") rather than using the direct address to the reader ("you") that Thomson herself uses. This transposition gives the argument a character that she obviously did not intend. In fact, it makes the argument a personal attack on Thomson's morality.

First, Finnis makes some changes to the analogy so that it will be more ac-curate—in his view. One of the changes he thinks should be made to the analogy to render it more like abortion is that the violinist, before being un-plugged, must be chopped up or killed in some violent way. He claims that to make it properly analogous to abortion, the violinist would have to have been "dead for six hours and had moreover been killed outright, say by drowning or decapitation."[10] Secondly, Finnis argues that the analogy be-tween the unplugging of the violinist and abortion is false, because the "phi-losopher" does the unplugging rather than a third party—for example, a doctor. Thirdly, Finnis asserts that the fetus owns its body as well. He believes that abortion is direct killing and the analogy should be amended to involve direct killing of the violinist by a bystander. Given the changes that he makes to the analogy, it is not surprising that the conclusion he reaches is that abor-tion is immoral.

Although Finnis rejects Thomson's conclusions, he sees it as important to respond in terms of Thomson's analogy, in particular, to decide whether it is a genuine analogy with abortion. Finnis also characterizes *other* people's arguments in terms of how they might respond to Thomson's analogy. Thus, he says Grisez "would, I think, say that Thomson could rightly unplug her-self from the violinist . . . even if 'unplugging' could only be effected by chop-ping the violinist in pieces."[11] Finnis's response to Thomson, in the way it transforms the image for his own purposes, supports Le Dœuff's view that images in philosophy are made to measure. His desire to persuade us that

9. Finnis, p. 125.
10. Finnis, p. 140.
11. Ibid., p. 136.

abortion is impermissible leads him to describe the unplugging of the violinist as a savage act.

Another alteration to the analogy concerned with the nature of killing is made by Baruch Brody. He begins his article, "Thomson on Abortion," with the comment "Professor Thomson unfortunately offers as her counterexample . . . her very problematic account of the violinist."[12] Brody considers Thomson's analogy to be false because abortion is not "a choice between using all or part of a woman's body to save her or the fetus" but a choice between "saving the woman by taking the life of the fetus and not taking the life of the fetus, thereby failing to save the woman."[13] Brody argues that her analogy fails to take proper account of the distinction between the not taking of a life and the saving of a life, and the fact that the duty not to do the former is much stronger than the duty to do the latter.[14] Perhaps he thinks that a more complex analogy needs to be given, to make this distinction more clearly. The distinction is one made famous by the doctrine of double effect, which says that certain evil actions, such as a death, may be acceptable if they occur as an unintended consequence of other actions.[15] The same point is made by those who rely on the distinction between acts and omissions. If this distinction were applied to Thomson's case it would suggest that although the woman has no duty to save the violinist, she does have a duty not to kill the violinist. He also tries to show that an abortion cannot be construed as a case of self-defense, because the fetus is not responsible for threatening the life of the woman.

In the end, Brody's amendment is similar to Finnis's—Thomson should have included murder of the violinist in her analogy. Michael Tooley points out that not all abortions involve direct killing—some, such as where premature labor is induced, could be indirect in that the death of the fetus is neither "a desired end or a means to any end."[16] Thomson herself says that she has only argued for the right to a fetal evacuation. However, the focus on the unplugging of the violinist, and the construal of abortion as self-defense, makes it easier for both Finnis and Brody to assert the opposite.

Brody does not actually commit himself on the case of the violinist, perhaps because he finds its force to be such that if he did, people would find his view less plausible. Tooley concludes that Brody must think it is morally

---

12. Brody, p. 335.

13. Ibid., p. 339.

14. Ibid.

15. A further condition is that the evil effect is not so evil as to outweigh the benefit that it brings about. Euthanasia, for example, is sometimes considered moral according to the doctrine.

16. Michael Tooley, *Abortion and Infanticide* (Oxford: Clarendon Press, 1983), p. 44. The indirectness of the death of the fetus in these cases would mean that abortion can be acceptable in terms of the doctrine of double effect.

wrong for the woman to unplug herself from the violinist, because, in his terms, it is a case of killing.[17] According to Tooley, if Brody accepts that unplugging from the violinist is a case of letting die, and so morally acceptable, he would also have to accept that certain means of abortion are morally permissible, such as drugs that induce miscarriage or premature birth.[18] So the analogy can be used against positions such as Brody's.

Brody's positive view relies on the principle that it is all right to kill someone to save another's life if you think that the first person was going to die anyway, the only situation where he believes an abortion would be permissible. What he takes to be the advantage of his view over one like Thomson's is that "It makes no appeal to any special fact about the fetus, the woman, or their relation"[19] and would apply equally to other situations.

It is significant that what Brody takes to be an improvement on Thomson's analogy is the elimination of any particular connection to abortion. This concern with promoting principles involves the construction of analogies even further removed than Thomson's from abortion, about killing in general.[20] The misleading idea that any position on abortion must be based on a principle that can apply to other situations is sanctioned and promoted by the use of analogies. This idea is further advanced by Thomson's construction of an analogy which attempts to assimilate abortion to self-defense. However, these considerations about the nature of self-defense and killing apply only to cases where the woman's life is threatened.

The Body as Property

In other kinds of cases, where the woman is not likely to die, Thomson requires a separate argument because she cannot rely on the idea of physical self-defense. Not surprisingly, a separate argument requires a separate analogy. Thomson argues, through her analogies, for the body to be understood as having the status of property. In acknowledging the limitations

17. Tooley, p. 43.
18. Ibid., p. 42.
19. Brody, p. 340.
20. For example, Brody gives this analogy for abortion: "X and Y are adrift in a lifeboat. Y has a disease which he can survive but which will kill X if he contracts it, and the only way X can avoid that is by killing Y and pushing him overboard. Surely X has no right to do this." Ibid., pp. 337–338. In her book on abortion, which is based on the violinist analogy, F. M. Kamm gives the following example: "Suppose many individuals had to drive cars, with each person having a low probability of either killing a pedestrian or being attached to him and having to kill him in order to be detached," hence suggesting that numbers should count "in violinist cases." Kamm, *Creation and Abortion: A Study in Moral and Legal Philosophy* (Oxford: Oxford University Press, 1992), pp. 61–62.

of the violinist analogy, she notes that: "Perhaps a pregnant woman is vaguely felt to have the status of a house, to which we don't allow the right of self-defense. But if the woman houses the child, it should be remembered that she is a person who houses it."[21] She also says that "what we have to keep in mind is that the mother and the unborn child are not like two tenants in a small house which has, by an unfortunate mistake, been rented to both: the mother *owns* the house."[22] The introduction of the notion of ownership is an attempt to make the woman's rights stronger in comparison to those of the fetus. Here, the woman is presented as defending her property rights over her body.

Thomson introduces another analogy in an attempt to cover cases where conception has occurred even though reasonable precautions have been taken against it. She asks us to suppose that:

> people-seeds drift about in the air like pollen, and if you open your windows, one may drift in and take root in your carpets or upholstery. You don't want children, so you fix up your windows with fine mesh screens, the very best you can buy. As can happen, however, and on very, very rare occasions does happen, one of the screens is defective; and a seed drifts in and takes root. Does the person-plant who now develops have a right to the use of your house? Surely not—despite the fact that you voluntarily opened your windows, you knowingly kept carpets and upholstered furniture, and you knew that screens were sometimes defective.[23]

Thus, the people-plants do not have the right to use the house. The protective mesh screens are supposed to be analogous to contraception, and the house analogous to a woman's body.[24] Thomson is attempting to show that women own their bodies, like a house, so therefore have a right to make decisions about what happens in and to their bodies. Her representation of the idea that our bodies are a kind of property which we own is a necessary supplement to her argument, to cover those cases where the fetus does not threaten the woman's life and where pregnancy occurs despite reasonable precautions.

This conception of the body is a liberal one, which can be traced back to Locke. To this extent a kind of Le Dœuffian "erudition" is required when assessing the *use* of images in analytic philosophy, despite the lack of scholarly antecedents for the image itself. In his *Two Treatises of Government*, Locke writes: "every man has a property in his own person; this nobody has any right to but himself."[25] The conception has a number of worrying conse-

---

21. Thomson, pp. 52–53.
22. Ibid., p. 53.
23. Ibid., p. 59.
24. Thomson also suggests that rape is like having a burglar break into one's house. Ibid., p. 337.

quences from a feminist point of view. Thomson's adherence to the idea that the body is a piece of property, like a house, is intended to support her argument that women have rights over their bodies. However, it endorses a common perception that women are just receptacles or incubators for fetuses. Another consequence which may even be unwelcome for a liberal is that we may sell or hire out our bodies and body parts as we wish. At its most extreme, this view implies an endorsement or at least acceptance of surrogacy, prostitution, and the traffic in body parts.[26] A third consequence is the notion of the self which is implied. If the body is a house, there is a further self which owns this house and directs what can happen in it. The obvious candidate for such a self is the mind, so the body as property view implies a view of the self as mind controlling the body. Thomson herself may be happy to accept some or even all of these consequences (though this is doubtful). However, they are at the very least problematic and difficult to defend, and furthermore, as Catriona Mackenzie argues, they "misrepresent both the nature of pregnancy and the woman-fetus relationship."[27] These consequences are indicative of a range of tensions underlying the analogy which will be explored further on in the chapter.

Another problem with Thomson's "house" analogy, which Steven L. Ross points out, is that it cannot cover circumstances where it is possible to remove the fetus from a woman and nurture it in some other way.[28] To put it in terms of its analogue, Thomson's analogy of the body as a house which we own entails that her argument can only apply to whether the fetus can continue living in the house, not whether it can live elsewhere. As I noted, Thomson is willing to accept the consequence that her argument only applies to fetal evacuation. However, such a limitation on the argument overlooks important aspects of the abortion issue and this problem has become more urgent with recent technological advances. It may become possible for a fetus to be removed from one woman and transferred to the uterus of another woman. In such cases, Thomson's analogy would be irrelevant and could not support an argument against such a procedure. Accepting the view of the body implicit in the violinist analogy and her other analogy of the house has important implications for the abortion issue, as well as wider ramifications in ethics and for our understanding of the self.

25. John Locke, *Two Treatises of Government* (New York: Hafner, 1956), p. 134.

26. Robert Nozick, in *Anarchy, State, and Utopia* (Oxford: Blackwell, 1974), shows how Locke's views of the body and property could justify selling oneself into slavery. If I own my body, I can do with it what I wish.

27. Catriona Mackenzie, "Abortion and Embodiment," *Australasian Journal of Philosophy* 70, no. 2 (1992): 150.

28. Ross, "Abortion and the Death of the Fetus," *Philosophy and Public Affairs* 11, no. 3 (1982): 238.

Rights

The parameters of the analogy are set up in such a way that the terms of the argument and certain presuppositions are built into it. The two individuals in the analogy are adult strangers with competing desires or interests. The violinist's is to live, and the woman's are to get out of bed and also to live. Furthermore, these two strangers have been forced into a relation with each other. Because of this particular construal of the problem, it seems natural to talk of competing rights. Like the idea of the body as property, it fits into a long tradition of liberal theory, where individuals with competing or opposed desires have to decide what to do, or others have to decide how to adjudicate between them.

The analogy makes it likely that we will see (and confirms the views of those who already see) abortion in terms of the woman and fetus as rivals, fighting for their lives. It also enables Thomson to question the idea that the right to life of the fetus automatically takes precedence over any other right. The precedence of a right to life over what are considered less important rights and moral considerations is assumed by the anti-abortionists. Their more recent name, pro-lifers, makes this point obvious. The violinist's right to life, taken as given, is weighed against the woman's right to her life in one version of the case. In another version, the violinist's right to life is weighed against her right to do what she wants with her own body, understood as a property right that needs to be defended. This way of construing the problem also brings in questions of the relative *value* of the two lives. For example, Finnis writes: "consider . . . the cases where the child's life seems so much more valuable, whether to itself or to others, than the life of its sick or old or low-born mother."[29]

The analogy strengthens the view that to argue for the permissibility of abortion is to assert the rights of the woman over the rights of the fetus, and to be against abortion is to assert the opposite. The debate is reduced to questions such as who has more rights, whether the fetus's right to life outweighs the property right women have over their bodies, and whether that property right extends to fetuses, as Finnis claims. By doing this, the debate is kept at the level of fairly simple for and against positions. It suggests that if one believes that abortion should not be legally or morally prohibited, one is interested in promoting abortions, when this is clearly not the case.

Furthermore, there is an asymmetry between the pro-choice and pro-life positions. Those who are against abortion are trying to prevent a whole range of actions. However, being "for" abortion does not mean trying to promote each of these actions, but trying to make choices possible. One is "for" the right to choose abortion or not, not "for" abortion itself as a particularly de-

29. Finnis, p. 132.

sirable part of one's life. Those who are pro-choice concerning abortion are often also in favor of free availability of contraception and sex education, stances which do not suggest the promotion of abortion. This asymmetry is obscured by Thomson's analogy, because it sets up the problem in terms of one set of rights against another. The analogy both reflects and reinforces an understanding of abortion in an adversarial way, both in making the woman and the fetus rivals and by presenting abortion as something you must be either for or against. The image is part of a methodology prevalent in ethical discussion in analytic philosophy.

Principles

Many analytic philosophers writing on abortion have used analogies to make their point, and there are other general features of the analogy which are characteristic of the analytic imaginary. Thomson's direct address to the reader in the analogy is clearly meant to suggest that it is a situation that *anyone* could find themselves in. It invites the reader to identify with the "you" position in the analogy. Yet one of the characteristics of pregnancy is that it is a situation that only women can be in, and even only women between certain ages and in certain circumstances. The need to make it seem like a common experience is yet another example of the limitations of the liberal framework and of reasoning based on the formulation of principles. This particular form of reason dictates that we can only make a decision in specific cases if it is based on principles that anyone could follow, at least in theory. Thomson's analogy incorporates the idea that there must be a general or universal principle under which abortion falls.

One reason for using analogies is to try and establish a principle which covers both the imagined case and the real issue. For example, Michael Tooley uses "wonder kittens" as an analogy for the fetus. The wonder kittens have been injected with a drug which gives them a mind like ours after a certain length of time, say, nine months.[30] Tooley says that if there were such kittens, we would not treat them differently from ordinary kittens until such time as they developed human characteristics. The principle behind this analogy is that having the potential to become a person should have no effect on present moral status.

R. M. Hare, in "Abortion and the Golden Rule," attempts to reject the methodology of Thomson and others, such as Tooley.[31] Hare says that

30. Tooley, p. 209.
31. R. M. Hare, "Abortion and the Golden Rule," *Philosophy and Public Affairs* 4, no. 3 (1975): 201–222.

Thomson writes as if the logic of moral concepts were not needed in moral philosophy, and claims further that "She simply parades the examples before us and asks what we would say about them."[32] He criticizes Finnis for falling into the trap of using examples and asking us what our intuitions are. Furthermore, he notes that Thomson's and Finnis's intuitions are widely differing, and asks: "Is it simply a contest in rhetoric?"[33] Hare rejects Tooley's wonder kitten as being too far-fetched, along with Thomson's violinist.

However, Hare himself retains one essential feature of the procedure of using analogies to discuss abortion. He says that instead of considering such strange possibilities, we should think about whether we are glad we were not aborted, and proceed from there. He wants to apply the general rule, "Do unto others as you would have them do unto you." Hare claims that when one applies this rule to abortion, one can conclude: "If we are glad that nobody terminated the pregnancy that resulted in *our* birth, then we are enjoined not, *ceteris paribus,* to terminate any pregnancy which will result in the birth of a person having a life like ours."[34] To Hare's way of thinking, this means a general principle against abortion is appropriate, as even those not glad to be alive would accept that if they had been glad to be alive, then they should not have been aborted. Some exceptions are allowed, such as if the woman would die or become sterile, or if the child would be "miserably handicapped."[35]

Hare's suggestion, although it is not an analogy, still relies on a methodology similar to Thomson's in important respects. As we have seen, Thomson's methodology itself is closely connected to principles. Her analogy provokes intuitions which are based on certain principles, in particular, principles originating in the liberal tradition. A further important respect in which Hare's and Thomson's approaches are similar is in their abstraction from the abortion decision. Hare's argument relies on the positing of a hypothetical situation which is at least as removed from the situation where a woman is contemplating an abortion as Thomson's. His case involves imagining what people might think about the question of whether they should have been aborted or not. In doing so, Hare constructs an imaginary case which has no relation to women or pregnancy and makes his claim about the morality of abortion dependent on that imaginary case. It also involves his assuming that everyone would think in the way that he does, which is especially bizarre in this case. First, it is odd to assume that one must adopt the position of the fetus in order to make a judgment on the issue of abortion,

32. Ibid., p. 201.
33. Ibid., p. 202.
34. Ibid., p. 208.
35. Ibid., pp. 211–212. The first two exceptions would seem to require a different justification from whether the fetus in question would be gladder to be alive.

and second, it is presumptuous to conclude that all people would share his views in relation to his wild counterfactual. There are a number of important issues relevant to abortion which the characteristic analogies and imaginary cases tend to misrepresent or neglect.

Abortion and Responsibility

One of the most important issues involved in abortion is the issue of responsibility, and Thomson's violinist analogy tends to obfuscate it. Mary Anne Warren in her paper, "On the Moral and Legal Status of Abortion," aims to clarify the issue by modifying the analogy. She prefaces her discussion with the comment: "[Thomson's] argument is based on a clever, but I think faulty, analogy."[36] She says that the analogy holds good for cases where the woman has been raped, but not for any other kind of case, because the fact that the woman had no choice in the matter of the violinist is an essential feature of the analogy. However, it could hold for any case where a woman did not actually decide to have a child. Warren attempts to make the analogy more apt by suggesting that "you" (note that she returns to addressing the reader) join a music lovers' society in which lots are drawn to save sick violinists, then your name is drawn, and you are kidnapped to save a violinist. This change is supposed to make the analogy closer to the circumstance of having sex knowing that there is a risk of becoming pregnant. She concludes that there is still a *prima facie* reason here for believing you should remain in bed with the violinist, because you have placed yourself in a position where you could be responsible for someone's life.[37] She concludes with the comment: "Thus the Thomson analogy cannot help us to produce a clear and persuasive proof of the moral permissibility of abortion."[38]

Her modification of the analogy is based on the common idea that if you have sex, then you must take responsibility for the consequences, whatever they may be. Warren's critique of Thomson's strategy is nevertheless structured by the analogy because she is willing to accept the drawing of lots as a good counterpart to the myriad circumstances that may be involved in becoming pregnant. She not only believes that Thomson's version of the analogy fails to provide a proof that abortion is permissible, she believes that her more satisfactory analogy provides a *prima facie* reason for not having an abortion.

36. Mary Anne Warren, "On the Moral and Legal Status of Abortion," *The Monist* 57 (1973): 48.
37. Ibid., p. 51.
38. Ibid., p. 52.

Joel Feinberg makes a similar point in his paper, "Abortion."[39] He argues that Thomson's analogy does not cover cases where a woman is "responsible" for the existence of the fetus, in that she made the choice to have sex. Thomson's people-seed analogy can be seen as an attempt to rectify this problem, because if accepted, it would cover cases where contraception had failed,[40] but still says nothing about all kinds of cases where people do not use precautions, for whatever reason. Furthermore, it does not take into account the different senses of responsibility involved, depending on whether "you" are a woman or "you" are a man.

There are several assumptions about responsibility, accepted by many on both "sides" of the debate, which are hidden by these analogies. One is that if a woman ever engages in sex without contraception, then she must take responsibility for the fetus.[41] More importantly, it is also assumed that if a woman is considered to have responsibility for the fetus, then the only morally responsible decision is to carry the fetus to full-term. This reasoning implies that the decision to have an abortion in these circumstances is always an irresponsible decision or one which abdicates responsibility. Yet such reasoning fails to take into account the complex factors involved in making the decision whether to continue the pregnancy or to have an abortion. It also fails to take into account the variety of reasons which may prevent a woman from using contraception, such as inadequate sex education or coercion, or the way in which a woman's circumstances may change after conception—if she is deserted by her partner, for example. The kinds of emotions women may feel about pregnancy are overlooked in a similar way.

Cutting One's Hair: Abortion and Emotions

Arguing for the permissibility of abortion using analogies, in terms of rights, seems to facilitate a disregard for women's emotional responses to the decision about abortion and the abortion itself. Many women who are pro-choice may still find it a difficult decision, one which is not taken lightly. The focus on rights fostered by the analogies tends to abstract from this response and make it seem that once something is considered a right, then little more thought need be given to it. Warren's comment that having an abortion is

39. Joel Feinberg, "Abortion," *Matters of Life and Death*, ed. Tom Regan (New York: Random House, 1980), pp. 602–611.

40. Mackenzie notes Thomson's attempt, but argues that she concedes "too much at the outset to the conservative notion of moral responsibility." I think Mackenzie refers to the notion that if you take the risk of getting pregnant, then you are committed to not having an abortion. Mackenzie, p. 139.

41. A different view is that assuming responsibility does not depend on whether contraception was used or not. Mackenzie, for example, argues that causal responsibility for becoming pregnant does not imply that an abortion is morally irresponsible. Ibid., p. 141.

not like "letting the violinist die, but rather is closer to being a morally neutral act, like cutting one's hair"[42] is a case in point. Likewise, her comparison of fetuses with fish,[43] and Tooley's comparison of fetuses with kittens,[44] suggest that little thought is given to an abortion decision.

However, Carol Gilligan, a psychologist who has interviewed women considering whether or not to have an abortion, has found that emotions are very important in making the decision. She shows that the decision involves the woman's own feelings and the feelings of others. The decision is based on caring for the feelings of all people likely to be involved in the life of the fetus if it were brought to full-term: for example, partners, family, and other children. So, construing the abortion decision as a purely individual or selfish one is inappropriate. Moreover, the decision involves taking into account the welfare of the fetus, both during pregnancy and after. One of the women interviewed by Gilligan expresses the difficulty like this: "The decision has got to be, first of all . . . a decision that the woman can live with, one way or another, or at least try to live with, and it must be based on where she is at and other significant people in her life are at."[45] Whatever decision is finally made, it is rarely an easy or simple process.

Some of the implications of the violinist analogy with regard to emotions have been spelled out by Steven Ross, who makes another attempt to improve the analogy. Ross says that the problem with the analogy is that the violinist is a complete stranger, whereas the fetus is "the object of a rather special range of emotions," involving "solicitous concern."[46] In his view this special relationship between the woman and the fetus cannot be captured by the violinist analogy. Thomson could not simply change the analogy to cover this, because it would (at least) make it much more difficult to talk in terms of individual rights. Consideration of these emotions are excluded by the use of the analogy, because there is no particular relationship between the woman and the violinist.

Thomson seems to have anticipated this objection to the analogy, because she says that a woman's relationship to the fetus is like that to a stranger, unless she has *assumed* responsibility for it. As we have seen, Thomson's view is that the question of responsibility relates to whether the woman tried not to conceive, or took the risk of pregnancy. For her, a woman's relation to a fetus

42. Warren, p. 52.

43. Warren writes: "a fetus, even a fully developed one, is considerably less personlike than is the average mammal, indeed the average fish." Ibid., p. 58.

44. Michael Tooley, p. 209.

45. Carol Gilligan, *In a Different Voice* (Cambridge, Massachusetts: Harvard University Press, 1982), p. 96.

46. Ross, p. 236. He does not try to defend abortion as a right of any kind but tries to explain why a woman would want to have an abortion rather than eventually having the child adopted.

is always like that to a stranger until after the birth, when she has taken the child home.[47] However, even if this were correct in legal and moral terms, it does not follow that women will necessarily regard the fetus as a stranger. The range of emotions a woman might feel concerning the fetus is not governed by legalistic notions of responsibility. Making the analogue of the fetus a stranger tends to promote the view that such emotions are inconsequential and ought to be disregarded.

Like Thomson, many involved in the abortion debate within analytic philosophy have avoided the whole issue of emotions relating to abortion. One reason for this is a certain kind of rationality which dictates that we should only consider the principles involved, and that emotions are irrelevant. Another reason is that philosophers who are in favor of abortion, including feminists, are afraid that by including a discussion of emotions that women have before and after abortions would lend support to the views of the anti-abortionists. It may seem important to argue that the abortion decision is trivial or without effect when arguing for the legality of abortion or arguing against anti-abortionists. Yet many women find it a difficult decision, and this should not be ignored in philosophical debate. It shows that women are not making a selfish decision, that they are considering the possible future welfare of the fetus, and that they are aware of the seriousness of the decision. Acknowledging that women may feel frightened before an abortion or guilty afterwards does not support an argument against abortion. It is not surprising that women find abortions traumatic in societies where abortion is at best tolerated, at worst prohibited. Yet any philosophical discussion of these emotions is precluded by a reliance on the analogies used in discussing abortion.

As I argued in the Introduction, emotions are seen as having no place in a rational philosophical argument, even at the level of describing relevant emotions. The analogy fosters that view, in this case, because it requires the reasoner to move from an unlikely case to the real issue of abortion, thus rendering specific and actual emotions irrelevant. An understanding of emotions involved in the abortion decision would increase the complexity of philosophical arguments about abortion, and bring women's concerns directly to bear on it. For example, pro-choice arguments would have to be more sophisticated in that they cannot rely on the claim that abortion is acceptable partly because it has virtually no psychological effects. On the other

---

47. Thomson, p. 65. Caroline Whitbeck says that Thomson's paper is almost a *reductio ad absurdum* of the idea that the best analogue of the fetus is an adult stranger. Caroline Whitbeck, "Women as People: Pregnancy and Personhood," in *Abortion and the Status of the Fetus*, ed. William B. Bondeson, H. Tristram Engelhardt, Jr., Stuart F. Spicker, and Daniel H. Winship (Dordrecht: D. Reidel, 1983), p. 254.

hand, anti-abortionists cannot claim that women who have abortions are just being selfish, nor that their psychology is similar to that of murderers'. This point is interesting, given the familiar philosophical mistrust of images, because of their appeal to emotions. While the violinist analogy, in one sense, relies on our emotional reaction for its force, in another sense it blocks any comprehension of the emotions central to the abortion issue. The relevance of emotions, obscured by analogies, is connected to the issue of the ways in which pregnancy is experienced.

Who's Pregnant?

The complexities and the uniqueness of abortion as a moral issue are often overlooked, and analogies like the famous violinist only serve to legitimate this abstraction and disguise its uniqueness. Nancy Davis argues that while it may be possible to think of analogies for some of the features of pregnancy, only pregnancy is *characterized* by these features.[48] This formulation is too weak because, while there are a number of situations where one person is dependent on another, there is no other situation where a being's existence depends on their continued nurturance by one particular individual. Janet Farrell Smith also draws attention to the fact that the fetus is dependent on the mother, and that "No other aspect of human life depends on one particular person in this way, which is why many analogies for pregnancy are misleading."[49] This special feature of the woman-fetus relation, and the facts and circumstances of pregnancy, are ignored in this debate. The changes women go through in pregnancy and the development of another self from the fetus means that pregnancy challenges traditional liberal notions of the self as a single, integrated individual. Thus, an understanding of the implications of pregnancy could lead to a radical reassessment of our notions of self. The use of an analogy such as the famous violinist, which tries to make pregnancy fit the liberal self, approaches the question the wrong way around. In the final section, I consider an approach which takes pregnancy seriously in its reflection on the morality of abortion.

The centrality of the conditions of pregnancy to the issue of abortion makes its neglect particularly distorting. Rosalind Hursthouse notes that no one could pick up the simplest facts about pregnancy by reading contemporary

48. Nancy Davis, "Abortion and Self-Defense," *Philosophy and Public Affairs* 13, no. 3 (1984): 201.

49. Janet Farrell Smith, "Rights-Conflict, Pregnancy, and Abortion," in *Beyond Domination: New Perspectives on Women and Philosophy*, ed. Carole C. Gould (Totowa: Rowman and Allanheld, 1983), p. 268. Susan Sherwin argues that the very existence of the fetus is relational. See Sherwin, "Abortion through a Feminist Ethics Lens," in *Living with Contradictions: Controversies in Feminist Social Ethics*, ed. Alison M. Jaggar (Boulder: Westview Press, 1994), p. 319.

philosophers' articles on abortion.[50] It is interesting that she uses a thought experiment to make this point:

> Imagine that you are an alien extraterrestrial anthropologist who does not know that the human race is roughly 50 percent female and 50 percent male, or that our only (natural) form of reproduction involves heterosexual inter-course, viviparous birth, and the female's (and only the female's) being preg-nant for nine months, or that females are capable of childbearing from late childhood to late middle age, or that childbirth is painful, dangerous, and emotionally charged—do you think you would pick up these facts from the hundreds of articles written on the status of the fetus? I am quite sure you would not. And that, I think shows that the current philosophical literature has got badly out of touch with reality.[51]

Clearly, Hursthouse is right about this neglect,[52] which is so pervasive that it suggests there is something odd about the treatment of abortion in gen-eral, an oddness which analogies like that to the violinist reveal in a partic-ularly striking way. It is not just the characteristics of pregnancy which are noticeably absent in this abortion debate. The special relation of women to abortion is also overlooked. Women's capacity to have children arguably means that only women can be in a position to judge whether they are able to continue with any particular pregnancy. Women will always have insights into the dilemma of abortion which men cannot have. Yet treatments of abor-tion in analytic philosophy seem to regard it as a general problem that can be decided by anyone, regardless of sex, using a few basic principles of rea-soning. The use of analogies such as Thomson's violinist perpetuates this misunderstanding of the issue. It may be precisely the uniqueness of abor-tion, and an attempt to deny that uniqueness, which leads philosophers to try to find analogies. The perhaps disturbing fact that it is an experience which only women can have may be what leads philosophers to reduce it to potentially more common experiences.

Philosophers often claim they can imagine themselves into any situation, thus considering that it is of little relevance who is particularly concerned in an issue. The particular framing, which is made evident by Thomson's di-rect address to the reader, highlights a general characteristic of the analytic imaginary that arises in relation to each of the images discussed in this

50. Rosalind Hursthouse, "Virtue Theory and Abortion," *Philosophy and Public Affairs* 20, no. 3 (1991): 237.

51. Ibid.

52. However, Hursthouse believes it is the use of principles which is the origin of the problem, whereas I argue that principles work in conjunction with analogies to abstract in a very extreme way from the actual context of abortion here.

book.[53] The appeal to an undifferentiated "you" is a typical attribute of this imaginary. This appeal is indicative of the idea that "one" can and should, through a mere act of will, imagine oneself in the position of another and on this basis make a series of ethical, political and philosophical judgments on their behalf. In the abortion debate in analytic philosophy, this characteristic of the analytic imaginary is reflected in the presumption of those who think they can take the position of the pregnant woman, and make decisions against abortion (and sometimes for) on her behalf. The analogy homogenizes the issue of abortion, which requires attention to a number of forms of difference: the differences between women and men in relation to such a decision, the differences between someone who could or has contemplated an abortion, and the differences between different women's situations. The presumption of virtually unlimited imaginative capacity and the equivalence in relation to moral and other issues of all human beings are a pervasive feature of the analytic imaginary, and in each chapter I discuss the particular form in which it appears. At the same time as the image neglects or covers over important features of pregnancy and abortion, it introduces a number of other considerations which would not have emerged if that particular image had not been used.

Irrelevant Details

The spelling out of the analogy's details brings even further removed questions into the argument. What might have begun as an incidental feature of the analogy is often treated as one of the most relevant or even essential features of abortion. Because Thomson used a famous violinist in her analogy, the discussion can easily shift from one about whether fetuses are persons or not, to one about whether any particular fetus is potentially an outstanding contributor to human advancement.[54] That this is a question without an answer has not prevented philosophers from discussing it. Of course, Thomson's aim in using a famous violinist can be interpreted as the desire to show that even if we did know that a particular fetus was destined to be an exceptional individual, this should not mean that abortion is out of the question.

53. In chapter 6 I discuss a questioning of this theme which emerges in the form of a direct address to the reader.

54. For example, Warren Quinn discusses the question of the loss of the fetus in relation to what Mozart would have written if he had lived longer. Warren Quinn, "Abortion: Identity and Loss," *Philosophy and Public Affairs* 13, no. 1 (1984): 45. A colleague remarked to me that when discussing Thomson's paper, students who love music are likely to think that the violinist should not be unplugged!

By making the analogue of the fetus an adult, Thomson has played into the hands of those who model the rights of the fetus on adult rights, therefore making it easier to claim that the fetus's rights outweigh those of the woman. Farrell Smith points out that the fetus's right to life is modeled on the adult sense of a right to life, but it should not be because the fetus is dependent on the woman and it is her responsibility to decide whether she is able to care for the fetus or not.[55] The relationship is asymmetrical, because of the fetus's dependence on the woman to survive. If the woman decides to continue the pregnancy, she has to nurture the fetus. The fetus, on the other hand, has no duties. Farrell Smith writes: "fetal 'duties' make no sense at all. The fetus has no "duty" of non-interference toward the woman."[56] Generally, rights are held to necessitate a corresponding duty. Therefore, "any right to life" of a fetus has to be of a very unusual kind, one which is vitiated by the circumstances of its development.

Davis makes an interesting point about Thomson's position in regard to the asymmetry between the woman and the fetus. According to her, Thomson's position relies on the asymmetry because the woman's superior moral claims only make sense in terms of such an asymmetry. However, Thomson's whole strategy is to assume that the woman and the fetus are moral equals.[57] In this sense, the violinist analogy contains these two inconsistent ideas in just the way Le Dœuff argues images generally cover a tension or gap in philosophical work. Furthermore, the analogy conceals the reliance on the unique nature of the woman-fetus relationship by making both the analogues adults.

Another side-effect of using an adult violinist is that the idea of the fetus as innocent victim is pushed to the background. Yet using an adult makes it more likely that the argument will be couched in terms of the fetus's interests. Even granted that it is appropriate to speak of fetuses having interests, another implausible assumption is that it will always be in the fetus's interests not to be aborted. The idea that in having an abortion a woman may be thinking sympathetically of the possible future life of any fetus is not even considered. Using an analogy often entails that certain features of the original case are over-emphasized, while others are excluded.[58] The violinist analogy ensures that issues of embodiment, responsibility, emotions and the actual considerations involved in making a decision about abortion are left out of the debate.

55. Farrell Smith, pp. 270–271.
56. Ibid., p. 268.
57. Davis, p. 201.
58. Drucilla Cornell notes that even the idea of waking up and "finding oneself" attached to the violinist obscures the way that: "the wrong in the denial of the right to abortion begins long before that." Drucilla Cornell, *The Imaginary Domain: Abortion, Pornography & Sexual Harassment* (New York: Routledge, 1995), p. 51.

Counterexamples

Although the violinist image is best understood as an analogy, it's worthwhile considering the view that it also works as a counterexample. The use of counterexamples in philosophy is rather a controversial issue. In "A Paradigm of Philosophy: The Adversary Method," Janice Moulton argues that philosophy is characterized by an adversarial style of argumentation. One of the features of the adversarial style is the use of counterexamples to defeat an opponent's argument. She uses Thomson's violinist analogy as a paradigm case of argument by counterexample. Moulton writes that Thomson

> did not show that abortion would, or would not, be wrong. There are many features beside personhood that are important to the people making a decision about abortion: That it is the result of sexual intercourse so that guilt, atonement or loyalty about the consequences may be appropriate; that the effects only occur to women, helping to keep a power-minority in a powerless position; that the developing embryo may be genetically like others who are loved; that the product would be a helpless infant brought into an unmanageable situation; that such a birth would bring shame or hardship to others.[59]

While one might not agree with the particular views expressed by Moulton here, that is not the important point. The point is that these issues are relevant to abortion, but the analogies that most philosophers use in discussing abortion make it difficult to raise them. Analogies also provide a mark of what is considered to be a properly philosophical way of discussing abortion, so that work which concentrated on the kinds of issues suggested by Moulton may not even be considered philosophical.

Moulton argues that any counterexample of this kind—which aims to defeat an opposing argument—will fail to address abortion as a personal issue or account for the kind of moral reasoning involved. Counterexamples fail because they can only show what is wrong with other arguments, and cannot provide "any positive reason for accepting a conclusion, [or] show how a conclusion is related to other ideas."[60] Moulton's points support my argument about these kind of analogies: not only do counterexamples structure the kind of answers that can be given, they are also part of a specific way of doing philosophy, "the adversary method," and so may blind us to other ways we may approach an issue. If we concentrate on responding to the analogy by modifying it, or supplying another, we may ignore, as in this case, the entire context of the issue involved.

59. Janice Moulton, "A Paradigm of Philosophy: The Adversary Method," in *Discovering Reality: Feminist Perspectives on Epistemology, Metaphysics, Methodology, and Philosophy of Science,* ed. Sandra Harding and Merrill Hintikka (Dordrecht: D. Reidel, 1983), p. 160.
60. Ibid., p. 161.

Reconceptions

To radically change the arguments about abortion, we should say that reasoning by way of analogies is inappropriate and unhelpful. While the sensitivity of the topic makes it unsurprising that philosophers have looked to analogies, the constraints and distortions of this method have made the need for a new one urgent. Moulton suggests two alternatives to the adversary method. One is to relate a specific argument to a larger system of ideas, and the other is to take experience into account. Some recent work on abortion has begun to take experience into account, and here is one approach which seems promising.

This approach uses phenomenological descriptions of pregnancy to provide a better understanding of the uniqueness of the experience of being pregnant and the relation between the woman and the fetus. For example, Catriona Mackenzie's article, "Abortion and Embodiment," gives an idea of how much more complex the abortion debate can and should be, unconstrained by odd analogies. Her criticism of Thomson's analogy, as well as those of other philosophers, is that they have "contributed to the representation of pregnancy as a mere *event* which takes over women's lives and with respect to which they are passive." She also argues that "they have focused philosophical and moral reflection away from the contexts in which deliberations about abortion are usually made and away from the concerns and experiences which motivate those involved in the processes of deliberation."[61] Mackenzie builds on Iris Marion Young's account of pregnant embodiment to show how pregnant women experience a unique relation between self and other that has implications for our understanding of abortion.

It is interesting that Young's description is one which aims to convey the experience only of those women who have decided, without pressure, to carry through a pregnancy. Yet Mackenzie says that her own description is "a normative and reflective apprehension of the way in which conscious experience is structured by our (bodily) situations, perspectives and modes of perception."[62] This goal is a significantly different one from Young's, which "presupposes that pregnancy can be experienced for its own sake, noticed, savored [..and so requires..] that the pregnancy be chosen by the woman."[63] A woman contemplating abortion has not made a choice yet,

61. Mackenzie, p. 155. Le Dœuff argues that successfully bringing a pregnancy to term is a demanding activity and that it is women who should make the decision about its continuation. *Hipparchia's Choice*, p. 276–277.

62. Mackenzie, p. 148.

63. Iris Marion Young, "Pregnant Embodiment: Subjectivity and Alienation," in *Throwing Like a Girl and Other Essays in Feminist Philosophy and Social Theory* (Bloomington: Indiana University Press, 1990), p. 161.

so is not usually in a position to notice and savor her pregnancy. Mackenzie overcomes this problem, using Young's empirical description of "the specific experience of women in technologically sophisticated Western societies"[64] to give a "normative and reflective" phenomenology of pregnant embodiment by abstracting the most general features of such experience. These general features concern the experience of self in relation to the fetus.

Young argues that a pregnant woman does not distinguish clearly between herself and the fetus. In her words, "Pregnancy challenges the integration of my body experience by rendering fluid the boundary between what is within, myself, and what is outside, separate. I experience my insides as the space of another, yet my own body."[65] This is the main point on which Mackenzie builds her account. In her view, the experience which is common to all pregnancies, whether they are wanted or not wanted, is the blurring of the boundaries between self and other. Mackenzie's point is that this blurring has the moral implication that at least in the early stages of pregnancy the welfare of the fetus is inseparably bound to the welfare of the woman. She argues that we can only understand abortion if we understand "the bodily and moral connection between the woman and the fetus."[66] This conceptualization of the relation makes it much clearer why women must be able to decide for themselves the issue of abortion. It also makes it possible to think about abortion in terms other than whether one is for or against it. One can see that a number of unique philosophical questions arise from the uniqueness of pregnancy itself.

An account of this kind will not fit well within a liberal framework, which treats the body as a kind of property and the woman's relation with the fetus as a kind of contract; and no analogy will eliminate this difficulty because there is no moral situation properly analogous with abortion. It is striking that there are so many analogies used in this area, not just Thomson's violinist and people-seed analogies, but also Michael Tooley's wonder-kittens and Warren's hair-cut. The suggestion that abortion is no more serious than a hair-cut, for example, is probably in part a response to the over-dramatization of abortion by anti-abortionists. If this supposition is correct, it supports the view that the adversarial nature of the discussion makes subtlety in argument less likely. In this case, working within the framework of analogies and using them uncritically leads to a stifling of thought on the complexities of abortion. We should also note that if we accept the analogy as a true one, then we will probably accept Thomson's conclusions. If we look at the replies,

64. Ibid.
65. Ibid., p. 163.
66. Mackenzie, p. 150.

we can see that no one actually says that Thomson's intuitions arising from the analogy are inappropriate, but only that her construction of the analogy is faulty.

Conclusion

As I argued in the Introduction, images may work simultaneously on a number of different levels of embeddedness. Two of the three levels I set out—persuasiveness and enframement—are particularly relevant here. Expressibility seems less relevant, as it is possible to describe the argument without using the violinist analogy, although a great deal of the force and point is lost. Thomson's violinist analogy works both at the level of persuasiveness and at the level of enframement. It works at the level of persuasiveness by encouraging only those intuitions necessary for Thomson's limited defense of abortion, while ignoring other intuitions. More importantly, the analogy works to elicit agreement with the fundamentals of Thomson's ideas about abortion, such as that abortion is a matter of competing rights. Whether Thomson's example of a famous violinist is a proper analogy or a false analogy now becomes the crucial point of the debate, rather than the real circumstances of someone struggling with the moral issues of abortion. The analogy distracts attention from these circumstances.

The analogy works at the level of enframement in two ways. The first is the way it constructs the immediate arguments. The fact that the violinist is plugged in against the woman's will and (in one construction of the example) that she will die, has implications for the conclusions open to someone who uses the analogy. It means that one can only conclude that abortion is permissible in cases where the woman has been raped, where the woman might die, and when she cannot be held to be causally responsible for the pregnancy. Thus, as Thomson herself admits, even if the argument were successful, it could only be used in a very limited set of cases. By accepting the premise, "the fetus is a person," and building that premise into her analogy, Thomson also accepts an argument conceived in terms of individuals' competing rights, rather than a woman's concern about her life or women's autonomy, and this fundamental idea is retained in the responses.

The second, and more important, way in which the analogy works at the level of enframement is the way it structures very general features of the abortion debate it engenders. In this debate the range of legitimate responses to abortion is restricted. The analogy reduces the complexity of abortion as a moral issue to logical problems and to questions of rights, self-defense, and ownership. It determines the kinds of argument which can be made about abortion, and obscures a number of tensions and unsatisfactory assumptions about the body, pregnancy, and the relation between the woman and the fetus. Using analogies of abortion in this way serves to exclude work which focuses on the emotions and experiences of women who are pregnant and contemplating abortion. The uniqueness of abortion in our moral life makes analogies specially inappropriate, and philosophical understanding of abortion will only increase when this methodology plays a less significant role in philosophical discussion of abortion.

Using analogies involves a denial of the uniqueness of abortion, and women's special relation to the question. This denial is tied very closely to what we will see is the most pervasive characteristic of the analytic imaginary: the fantasy that it is always possible to imagine oneself into the position of another human being, and make judgments on that basis.

3

Experimenting with Persons

The imagery of the debate concerning personal identity in analytic philosophy reveals a great deal about its presuppositions and methodology. As Michèle Le Dœuff argues, the images in philosophy work both for and against the philosopher who uses them. They work for the philosopher in that they can conceal tensions and elicit agreement from the reader. However, on careful examination, the more questionable assumptions operating in the text are exposed. In that sense, they can work against their authors. These features, so characteristic of philosophical metaphor and analogies, are also characteristic of thought experiments in contemporary analytic debates on personal identity. An understanding of the tensions integral to the thought experiments makes their philosophical role clearer.

Thought experiments are not images in the sense of being tropes or figures of speech. However, they are striking and effective images in the broader sense I use here. They function in importantly similar ways to the other images examined so far and contribute to our understanding of the nature of the analytic imaginary. Thought experiments are controversial philosophical tools, even within analytic philosophy. Analytic philosophers are divided over their usefulness and legitimacy, particularly in the personal identity debate. This controversy introduces yet another level of discussion. There is the personal identity debate itself, the debate within analytic philosophy over thought experiments' utility in producing results, and my own approach, which contrasts with both of these by showing a number of broader implications of the use of thought experiments.

Thought experiments play a predominant role in analytic philosophy, in spite of the debate about their usefulness. A thought experiment is a hypothetical exercise which is impossible to carry out or test in reality and can range from a simple "What would happen if everyone were to do that?" to detailed descriptions of imaginary scenarios. It is generally accepted that Plato was the first Western philosopher to use a thought experiment: the story in the *Republic* of the ring of Gyges. A shepherd, Gyges, finds a ring which makes him invisible and takes advantage of his invisibility to act unjustly—to get access to the king and take his place. This thought experiment is supposed to show that no-one would act justly if they could act unjustly with impunity, though none of the participants in the dialogue believe that the thought experiment successfully proves this.[1] Thought experiments are also used a great deal in discussions of ethics in analytic philosophy. Well-known thought experiments used in ethics include the experience machine, used by Robert Nozick[2], Joel Feinberg's nowheresville,[3] and Bernard William's Jim in the jungle thought experiment.[4] Some of these thought experiments are used to convince us of things it could well be very easy to persuade us of without them. The experience machine, which is introduced by Nozick to demonstrate that there is more to life than hedonism, is like this. Thought experiments of the most simple, practical kind are both unavoidable and useful. However, these kinds of thought experiments are far less important for my purposes than the personal identity thought experiments, because these are more distinctive of analytic philosophy and play a much more substantive role in argument.

To see how these thought experiments operate in the arguments about personal identity, it is best to concentrate on three of the most common and most significant thought experiments for determining the fundamental link in personal identity. The thought experiments are brain swapping, used by a number of philosophers including Sydney Shoemaker and Bernard Williams, tele-transportation, and fission (dividing like amoebae), the two thought experiments made famous by Derek Parfit. Certain forms of these three are the main thought experiments to which any student of the topic will be introduced. Le Dœuff argues that while it is often claimed that images are good pedagogic devices, it is at least as difficult to teach the significance of the images as to explain the intricacies of the argument.[5] It is

1. Plato, *Republic*, in *Collected Dialogues*, ed. Edith Hamilton and Huntington Cairns (Princeton: Bollingen, 1999), pp. 607–608; 359c–360d.

2. Robert Nozick, *Anarchy, State, and Utopia* (Oxford: Blackwell, 1974).

3. Joel Feinberg, "The Nature and Value of Rights," in *Ethical Theory: Classical and Contemporary Readings*, ed. Louis P. Pojman (Belmont: Wadsworth, 1989), pp. 602–611.

4. Bernard Williams and J. J. C. Smart, *Utilitarianism: For and Against* (Cambridge: Cambridge University Press, 1973).

5. Le Dœuff, *The Philosophical Imaginary*, trans. Colin Gordon (London: Athlone Press, 1989), p. 173.

thought-provoking to consider the value of these particular manifestations of the analytic imaginary as pedagogic devices.

By exploring the analytic imaginary as it emerges in the personal identity debate, the assumptions behind the thought experiments which are shared, regardless of the conclusions they are supposed to support, become clear. Thought experiments work strongly on the level of persuasiveness, and this feature is closely connected to the question of their pedagogic import. They also work on the level of enframement, by defining the debate within a narrow set of questions. Thought experiments in these particular cases come close to working at the level of expressibility, in that they are needed for the particular questions considered to be taken seriously. Questions concerning the relevance of gender to personal identity, how other kinds of differences between persons may affect conclusions about personal identity, and how we should understand the relation between mind and body, are forestalled before the project even begins. In order to bring feminist and other questions into the debate, we need to see how the analytic imaginary in this case works to maintain the view that such questions are irrelevant without ever actually saying so. But first the thought experiments should be placed in context.

Personal Identity and Thought Experiments

The personal identity debates in analytic philosophy relates to questions about the concept "person." This concept, rather than concepts of man, self, or human being, has only been of special interest to philosophers since Locke made the philosophical distinction between a human being and a person.[6] The most dominant and prolific strand of the analytic literature, which is concerned with distinguishing individuals from each other and over time,[7] is a very rich source of imagery, especially in the shape of thought experiments.[8]

6. John Locke, *An Essay Concerning Human Understanding* (Oxford: Oxford University Press, 1979), p. 335. Ross Poole argues in "On Being a Person," *Australasian Journal of Philosophy* 74, no. 1 (1996): 38–56, that Locke's promotion of the concept "person" led philosophers astray, as being a person is only one, and not the most important, of our possible identities. In his view, the concept "human" better serves the purpose of representing what we essentially are.

7. There are a number of related questions. Amélie Rorty lists three others: (1) Class differentiation—distinguishing persons from other kinds of beings. (2) Individual differentiation—distinguishing individual persons from each other. (3) Individual identification—determining the essential characteristics of a person. Amélie Oksenberg Rorty, introduction to *The Identities of Persons* (Berkeley: University of California Press, 1976), pp. 1–2.

8. Philosophers who write on personal identity using thought experiments include: David Lewis, Harold Noonan, Robert Nozick, Derek Parfit, John Perry, Anthony Quinton, Sydney Shoemaker, David Wiggins, and Bernard Williams.

Since the inception of this debate, attempts to answer these questions have involved the use of unusual metaphors and thought experiments. For example, Hobbes discusses the "Ship of Theseus," which has all its planks replaced over a period of time, to answer the question of whether it is still the same numerical ship or not. He points out that if someone had reconstructed the ship out of the old planks, it would appear that there are two numerically identical ships. Hobbes concludes that the matter (the material) of the ship is important to its identity, so if all of its planks are replaced, a different ship is made.[9] In *An Essay Concerning Human Understanding,* Locke relates an amusing story of a parrot who engages in conversation. The point of the story is that we should call it an intelligent parrot, rather than a man, because a particular kind of body is important to the idea of being a man.[10] Locke also introduces a thought experiment concerning a prince's soul entering the body of a cobbler to suggest the importance of consciousness to personal identity as well as the distinction between "man" and "person." He argues that although others might not think the *man* has changed, "every one sees he would be the same person with the prince, accountable only for the prince's actions."[11] Following Hobbes's and Locke's precedents, the contemporary literature is characterized by the use of thought experiments and puzzle cases, which often do not involve recognizable human beings. These thought experiments take the form of asking us to imagine (for example) that everyone is able to split into two people like amoebae, and then asking us for our reactions. Naturally, my concern here is with the underlying functions of these thought experiments, rather than with the particular views on personal identity of the authors concerned.

The Brain Swap

The brain swap, like the other thought experiments, is a case where we arrive at different conclusions depending on how the thought experiment is presented. This is suggested by the many names used to cover similar thought experiments: brain transfer, body swap, or mind swap. Sydney Shoemaker first presents the brain swap thought experiment as one that is used to support a psychological continuity theory (the view that the criterion for reidentifying a person over time is continuity between brains/mental states). He describes the case like this:

---

9. Thomas Hobbes, *The Metaphysical System of Hobbes,* ed. Mary Whiton Calkins (Chicago: Open Court, 1910), pp. 84–86.
10. Locke, *Essay,* pp. 333–334.
11. Ibid., p. 340.

Two men, a Mr. Brown and a Mr. Robinson, had been operated on for brain tumors, and brain extraction had been performed on both of them. At the end of the operations, however, the assistant inadvertently put Brown's brain in Robinson's head, and Robinson's brain in Brown's head. One of these men immediately dies, but the other, the one with Robinson's body and Brown's brain, eventually regains consciousness. Let us call the latter "Brownson" . . . He recognizes Brown's wife and family . . . and is able to describe in detail events in Brown's life . . . Over a period of time he is observed to display all of the personality traits, mannerisms, interests, likes and dislikes, and so on that had previously characterized Brown, and to act and talk in ways completely alien to the old Robinson.[12]

Shoemaker accepts that most people would be inclined to say that Brownson is really Brown and takes this to imply that they are using the psychological criterion of personal identity. Thus, this thought experiment is used to convince people that psychological continuity is the correct criterion. Shoemaker notes that the intuition behind this argument can be strengthened further by recasting the thought experiment from our own point of view. Were a mind/brain swap to be performed on us, we would, supposedly, identify quite readily with the mind/brain, since it retains all the memories of our past life. However, all this can show, Shoemaker later argues, is that people do not regard bodily identity as the decisive criterion in all cases.[13] The move to a first person narrative merely functions to restrict the extent of the thought experiment's conclusion. In this way, one basic thought experiment is made to do different philosophical work, to support either a bodily or a psychological continuity view of personal identity, depending on how it is presented.

Since this particular thought experiment became very popular in the literature, it is worthwhile to trace one or two of its transformations. In "The Importance of Being Identical," John Perry argues that the concern which we feel for ourselves in the future in these kinds of thought experiments needs to be explained.[14] The puzzle then becomes one where we have to decide how we would feel or how Brown would feel about our/his brain being put in someone else's head. This yields the conclusion that so long as, say, Brownson was going to do most of the things that Brown was going to, Brown would feel the same way about Brownson's future as about his own.

Yet the same thought experiment can be presented differently again. In "The Self and the Future," Bernard Williams gives a description of an ex-

12. Sydney Shoemaker, *Self-Knowledge and Self-Identity* (Ithaca: Cornell University Press, 1963), pp. 23–24.
13. Ibid., p. 247.
14. John Perry, in "The Importance of Being Identical," in *The Identities of Persons*, p. 74.

periment (an updated version of Shoemaker's) where two people enter a machine which extracts all the information from one person—A's—brain and puts it into B's brain, and the information from B's brain is put into A's. Williams imagines the reactions of A and B if they thought, for example, that the A-body was going to be tortured. Looking at the case from the third-person point of view, it might seem that a body swap has occurred, because A would rather have their memories transferred to the B-body. But, argues Williams, if we think it is us whose body is going to be tortured and some-one else's memories put in our brains, then we would regard the situation with fear, it being no consolation that our memories were put into someone else's body.[15]

There are a number of possible responses to these thought experiments. We could happily accept "we" were being put into another body, we could believe we would be killed, or we could be frightened by either alternative, or we might be completely confused about what to say. Our reaction would probably depend on how influenced we were by the way the thought ex-periment is described. These philosophers appear to make a judgment about what people would think if presented with these thought experiments, and use this judgment to support their conclusions. Two other thought experi-ments reveal similar features of the analytic imaginary.

Tele-transportation

In *Reasons and Persons,* his book on personal identity and ethics, Derek Parfit uses a number of thought experiments, including tele-transportation and fission. One of Parfit's most important thought experiments is tele-transportation, which is used to introduce his discussion of personal identity. A clone of him-self is sent to Mars, while his own brain and body are destroyed. Here is an abridged version: "I enter the Teletransporter . . . The Scanner here on Earth will destroy my brain and body, while recording the exact states of all my cells. It will then transmit this information by radio. Traveling at the speed of light, the message will take three minutes to reach the replicator on Mars. This will then create, out of new matter, a brain and body exactly like mine. It will be in this body that I shall wake up."[16] Then a new Scan-ner is developed, which records the blueprint without destroying his brain and body, so he can see and talk to himself on Mars. There are some prob-lems with the new Scanner, and one day Parfit finds that his replica on

15. Bernard Williams, "The Self and the Future," in *Problems of the Self: Philosophical Papers 1956–72* (Cambridge: Cambridge University Press, 1973), p. 56.
16. Derek Parfit, *Reasons and Persons* (Oxford: Oxford University Press, 1986), p. 199.

Mars is going to continue living, while he on earth is going to die of cardiac failure. He wants to persuade us that if we were about to die but knew that our replica would live for another forty years, we should think of this as about as good as ordinary survival. Parfit uses the tele-transportation thought experiment to convince us that personal identity is not what matters in survival, and we should think about survival in a different way. Having managed to convince himself, at least, that if we had a replica of ourselves made this would be more than a great consolation on our deathbed, Parfit concludes that with regard to survival, personal identity is not "what matters."[17]

Thus, we can see that there is much more being done with the trip to Mars than finding out what our beliefs are about it. Parfit believes that after considering the tele-transportation thought experiment, most people would accept that the views of common sense are inadequate, because they fail to account for the now demonstrated "fact" that we would feel that having a replica made of ourselves would be nearly as good as continuing to live ourselves. Paul Ricoeur argues that the question of personal identity remains in the tele-transportation thought experiment. He declares, "how can we ask ourselves about *what* matters if we could not ask *to whom* the thing mattered or not?"[18] The tele-transportation thought experiment relies on our confusion about the issue of who it matters to. If we are confused about whether the replica is Parfit, we will be more likely to concede that perhaps the death of the original does not matter.

Parfit's thought experiments are unusual, in a sense, because he wants to show us that personal identity is not all-or-nothing, but a matter of degree. He tries to show this by presenting us with thought experiments where the situation is so strange we are not sure how to respond. Yet he also wants to convince us that we should think of personal identity in terms of shifting, changing selves. To convince us of this he needs another truly bizarre thought experiment—fission.

Fission

Parfit's version of the fission thought experiment is where people divide like amoebae. This thought experiment is so unclear and so badly spelled out that it is hard to see why or how anyone could use it to support conclusions about personal identity. Nevertheless, Parfit attempts to do just that, so it is worthwhile seeing what role it plays in his argument. Parfit writes: "Consider

17. Ibid., p. 215.
18. Paul Ricoeur, *Oneself as Another,* trans. Kathleen Blamey (Chicago: University of Chicago Press, 1992), p. 137.

next some more imaginary people. These are just like us except for their method of reproduction. Like amoebae, these people reproduce by a process of natural division."[19] This process means that one life (person) will become the beginning of a tree-like formation of connections, where one becomes two, two four, four eight, and so on. Parfit calls the first person to undergo this process Eve, the next two Secunda and Tertia, and so on down to the fiftieth person, Quinquagesima. Parfit suggests that these people would refer to the others in the Tree as "my past selves" and "my future selves," and he argues that this manner of speaking can also cover cases where half his brain is transplanted into another body similar to his.[20]

The purpose of introducing this thought experiment (and others like it), is to make familiar the idea of talking in this way about past and future selves, which have relations of what Parfit calls "psychological connectedness." Furthermore, they are supposed to enable him to argue that analogously, in ordinary life, we should refer to things we have done in the past as things done by an earlier self, and things we might do in the future as things that will be done by a future self. Parfit thinks that we should talk like this when there has been "a significant change of character, or style of life, or of beliefs and ideals."[21] He argues that we would find it a useful way of speaking in our own lives and gives quotations from Marcel Proust and Alexander Solzhenitsyn to support his view. The examples focus on the experience of falling out of love, and in Parfit's view we can be in love with someone's earlier self. However, this is just a rather artificial and inaccurate manner of speaking, and Parfit himself warns against taking it too literally. He tries to support his views by real-life or literary examples, but they do not provide support, unless we already accept the conclusions based on his thought experiments. If Parfit's view of the self were accepted, it could have serious moral and legal implications. For example, such a view could be used to excuse the past actions of a criminal, or to ignore the past sufferings of a victim. Although there may be situations in which it is appropriate to think of persons in this way, it does not take into account the way past actions and events affect the overall narrative of a person's life, or the person's self-understanding.

There is a tension between Parfit's explicit statements about the purposes of the thought experiments, which he says are simply to clarify different positions, and the purpose of his entire project, which is to convince people to reject their usual views on personal identity. This tension can only be resolved if we take the actual purpose of the thought experiments to be something quite different from simply clarifying positions.

19. Parfit, p. 299.
20. Ibid., p. 302.
21. Ibid., p. 305.

Parfit is well aware of the view that a thought experiment of the kind he uses teaches us little about persons, and he notes remarks by Ludwig Wittgenstein and W. V. O. Quine, whom he quotes: "The method of science fiction has its uses in philosophy, but . . . I wonder whether the limits of the method are properly heeded. To seek what is 'logically required' for sameness of person under unprecedented circumstances is to suggest that words have some logical force beyond what our past needs have invested them with."[22] Parfit admits that the thought experiments he uses are "deeply impossible," because they "contravene the laws of nature" and could never occur, no matter what technological progress is made in science.[23] However, he says, thought experiments can be useful even in science, citing the case of Einstein's famous thought experiment about the speed of light. Parfit further argues that thought experiments are important because of the strength of our reactions. He believes that they reveal, in a clearer way than our reactions to actual cases, what our beliefs about personal identity over time are.[24] It is noteworthy that this is the reason Parfit gives for using thought experiments, because, as we have seen, his project is to convince his readers that most people's views about personal identity are wrong. These "Common-Sense" views, apparently, are that we are "separately existing entities" (apart from physical and mental characteristics), that our identity is determinate, and that personal identity is what matters. Parfit believes that all these views are wrong, and he says explicitly that he is trying to show that "most of us have a false view about ourselves, and about our actual lives."[25] Thus, if his thought experiments really reveal the views we already have more clearly, it seems that using these imaginary cases would be exactly the wrong way to go about getting us to change our mind. We may ask why the experiments are necessary to reveal the need for change in our views on personal identity. Furthermore, we can ask whether this need really exists, if it can only be revealed by looking at strange cases.

Parfit's use of impossible thought experiments has its critics within the analytic philosophical community. Kathleen Wilkes argues that thought experiments are much more acceptable in science than in work on personal identity, because in science there is greater control over the variables. While finding science fiction examples fun, she argues that they are "highly

22. For W. V. O. Quine's review of *Identity and Individuation* as edited by Milton K. Munitz, see *The Journal of Philosophy* 69, no. 16 (1972): 490. Parfit, p. 200.

23. Ibid., p. 219.

24. Ibid., p. 200.

25. Ibid., p. 217. I think that it is questionable whether there really is consensus on these matters.

problematic in general and, for this topic in particular, highly misleading as a philosophical tool."[26] Wilkes accepts the claim made by Parfit and others that the purpose of these thought experiments is to find out what our actual concepts of a person are. Nonetheless, in her view the problem with thought experiments is that they fail to do this, because the relevant information is not given in the experiment.

Parfit's concession to those who agree with Wilkes is to admit that the impossibility of some thought experiments might render them irrelevant, depending on the questions they are designed to address. However, he does not say what these questions are. Instead he continues to use an array of deeply impossible thought experiments, without considering whether they are appropriate, well-designed, or exactly which questions are being answered. The tele-transportation and amoebae thought experiments do not conform to any special experimental design. The amoebae thought experiment is a wonderful illustration of the lengths to which philosophers writing on personal identity will go to convince us of their ideas. Wilkes cites the example of what we might think if we all split like amoebae, and says that we would need to know the answers to questions like: "How often? Is it predictable? Can we control it? What would society be like under such circumstances? and Would pregnant women be debarred from splitting?"[27] Not surprisingly, Parfit and others who use thought experiments to discuss personal identity do not give the answers to these kinds of questions. Examining the role of these thought experiments in philosophical methodology reveals more clearly the nature of the analytic imaginary.

Pedagogy or Perplexity?

A most important question is how thought experiments function pedagogically. Wilkes is against the use of thought experiments on the grounds that they fail to produce substantial results. She concludes that since we do not know the answers to questions about the nature and consequences of, for example, amoebae-like splitting, we cannot say what we think the experiment tells us about our concept of a person. She believes that we discover nothing about persons or our real views of personal identity by considering these thought experiments, but that we remain simply perplexed.

My view differs from Wilkes's in that I do not see the thought experiments as simply entertaining and amusing diversions, but as playing a role that is

26. Kathleen V. Wilkes, *Real People: Personal Identity without Thought Experiments* (Oxford: Clarendon Press, 1988), p. 1.
27. Ibid., p. 12.

even more significant than the philosophers using them admit. The philosophers concerned may not be aware of how much their position relies on the thought experiments. Certainly, these philosophers underplay the significance of the thought experiments in claiming they are merely used to refine our concepts and discover our deepest intuitions. My view is that thought experiments do much more than this: they hide important assumptions, obscure relevant questions, and demand our complicity in certain methods and conclusions. It is not just the impossibility of the thought experiments that is a problem, but the ways in which they obscure understanding of the concept of the person and exclude important aspects of identity.

These exclusions operate partly by eliciting our agreement to certain conclusions. While it is true that we are often not sure how to react because the cases are too remote from our everyday experience, a reaction is nonetheless expected, so we go the way we are led. Daniel Dennett calls such thought experiments "intuition pumps."[28] He contends that they force us to come up with an intuition which validates the writer's views. Perhaps we should not even use the word "intuition" here, as our responses to these cases are not views that spring to mind independent of reasoning. Rather, our response is the conclusion we accept if we follow the reasoning incorporated in the thought experiment.

In one sense, the thought experiments only work *for* the writer concerned, if the thought experiment is viewed uncritically, and the reader agrees with the conclusion being put forward. They work *against* the philosopher's aims because we can recast the thought experiment to draw conclusions opposed to those being forwarded. We can then claim that these views are justified by their own thought experiment, or at least a variation on that experiment. Thought experiments leave philosophers open to the kind of treatment Williams gives the brain swap thought experiment, or to the possibility that someone will simply assert that they have the opposite reaction to the hoped-for one.

Nonetheless, our response to these thought experiments will be severely restricted by the way the thought experiment is spelled out—from first or third-person viewpoints, what it is said the "persons" involved can remember, how they act, and so on. If we accept the use of the thought experiment as legitimate, we might just agree with the author or choose one of the other alternatives offered. What is difficult to do, however, is revise the questions or raise different views of the self. All the thought experiments of the type discussed here share this feature: they restrict the range of views that may be readily advanced or investigated. They also shape the intuitions they provoke,

---

28. Daniel Dennett, *Consciousness Explained* (Boston: Little, Brown and Company, 1991), pp. 399–400.

these being as much dependent on the way the thought experiments are described as on our prior concepts. Derek Parfit's thought experiments show perhaps most clearly how thought experiments can work to support a position that would otherwise be untenable and to induce our agreement to this position.

If philosophers want to know about our concept of a person, why do they not just ask themselves and other persons? Yet philosophers for the most part do not conduct empirical surveys. Accordingly, they need to assume what most people's response is likely to be or to ensure that a particular response is likely. Thought experiments are supposed to reveal to us our deep-seated ideas about personal identity in ways that might even be quite startling to ourselves. However, intuitions about far-fetched thought experiments are probably more vulnerable than any other. These thought experiments instead reveal the views of the particular philosopher who invents them, and they urge or seduce us to agree with those views.

As a pedagogic technique, these kind of thought experiments are more likely to bewilder and confuse than to clarify, so that the student is put in the position of having to ask or guess what they are expected to conclude rather than coming up with genuine insights. The way the thought experiments are presented as introductions to the topic makes it easier to cover over the presuppositions behind their use. As Le Dœuff argues, philosophical images are not transparent, and need to be explained and taught, just as concepts do.[29] On the other hand, images work by a form of induction: the reader or student, introduced to the topic via its images, accepts fundamental assumptions, possibilities, and implications before thinking about the broader issues involved in the topic. This peremptory aspect of the thought experiments means that they work near the level of expressibility as well as at the level of persuasiveness. Although it would be possible to present the conclusions without the thought experiments, they are needed to convince the reader or student that certain questions of philosophical significance must be answered.

Therefore it is clear that the thought experiments are doing much more philosophical work than it is claimed that they are doing. The thought experiments are not just being used to discover our intuitions, to clarify a point, or to "sharpen up" our theories. They function to change our views, to force or persuade us to agree and to help us to ignore the underlying assumptions involved. Yet these functions are not adequately acknowledged. Part of this lack of acknowledgment can be located in the perception of the thought experiments as scientific tools, rather than persuasive ones. This perception is linked with the scientism of the analytic imaginary.

29. Le Dœuff, *The Philosophical Imaginary*, p. 173.

Philosophy in the Laboratory

The use of thought experiments in philosophy can usefully be interpreted as an attempt to imitate the methods of science, which are perceived as being more precise than other methods. It is often claimed that it is legitimate to use thought experiments in philosophy because they are used in science.[30] They may have been used in science on occasion with some success, but in philosophy their role is more ambiguous. In the area of personal identity, philosophers seem concerned to match the methods of science, although I do not believe that they succeed in this.

As we saw in chapter 1, Le Dœuff argues that philosophy transforms the images it borrows from other disciplines and makes them part of a specific philosophical imaginary.[31] This transformation is especially apparent in the attempt to apply a methodology of thought experiments to the question of personal identity. It is interesting to note, in this connection, that in the attempt to become more scientific, philosophical discussion of personal identity borrows not from science itself, but from imaginary science, science fiction. For example, Derek Parfit's tele-transportation thought experiment is reminiscent of "beaming up" in the "Star Trek" films and television series. He notes that "Simple Teletransportation, as just described, is a common feature of science fiction."[32] The thought experiment is transformed by the role it plays in Parfit's argument because it is being used in support of his view of personal identity.

We can understand this purported connection with science by looking at philosophers' specific claims about it. For example, a philosopher who tries to present a case for the value of thought experiments on the grounds of their scientific credentials is Daniel Kolak. He thinks that there are only two ways we can think about personal identity: either by accepting the dictates of common sense or by using thought experiments. One of the justifications of thought experiments Kolak gives is that because the perception of the metaphysical significance of physiological and psychological "borders" varies between persons and cultures, "we must, necessarily, turn to conceptual analysis via thought experiments."[33] Presumably we should do this in order

---

30. Mark Johnston notes this claim in "Human Beings," *The Journal of Philosophy* 84, no. 2 (1987): 59–83. He argues that we cannot draw any worthwhile conclusions from the puzzle cases, and believes that the use of "the method of cases" is more problematic in personal identity than in epistemology. Philosophers probably apply the method because it seems useful in other areas, and it has what is seen as the advantage of simplifying what is a difficult, complex and messy topic. However, I argue that it results in over-simplification.

31. Le Dœuff, *The Philosophical Imaginary*, p. 4.

32. Parfit, p. 200.

33. Daniel Kolak, "The Metaphysics and Metapsychology of Personal Identity: Why Thought Experiments Matter in Deciding Who We Are," *American Philosophical Quarterly* 30, no. 1 (1993): 43. One other way to understand the purpose of the thought experiments is that they

to gain a non-culture-specific view of personal identity. However, the claim that thought experiments like Derek Parfit's, where people have replicas made of themselves and sent to Mars, are not culture-specific, is a dubious one.

It is worth noting that Parfit's views bear remarkable similarities, in some respects, to the Buddhist view of personal identity. Parfit quotes from Buddhist texts in an appendix, and claims that "*Buddha would have agreed*" with him and that his view "may be . . . the true view about all people at all times."[34] Finding one example of a similar view of personal identity does not make his view universal. His claim that it is seems obviated by his reliance on what seem to be culture-specific thought experiments that are supposed to reveal or to test what philosophers and people in general really believe personal identity consists in or sometimes more strongly, what personal identity actually consists in. Rather the thought experiments are designed to give spurious credence to the arguments made about personal identity.

Kolak uses an analogous thought experiment to explain why he thinks thought experiments are useful: "Say I want to find out whether physical or psychological intercourse better preserves my marriage long-term; considering imaginary cases where for the rest of my life I can make love to my wife but only without ever talking with her, and vice-versa, could then help me see what I care about more and what better preserves my marriage."[35] Kolak's thought experiment about his marriage partner mirrors the rather crude separation of the physical and the psychological we see in personal identity thought experiments. The idea that the physical aspects of relations between people can be accounted for by making love, and the psychological by talking, is extremely reductive, and thought experiments tend to promote these kinds of reductions.

As other philosophers have argued, Kolak's main attempt to justify the use of thought experiments is to reiterate the common claim that in thought experiments one variable is isolated and therefore tested. However, as the above thought experiment demonstrates, in a way similar to the thought experiments he is defending, it is not possible to genuinely isolate the variables. Kolak says that these kind of imaginary thought experiments are all right if we set them up properly[36] but he gives us no idea as to how they could be or should be set up. As we have seen, there are no guidelines on this point

---

are to show that certain views about personal identity are not necessarily true, because they can possibly be false under the conditions of the thought experiment. However, I think that although the thought experiments may be logically possible, they are not meaningfully possible.

34. Parfit, p. 273.
35. Kolak, p. 46.
36. Ibid., p. 47.

in the philosophical literature on personal identity. One of the most untenable assumptions Kolak makes is that without thought experiments we are stuck with a commonsense view.[37] In doing so, he disregards the variety of other ways in which work on personal identity may be done and assumes a homogeneity of common sense.

Kolak argues that using thought experiments is both more philosophical and more scientific than either common sense *or* philosophy that deals with actual cases, because it describes abstract, metaphysical persons, and because thought experiments produce visions of personal identity that are more in keeping with contemporary science.[38] These remarks make clear that much is being hidden behind Kolak's claims about the relation between science and philosophy. Kolak implies that philosophers can choose and design thought experiments at will, and that there are not any constraints on the type of thought experiment used. The underlying thought seems to be that although philosophy can employ a method drawn from science, it is not subject to the constraints of scientific knowledge or practice. A link is also made between the abstract, the metaphysical, and the scientific, a contentious link that I will have occasion to return to in the next chapters. Now that we have examined the thought experiments, it is difficult to accept that using thought experiments can produce the amazing results Kolak claims for them. Philosophy here does not take place in a laboratory either real or imagined. Nonetheless, it is clear that the perceived connection between thought experiments in personal identity and the methods of science is a key feature of the analytic imaginary.

Self-Generation

There are other interesting aspects of the analytic imaginary revealed by a close reading of the thought experiments. Those who use thought experiments assume that they are a valuable means of clarifying concepts, but once we have seen that they are used to elicit acceptance of the terms and conclusions of a debate, their value appears to be quite different. This value is connected to the notion of self-generation. The thought experiments are self-generating or self-founding in two connected senses—they justify the existence of the debate in the first place, and they create a fable of male self-reproduction.

The first sense of self-generation is that these thought experiments work to create much of the interest in the questions and to keep the discussion

37. See ibid., pp. 44–45.
38. Ibid., p. 49.

going in spite of the lack of progress in the debate. These bizarre imaginings do not bring to the surface our intuitions about personal identity. Instead they manufacture a controversy. As the debate continues, the examples proliferate and become increasingly removed from the so-called object of inquiry—"persons." The points made by Janice Moulton about the usefulness of counter-examples, discussed in relation to the violinist analogy, are relevant here. Often the aim of work on personal identity is to show how another philosopher's thought experiment can be rewritten to establish a different conclusion, rather than to establish a positive view.

A further point, which we observed in regard to much philosophical work on abortion, is that the methodology used leads to what Le Dœuff calls "closed philosophy." While the debate may be lively and interesting for those concerned, the thought experiments constrain possible responses, rather than lead to fresh insights. It is difficult to see how the debate can progress further beyond an endless proliferation of increasingly unlikely thought experiments which can always be redescribed in order to come up with opposite conclusions.

The implications of Wilkes's questions about pregnancy in relation to Parfit's amoebae thought experiments points to the second sense of self-generation which emerges. Cloning, fission, and even mind swaps are all methods of reproducing new persons either without women being involved or without actual human reproductive processes. Again, there is a Lockean precedent: in *An Essay Concerning Human Understanding*, he uses the example of seeds in a parsley bed to argue that we can understand the concept brother without understanding the concept of birth, in the context of an argument for the point that we can understand an idea of relation as clearly, or more clearly, than we can understand the things in relation. He writes: "For if I believed that *Sepmpronia* digged *Titus* out of the parsley-bed (as they used to tell children) and thereby became his mother, and that afterwards in the same manner she digged *Caius* out of the parsley-bed, I had as clear a notion of the relation of brothers between them, as if I had all the skill of a midwife."[39] Locke apparently thinks that an understanding of brotherhood is prior to an understanding of childbirth, that this notion is equivalent to having the skill of a midwife, and that motherhood is a passive state following on from the (male) child: he comes out of the parsley bed, she becomes his mother. Of course, Locke's homespun example is very different from the futuristic science fiction of analytic philosophy, but it does invoke the theme of male self-generation. Personhood develops in the context of birth, life,

39. See John Locke, *An Essay Concerning Human Understanding*, p. 361. Le Dœuff discusses this example in "On Some Philosophical Pacts," *Journal of the Institute of Romance Studies* 2 (1993): 395–407.

relations with others, and death. These thought experiments, by imagining male self-reproduction, have become remote from these realities in a way that affects the worth of their imaginings. The fantasies of reproduction enable the entire question of bodily differences between men and women to be overlooked. This sense of self-generation is connected to a number of tensions concerning the mind and body and the question of differences between persons in general.

Mind or Body?

There are a number of problematic assumptions involved in these kind of thought experiments: one set concerns the relations between mind and body. It is presupposed that mind and body are separate and independent, although paradoxically the mind is somehow contained in the brain, which is a part of the body. The thought experiments assume that the body has little effect on mental life, apart from being a kind of "house" for the brain and mind. These conceptions relate quite closely to the conceptions of self encapsulated in the violinist and people-seed analogies. Psychological continuity theories are more popular than bodily continuity theories because it is thought that it is the mind which controls the body, the mind which will suffer, and the mind which takes responsibility for actions.[40]

Whatever one thinks about the importance of mind or body, it is the relation between the two which the thought experiments exclude from proper consideration. Amélie Rorty notes that there are kinesthetic factors involved in connection with Shoemaker's thought experiment. She argues that the body will affect the brain (and the memories) and vice-versa: "suppose that Robinson limps painfully. Won't Brown's passion for dancing the flamenco be affected by the discomfort of expressing it in Robinson's hulking, lumbering body? Suppose Robinson's body suffers from an overproduction of adrenalin: will Brownson's memories take on an irascible tone? How can we establish the identity of tastes and memories under different emotional tonalities?"[41] These remarks illustrate the difficulties of thought experiments that incorporate the idea that either psychological or bodily continuity by themselves are sufficient for identity. They also point to the absurdities that can arise from simply assuming we have to choose between these two views.

40. Supporters of the psychological/mental continuity view include John Locke, David Lewis, John Perry, Anthony Quinton, Sydney Shoemaker, and Richard Swinburne. Parfit, as we have seen, argues for psychological connectedness. Supporters of the bodily continuity view are David Wiggins and Bernard Williams.

41. Rorty, p. 3.

Certain views of the relation between mind and body are taken for granted, and recent scholarship on the social construction of bodies, and on the mind-body problem, is ignored and excluded. If you describe a thought experiment based on the question, "Which is more important in personal identity, bodily or psychological continuity?" there is no space for someone to argue, for example, that we cannot separate the two in this way. When Maurice Merleau-Ponty considers the possibility of psychological continuity without bodily continuity, he responds: "It will perhaps be objected that the organization of our body is contingent, that we can 'conceive a man without hands, feet, head' and *a fortiori*, a sexless man, self-propagating by cutting or layering. But this is the case only if we take an abstract view of hands, feet, head or sexual apparatus, regarding them, that is, as fragments of matter, and ignoring their living function."[42] The personal identity thought experiments are based on precisely the view that Merleau-Ponty describes here. They take an abstract view of all aspects of persons, and ignore their living function. The fragmented nature of the debates themselves, where questions of personal identity are separated from other related questions, is partly responsible for these problems. The thought experiments promote and accentuate this fragmentation. A phenomenological account like Merleau-Ponty's arguably gives a much fuller description of experience, by showing how we always experience ourselves and relate to others both physically and psychologically. While Merleau-Ponty may not have a fully articulated account of personal identity, a theory that incorporates his insights might be more promising than one based on thought experiments. In any case using the thought experiments ensures that these kinds of considerations cannot be raised. Furthermore, the abstraction of the thought experiments obscures a number of other questions in addition to mind-body relations.

Abstracting Persons

The thought experiments involve a number of fundamental assumptions about the nature of persons and thus the philosophical literature on personal identity should be of particular interest to feminists. In philosophical discourse, women have often been classified as inferior beings. For example, Aristotle's description of "man" as a rational animal does not include women, because he thinks that women's reason is limited.[43] Personhood has often

---

42. Maurice Merleau-Ponty, *Phenomenology of Perception*, trans. Colin Smith (London: Routledge and Kegan Paul, 1962), p. 170.

43. Aristotle, *Politics*, in *The Complete Works of Aristotle*, ed. Jonathan Barnes, vol. 2 (Princeton: Princeton University Press, 1986), p. 1999; 1260a10–15.

been defined in terms of characteristics or activities which are (at the time) possible only for men, such as ownership of property or acting in the public sphere, and "personhood" has been linked to rationality in a way which excludes women.[44] However, it is clear that explicitly feminist issues have been given little or no place in the personal identity debates and that conceptions of persons remain problematic in feminist terms.

There are a number of different reasons why feminists and other philosophers should find the philosophical literature on personal identity particularly problematic. One is that it constructs a kind of reason which abstracts and displaces from any ordinary context in order to create a discourse that is supposedly neutral and universal, yet which is really value-laden and specific. It is value-laden for two main reasons. First, because the thought experiments are influenced by Western science fiction, they incorporate the high value placed on technological manipulations and the notion that persons can go through almost limitless changes without altering their basic personhood. The use of thought experiments is premised on the idea that the most important question about personal identity is: What are the minimum necessary conditions for personhood? It is assumed that this question can be answered by looking at strange thought experiments which ignore features of everyday life.

Secondly, because questions of gender and cultural identity, for example, are not taken into account, they promote the view that such characteristics are trivial and contingent. One might think that philosophers writing on personal identity would discuss different people in ordinary contexts, but instead we get a variety of science fiction thought experiments involving As and Bs, men with plain "Anglo" names like Brown and Robinson, and often the philosophers themselves in impossible contexts. Parfit, for example, tends to write from the first-person viewpoint, as in the tele-transportation thought experiment, and responses to his work refer to Parfit's possible lives, and so on. The imaginary of science fiction is a culture-specific one, and the characters of this fiction are usually, though not always, men. Making the subjects of the case two under-described adult males effectively eliminates any questions that would arise if differences of sex, ethnicity, age, character and style or manner were taken into account. The thought experiments make it difficult to consider how the questions and the debate would be

44. See, for example, Jean Grimshaw's discussion of Aristotle's, Kant's and Locke's views on women's inherent inability to reason fully, be of moral worth, or consent to government, respectively, in *Feminist Philosophers* (Brighton: Wheatsheaf Books, 1986), pp. 38–51. Also see Susan James's argument that the feminine is marginalized in personal identity debates: "Feminism in Philosophy of Mind: The Question of Personal Identity," in *The Cambridge Companion to Feminism in Philosophy,* eds. Miranda Fricker and Jennifer Hornsby, (Cambridge: Cambridge University Press, 2000), pp. 29–48.

restructured if we thought of "persons" as essentially sexually embodied be-ings. As we have seen, even to ask these questions, as Rorty and Wilkes do, reveals the absurdity of the thought experiments.

Another basic assumption, which applies to all the philosophers working in this strand of the personal identity debate, is the assumption of radical in-dividualism, that the self can be understood in isolation from group identi-ties. Rorty argues that the question of identity has even more force when we ask what Brown's and Robinson's wives [we could add, and children] have to say about it.[45] The thought experiments fail to take into account individ-uals' relations with others, in the sense of intimate others or as groups to which they may belong. This individualistic concept of the self is related to the fundamental characteristic of the analytic imaginary, that each individ-ual can imagine themselves in another's place. If this is accepted, so is the idea that any thinker can determine how they might regard any situation, even impossible ones. On the basis of this assumption, it is not necessary to consider particular details of a person's existence to understand what is es-sential to it. This assumption works in conjunction with the view that the only proper philosophical way to understand persons is as abstract, disembodied beings.

Reconceptions

Personal identity is a complicated area, because it potentially involves many different kinds of questions. While it could be argued that thought experi-ments are part of a focus on certain questions, it is clear that they are not successful even in their limited aims, and that research would benefit from broader studies. There are a number of different ways we could approach topics related to personal identity, if we want to step outside the debates gen-erated by strange and impossible thought experiments or puzzle cases.

We could explore the possibilities without the use of imaginings that in-volve our losing our particularity, by looking at actual experiences of self. Another method is that already used by some writers on personal identity, for example, Wilkes and Jonathon Glover who look at actual examples rele-vant to the issue, such as people with so-called "split personalities" or men-tal illness, and who examine our concept of a person in the light of these is-sues.[46] However, these studies still tend to ignore class, ethnicity, and sex differences, and the way identity is formed through relations with others. Yet

45. Rorty, p. 3.
46. Jonathan Glover, *I: The Philosophy and Psychology of Personal Identity* (London: Allen Lane, 1988).

another approach is to compare concepts of personal identity cross-culturally or historically, and to use work from disciplines apart from philosophy. A further possibility is to do more research based on the work of theorists, such as Merleau-Ponty, who do not presuppose a reductionist or dualist account of mind. Various kinds of relations between physical and mental qualities need to be taken into account. Another way is to look at a variety of distinctive experiences of self.

In her book, *Volatile Bodies: Toward a Corporeal Feminism*, Elizabeth Grosz combines the last two approaches by developing a non-dualist, non-reductionist account of the body and subjectivity premised on an acknowledgment of sexual difference. While Grosz does not concentrate specifically on the question of personal identity, it is useful to recognize her criticisms of dualism and monism, some version of which is generally assumed by the personal identity theorists. The main problems she finds with both dualism and monism is that they leave mind-body interaction unexplained, and that they tend to privilege the mind.[47] It is also worthwhile to consider ways in which we could think about whole persons. In order to do this it is necessary to focus on the body, partly as a counterbalance to the overwhelming philosophical concentration on the mind. She argues that the body itself is as much a cultural and historical product as the mind.[48]

Grosz's model of the self or subject is a Möbius strip, which she believes represents the way the body is imbued with subjectivity and the way subjectivity is material. She writes: "The strip has the advantage of showing the inflection of mind into body and body into mind, the ways in which, through a kind of twisting or inversion, one side becomes another. This model also provides a way of problematizing and rethinking the relations between the inside and the outside of the subject, its psychical interior and its corporeal exterior, by showing not their fundamental identity or reducibility but the torsion of one into the other, the passage, vector, or uncontrollable drift of the inside into the outside and the outside into the inside."[49] Mind and body cannot be separated, because if we try to map the effects or structure of one, we will soon begin to map the other. An example of the way she thinks the mind and body twist into one another is in the sense of touch, where one can be both the subject and object of touch.[50] Her idea of the role of the body is as neither just a completely pliable thing nor as a biological given. The body is not inert matter, nor do we experience it as such. We live our bodies in one way through a psychical body image that is influenced through

47. Elizabeth Grosz, *Volatile Bodies: Toward a Corporeal Feminism* (Sydney: Allen and Unwin, 1994), pp. 6–7.
48. Ibid., p. 187.
49. Ibid., p. xii.
50. Ibid., p. 36.

social, cultural and historical factors. The famous phantom limb cases are examples of this, or where prosthetic limbs or tools we use become part of our body image. Hysterical paralysis is yet another striking illustration. These points can be related to the remarks Rorty makes about the brain swap example in the sense that calling certain characteristics "kinesthetic" is to suggest a more complex understanding of mind-body relations than most of the thought experiments employ. Body image involves our understanding of our physical relation to space, other people, and the world. These points are well summarized by Grosz: "the subject's psychical interior can be understood as an introjection, a form of internalization of (the meaning and significance of) the body and its parts, and conversely, how the body is constituted through projection as the boundary, limit, edge, or border of subjectivity, that which divides the subject in the first instance from other subjects and in the second, from the world."[51] From the other side of the Möbius strip, she argues that bodies' interactions with the world create all the impressions of subjectivity or consciousness.[52] We internalize the constraints and pressures on our bodies. For example, torture and punishment are inscribed on our body, but also lived. The body is also marked by clothing, grooming, gait, exercise, drugs, and nutrition.

Grosz argues that one's sex and sexuality are important to identity, because different bodies interact differently with the world, and because we live the cultural meanings prescribed for our bodies because of our sex. For example, we live our bodies differently under a system of oppression. We hold, move, and inscribe our bodies in relation to cultural prescriptions for the particular body and live physiological functions in accordance with these prescriptions. She thinks that sexual difference is non-contingent in a way that eye-color, for example, is not. She argues that one's sex affects the meaning of every biological, social, and cultural function.[53] This aspect of identity is perhaps recognized but not acknowledged by writers on personal identity, because the various swaps of minds, brains, and bodies, always go on between two persons of the same sex, almost always men.

Grosz points out the limitations of her own model. She notes that: "For one thing, utilizing the Möbius model limits our understanding of the subject in terms of dualism but links it to a kind of monism, autonomy, or self-presence that precludes understanding the body, bodies, as the terrain and effect of difference."[54] In any case, this brief presentation of Grosz's views is not intended to offer a theoretical end-point. Rather, it suggests some of the ways in which personal identity could be understood if we took the conjoining of mental

51. Ibid., p. 115.
52. Ibid., p. 116.
53. Ibid., p. 22.
54. Ibid., p. 210.

and physical seriously, and recognized sexual difference. Our understanding of personal identity would be more complex, subtle, interesting and accurate if these kinds of approaches were taken into account. The analytic imaginary would be enriched by these considerations. There is not just a stark choice between common sense and thought experiments: there are other ways to do philosophy. We can use other kinds of images and examples, and different questions can be asked. By relying so heavily on thought experiments, analytic philosophers in this area have cut themselves off from many sources of insight.

Conclusion

Like the analogy we considered in the previous chapter, thought experiments in personal identity work on a number of levels. One is at the level of enframement. First, thought experiments provide the framework and terms of the debate. If we want to participate in the debate on personal identity we must accept the thought experiments and a divided self, either split into two by the bodily versus psychological continuity theorists, or in Parfit's case, split into infinitely many fragments. The bodily and psychological continuity theorists presuppose that the mind and body can be separated, and that we can decide which one is more important than the other. It is particularly odd when we consider that the mind is often treated as identical to the brain, even though the brain is a part of the body. An even deeper assumption is the individuality and isolation of the self, as one that lives and reproduces outside human communities and natural processes. This self is interchangeable with other (similar) selves. Accepting the thought experiments means accepting a pseudo-scientific methodology in philosophy. Philosophers need to reassess methods of reasoning that include thought experiments in order to discover repressed assumptions, both about the content under discussion, and reason itself.

The fact that it is difficult for feminists to get involved in this area suggests that questions of interest to feminists, such as the relations between gender and identity, and persons as sexed and in particular contexts, are excluded. By using thought experiments focused on questions of psychological continuity, historical and social context can be ignored. Certain problems and ways of thinking are excluded by arguing that we must make a decision in impossible thought experiments. In the debate on personal identity predicated on thought experiments, there is no room for a profound reconception of "persons," no possibility of using accounts of embodiment or the social and cultural construction of bodies. The possible effects of the body on the mind are disregarded. Until philosophers begin seriously to attend to these questions, the debate will not make any progress.

The thought experiments operate very strongly on the persuasive level, because they are used to introduce the topic or question. Then one is asked to choose, generally, between only two possible alternatives, such as between mind and body, or brain and body, in terms of psychological and physical continuity or connectedness. Furthermore, the choice we are likely to make is constrained by the peculiarities of the particular thought experiment. However, thought experiments are also vulnerable at this level, because they are so readily recast in ways which induce contrary conclusions. Thought experiments work very near the level of expressibility as well. They do this not because it is impossible to express analytic theories of personal identity without recourse to thought experiments, but because theories thus expressed are unlikely to mean anything to anyone.

By constraining debates through thought experiments, a community of personal identity theorists is able to repel innovation and maintain its borders. These thought experiments are a good example of Le Dœuff's observation that images are "the language of the corporation."[55] Images and thought in images, such as thought experiments, should help to open up debates, not close them off. If we use the kind of puzzle cases and thought experiments discussed above, we are accepting much more than bizarre possibilities. We are accepting the assumptions behind the thought experiments and a type of philosophical reasoning which makes demands upon our intuitions about thought experiments in an attempt to elicit our agreement with desired conclusions.

55. Le Dœuff, *The Philosophical Imaginary,* p. 171.

4

Contractarian Myths

The image of the social contract structures debates about justice in contemporary political philosophy. In some respects, it is more complicated than the violinist analogy or the personal identity thought experiments because the characterization of the image itself is a matter for debate. The image of a social contract first emerged in the work of Hobbes, Locke, and Rousseau and some of the most influential political philosophy in the last three decades has involved a reworking of this image. While different social contract theorists have come to quite different conclusions, the image they share effects similarities in the structure of their thought.

My focus here is the contemporary recasting of the image of the social contract in the work of John Rawls and his defenders and critics, including Thomas Nagel, Will Kymlicka, Susan Moller Okin, Iris Marion Young, and Carole Pateman. In order to investigate this use of imagery, we must ask first whether the social contract is a concept, a theory, a doctrine, a metaphor, a device, an allegory, or myth. Before giving an answer, it is important to present Rawls's version of the image and see how it has been described. I argue that the social contract and its accompanying images are best understood as myths. Assumptions about political organization, human nature and moral reasoning are incorporated into the image itself and its formulations, assumptions that reveal the nature of the analytic imaginary. Furthermore, a number of tensions in the image emerge in relation to women and the family. These tensions re-emerge in the work of feminist philosophers who attempt to use the image for their own purposes.[1] The myths of contract provide a frame within which questions about sexual and ethnic differences are understood, as well as persuading readers of the justifiability of that framework. We will see how myths of contract can exclude recognition of difference and even prevent alternatives from being developed.

The Social Contract

The philosophers who first used the social contract image wrote as if they were discussing a historical event, but in recent years Rawls and other analytic philosophers admit the speculative or hypothetical nature of the contracts they set up. Most constructions of the social contract depend on an accompanying image, the state of nature, an age when there was no political organization, which takes various forms. How this image is presented provides some of the conditions for acceptance of the final contract. For example, Hobbes's description of the state of nature as one of violent conflict, where life is "solitary, poore, nasty, brutish, and short" makes the idea of autocratic government he wants to justify, "a common Power to keep them all in awe," seem more legitimate.[2] The basic idea of a contract is as a kind of promise made by two parties to each other. Alternatively, it can be thought of as a bargain, or an exchange. A contract is supposed to be made between equals who want to come to an agreement, or between two parties who have some kind of property of roughly comparable value which they wish to exchange. For example, a contract may be made to exchange goods or labor for money.

However, the kind of exchange that is involved in a social contract is less tangible. The early social contract theorists thought of the social contract as a kind of exchange of natural freedom for a protected freedom. Often, it is claimed, there is an explicit or implicit agreement made by members of a society to the system of government under which they are living. However, the "social" aspect of the contract is varied depending on which philosopher is presenting it, because it may be a contract between, say, the individuals in a society and the state, or between each individual and the rest of society. This is why the parties to the contract can be so diverse: Hobbes's

---

1. I will show a similar effect in the use of visual metaphors by feminist epistemologists in chapter 5.

2. Hobbes, *Leviathan* (London: Aldine Press, 1953), pp. 185–186.

monarch and the people; Locke's government and the people; or Rawls's group of individuals.[3]

The images of the social contract and the state of nature, as characterized by Rawls, work to make certain assumptions about the parties to the contract, the conditions of the contract, and moral reasoning, in general, seem plausible, and certain conclusions about the nature of social organization seem inevitable. These assumptions are central to the analytic imaginary.

Reinventing the Social Contract: Rawls

Rawls's work in political philosophy has developed, over more than thirty years, from the extremely influential *A Theory of Justice* to his more recent book, *Political Liberalism*. The contract in Rawls's work is quite different from that of the classic social contract theorists, although he says he is influenced by Kant, Locke, and Rousseau and wants to use social contract doctrine. He clarifies that he is not referring to any original, historical contract made by members of a society, to forestall the obvious objection that no such contract was made, and therefore no appeal to a social contract can have legitimizing power. Thus, Rawls's social contract is a hypothetical one, not an actual promise or exchange, to be used as a model for determining principles of justice.

Rawls wishes to use the language of contract for a number of reasons, even though his is a contract in only a derivative sense. He believes that links with the contract tradition help to define ideas and suggest principles that are chosen in a well-defined situation. As he puts it, "The merit of the contract terminology is that it conveys the idea that principles of justice may be conceived as principles that would be chosen by rational persons, and that in this way conceptions of justice may be explained and justified."[4] Thus, Rawls is acutely aware that the notion of a contract is one which brings in certain assumptions right from the start. Distributive justice, consensus, and a theory based on rational choice become part of the accepted basis for political justice and moral reasoning. Rawls's claim is that these assumptions are quite trivial and would be accepted by most people. However, these and further assumptions introduced by the original position are in fact controversial. We should look at the images to understand how they work to make these controversial assumptions more acceptable.

---

3. Hobbes, p. 90; John Locke, *Two Treatises of Government* (New York: Hafner Publishing Company, 1956), p. 187; and John Rawls, *A Theory of Justice* (Cambridge: Harvard University Press, 1971), pp. 12–13.

4. Rawls, *A Theory of Justice*, p. 16.

A Story of Origins: The Original Position
and the Veil of Ignorance

Rawls insists that he is not presenting a story of origins, yet he makes use of such a story within the central image of the social contract: this is the "original position," the starting point for moral reasoning. The original position is a hypothetical situation, where a group of people is supposed to meet to discuss and unanimously agree upon the principles of justice which will form the basic structure of society. Rawls describes the original position like this:

> [M]any individuals coexist together at the same time on a definite geographical territory. These individuals are roughly similar in physical and mental powers; or at any rate, their capacities are comparable in that no one among them can dominate the rest. They are vulnerable to attack, and all are subject to having their plans blocked by the united force of others. Finally, there is the condition of moderate scarcity understood to cover a wide range of situations. Natural and other resources are not so abundant that schemes of cooperation become superfluous, nor are conditions so harsh that fruitful ventures must inevitably break down. While mutually advantageous arrangements are feasible, the benefits they yield fall short of the demands men put forward.[5]

These are what Rawls calls the *objective* circumstances of the original position. The most important subjective condition is that the parties will not be interested in each other's interests. It is taken that they are the heads or representatives of families, which is meant to ensure a concern for future generations.

The participants in the original position are to work out which principles of distribution of certain goods would ensure a just society, in a situation that guarantees fairness. Rawls gives a list of the social primary goods that he thinks need to be distributed fairly: "things that every rational man is presumed to want."[6] They are rights and liberties, powers and opportunities, income and wealth, and self-respect. He notes that there are other primary goods such as health and intelligence, but says they are natural goods which cannot really be controlled by the principles of justice.

Another important image Rawls employs is the "veil of ignorance," an aspect of the original position used to convey the unawareness of the reasoners of certain facts about themselves and their position in society. He describes the veil of ignorance thus:

5. Ibid., pp. 126–127.
6. Ibid., p. 62.

First of all, no one knows his place in society, his class position or social status; nor does he know his fortune in the distribution of natural assets and abilities, his intelligence and strength and the like. Nor, again, does anyone know his conception of the good, the particulars of his rational plan of life, or even the special features of his psychology such as his aversion to risk or liability to optimism or pessimism. More than this, I assume that the parties do not know the particular circumstances of their own society. That is, they do not know its economic or political situation, or the level of civilization it has been able to achieve. The persons in the original position have no information as to which generation they belong.[7]

To summarize, behind the veil of ignorance, people do not know their class, social status, age, cultural background, natural gifts and talents, their own conceptions of the good, or their own psychological characteristics. Rawls does not mention whether their sex is one of the things the participants in the original position do not know, but it is fairly clear that he considers it to be a contingent and morally irrelevant characteristic as it is not mentioned as one of the things they *do* know. He clarifies the point much later in *Political Liberalism,* stating that the parties will not know their sex or gender.[8]

This ignorance is supposed to ensure that no-one will be advantaged or disadvantaged by choices based on contingent facts, and so the principles of justice will result from a fair agreement. He believes that if people knew their position in society, they would not be able to arrive at fair principles, but would simply devise principles that put themselves in the most advantageous position. The veil of ignorance is a "thick" one, which means, "the parties are not allowed to know . . . the particular comprehensive doctrine of the person each represents."[9] In other words, the parties do not know their moral or political views. However, Rawls allows that they will have certain "facts" at their disposal, such as the facts of psychology, sociology, politics and economics.

In describing the situation in the original position, Rawls makes a number of explicit assumptions about the way people will reason, which he calls the circumstances of justice. It is assumed that people behind the veil of ignorance

7. Ibid., p. 137. Veils have had a number of different significations in literature and philosophy. One important meaning is preventing access to science and enlightenment, while another is as a protection from dangerous knowledge. It is interesting that the meaning of Rawls's veil appears closer to the latter. For a fascinating discussion of the history of this image, see George Armstrong Kelly, "Veils: The Poetics of John Rawls," *Journal of the History of Ideas* 57, no. 2 (1996): 343–364.

8. John Rawls, *Political Liberalism* (New York: Columbia University Press, 1993), p. 24.

9. Ibid.

will be concerned only with their own interests, and they are rational in that they know the most effective means to achieve ends. As we have seen, the participants in the original position have no moral ties to each other: they are mutually disinterested. This does not mean that their interests are necessarily opposed, but they are not particularly concerned about each other's interests. The method of coming to agreement in the original position is unusual, because rather than discussing conflicts and problems, Rawls dictates that each participant will reason privately about how they would like things to be, and then come to agreement with the others. He says we can "imagine that the parties are required to communicate with each other through a referee as intermediary, and that he is to announce which alternatives have been suggested and the reasons offered in their support . . . But such a referee is actually superfluous, assuming that the deliberations of the parties must be similar."[10] The principles of justice that the parties compare are weighed up against considered moral judgments, and altered if they do not correspond with them. The outcome of the balancing of principles against judgments is called "reflective equilibrium." This process is supposed to be analogous to scientific method—where theories or hypotheses are judged against particular observations.[11] Like the thought experiments of the previous chapter, Rawls's use of reflective equilibrium is an example of an attempt to make theories appear more scientific.

Rawls argues that the results of deliberation in the original position will be two principles of justice. The first is the principle of basic equality of liberty. The second is a two-part principle: fair equality of opportunity, and the difference principle. The difference principle states that social and economic inequalities must "enhance the opportunities of those with the lesser opportunity."[12] The first principle has priority over the second. According to Rawls, any society will be judged to be fair, therefore just, if it is organized around these principles.

Rawls is quite open about his reasons for using the original position to reach the conclusions he does, as he admits that the point of the original position is to "get the desired solution."[13] However, he argues that the assumptions he makes are innocuous ones, which free, rational, self-interested persons would accept, and that the original position best models an ideal situation of fairness. These assumptions will be examined further, but at this stage, it is important to make clear why I think that the original position works as a myth, rather than as, say, a device or metaphor.

10. *A Theory of Justice*, p. 139.
11. Ibid., p. 49.
12. Ibid., pp. 302–303.
13. Ibid., p. 141.

Methodological Devices?

First, the term "device" is a misleading characterization of these images. Early responses to Rawls's work accepted his characterization of the original position and the veil of ignorance as "simplifying devices."[14] This rather neutral term is meant to refer to hypothetical explanations that provide much of the drive for certain theories. However, Rawls's commentators do not necessarily believe that the devices justify his principles. Thomas Nagel argues that Rawls makes a number of additional assumptions about how the parties will reason in the original position. For example, he thinks that there is no reason to suppose that the parties will choose conservatively because they are concerned about the possibility of being in the worst-off group; people are just as likely to gamble and arrive at a principle that allows much greater inequalities than the difference principle. In Nagel's view, the original position, and the contractual basis of Rawls's theory, is even more likely to be rejected than the principles themselves, as they rely on presumptions rather than offering independent support to his conclusions. As he puts it: "The egalitarian liberalism which he develops and the conception of the good on which it depends are extremely persuasive, but the original position serves to model rather than to justify them."[15]

Another commentator, Alan Brown, also feels that the original position does not justify the principles of justice. Furthermore, he argues that Rawls's theory is not a contract theory at all, and does not involve genuine bargaining, because the parties involved do not know their own interests.[16] He says: "the methodological devices employed by Rawls are at best irrelevant and are more likely destructive of any sound philosophical construction."[17] What Brown means is that the original position does not provide an adequate justification for Rawls's liberal views. More strongly, he says that the original position actually supports the utilitarian view that Rawls is so anxious to give an alternative to—the parties could well decide that it is in their interest to opt for highest average utility, with the restriction that the situation of those at the bottom cannot go below a certain point.[18] The further device of reflective equilibrium is designed to make good some of these deficiencies. However, reflective equilibrium presupposes liberal views, because

14. Ibid., p. viii.

15. Thomas Nagel, "Rawls on Justice," in *Reading Rawls: Critical Studies of A Theory of Justice,* ed. Norman Daniels (Oxford: Blackwell, 1975), p. 15.

16. Alan Brown, *Modern Political Philosophy* (London: Penguin, 1986), p. 64.

17. Ibid., p. 78.

18. David Lyons, "Nature and Soundness of Contract and Coherence Arguments," in *Reading Rawls,* p. 166, also argues that the principle of utility might be chosen in the original position, as it is no more risky than Rawls's principles.

the "considered moral judgments" Rawls refers to are liberal judgments, and in searching for a reflective equilibrium the original position is altered until it offers maximum support to liberal conclusions. Thus, the characterization of Rawls's images as devices tends to lead to an underestimation of their role in his argument.

A more sophisticated description of the role of the contract image has been given recently by Will Kymlicka. He is an enthusiastic liberal, but believes that the original position, like all uses of what he calls the contract device, does nothing to generate or defend liberal arguments. He accepts that views about justice are presupposed in the setting up of the contractual situation. However, he argues that it serves a number of useful purposes, such as rendering political judgments more determinate and more vivid, and dramatizing the commitment to impartiality.[19] In *Political Liberalism,* Rawls himself conveys a similar view when he says that we should think of being behind the veil of ignorance like acting a part in a play.[20] However, Rawls would probably not accept that this dramatizing impartiality is *all* that the veil of ignorance does.

Kymlicka's claims about the role played by contract "devices," like the original position, are more convincing than Rawls's own. However, for a number of reasons, their role is actually more substantial than he allows. Although Kymlicka says that the contract is redundant, it continues to be used—Rawls himself shows no signs of giving it up. The reluctance of theorists to relinquish contract images shows that they have a continuing resonance in the analytic imaginary. Contractarian images are used for purposes other than dramatic or illustrative ones. First, these images retain rhetorical force as a foundational myth for liberal thought and the philosophical notion of impartiality. The original position and the veil of ignorance not only make these ideas vivid, but also persuade people of their validity. Furthermore, they enable many of the implications of impartiality and liberalism to be overlooked in a way that they might not be if these so-called devices were not used. The images also give a frame and substance to certain liberal views, and to debates about political organization. Robert Nozick, for example, acknowledges the depth of analytic philosophy's commitment to Rawlsian images when he claims that "Political philosophers now must either work within Rawls' theory or explain why not."[21] In other words, political philosophers within the analytic tradition must either use the contractarian image or explain why not.

19. Will Kymlicka, "The Social Contract Tradition," in *A Companion to Ethics,* ed. Peter Singer (Oxford: Blackwell, 1991), p. 193. I will say more about the concept of impartiality further on in this chapter.

20. *Political Liberalism,* p. 27.

21. Robert Nozick, *Anarchy, State, and Utopia* (Oxford: Blackwell, 1974), p. 183.

The social contract, original position, and the veil of ignorance are best described as myths. It is clear that Rawls's contract is not a contract in an actual historical or conceptual sense. The term device, as we have seen, is too neutral and does not convey the manner in which the images work. Metaphor is incorrect, because the images are not referring to one thing as something else, although the original position and the veil of ignorance are *metaphorical* in the sense of being evocative. The term thought experiment, used by Bruce Ackerman to describe the veil of ignorance, only conveys its hypothetical nature.[22] It does not function the way the thought experiments of chapter 3 do. Paul Ricoeur's suggestion that the veil of ignorance is an allegory is quite attractive, but it implies that there is or could be a real situation for which the veil of ignorance stands.[23] The term myth is preferable because it expresses the fictitious nature of the images, as well as alluding to the idea of origins and its purported explanatory and justificatory role. Rawls's myth tells a story about a group of people founding a state; this story can act as both a spur to change in political organization and to explain and justify the general outlines of current political organization in some states. A number of writers argue that the social contract is a kind of myth, a myth of origins that justifies the dreams of the political philosopher.[24] While the original position and the veil of ignorance are not myths about how society began, they are myths about how we should think of society as beginning. Myths are common in political thought, just as the other images looked at so far are common in their areas. The reasons for regarding these images as myths should become even clearer as we go on and look more closely at how the myths of the social contract, the original position and the veil of ignorance work for Rawls.

Participating in the Original Position

First, the myth of the original position partially conceals a number of problematic assumptions. Some of these assumptions have been exposed by the feminist philosopher, Susan Moller Okin, although there are others, which

---

22. Bruce Ackerman, "Political Liberalisms," *The Journal of Philosophy* 91, no. 7 (1994): 368.
23. Ricoeur, p. 231. He also calls it a fable.
24. For example, Carole Pateman, *The Sexual Contract* (Stanford: Stanford University Press, 1988), p. 219, and Iris Marion Young, *Justice and the Politics of Difference* (Princeton: Princeton University Press, 1990), p. 104. I will discuss both their views in more detail further on this chapter. See Terence Ball, *Reappraising Political Theory: Revisionist Studies in the History of Political Thought* (Oxford: Clarendon Press, 1995), pp. 281–285. He argues that the original position is a version of a distinctive myth of an American Adam first put forward by Thomas Paine.

I shall discuss. Even more importantly, when Okin tries to use the original position for her own purposes, the image subverts her intentions. Just as images can constrain debates in applied ethics and personal identity, and metaphors interact with certain concepts (as will become clear in chapter 5), in this case, images subvert critique.

One of the first questions of importance concerning the assumptions embodied by the original position is: Just who are the participants in the social contract? Given the abstract nature of the original position, the participants seem to be not much more than reasoning entities. Rawls argues that fair principles of justice can only be reached by parties who know nothing of their particular psychologies, interests, or situation in life. But we are given *some* information about these entities and this can enable us to get a clearer idea of the kind of people Rawls really has in mind. In her paper, "John Rawls: Justice as Fairness—For Whom?," Okin explores the implications of Rawls's original position for justice in the family.[25] As noted earlier, in the original position the parties concerned do not know their own sex, it being one of those contingent characteristics it is not necessary to know.[26] Yet they do know that they are heads of families, and also, Okin believes, that there will be an institutionalized system of sexual discrimination in the society they are part of. This claim is surely correct, because the parties are supposed to know facts about sociology and politics. Thus, they must know they are men, or otherwise they could not be heads of families.[27]

In *A Theory of Justice*, Rawls says that the family is one of the basic social institutions which will need to be tested by the theory of justice, but he does not discuss the family at all in that book, and in later articles he places the family in the category of private arrangements, not subject to the criteria of justice.[28] As Okin notes, Rawls needs to make his reasoners heads of families in order to ensure a concern for future generations. Given the importance of that concern, it seems that he is in an extremely difficult position. On the one hand, he is relying on family connections for an essential part

25. Susan Moller Okin, "John Rawls: Justice as Fairness—For Whom?" in *Feminist Interpretations and Political Theory*, ed. Mary Lyndon Shanley and Carole Pateman (Cambridge: Polity Press, 1991), pp. 181–198.

26. Okin notes that Rawls is silent on this question in *A Theory of Justice*, but later "made it clear that sex is one of those morally irrelevant contingencies that is hidden by the veil of ignorance." Ibid., p. 183.

27. Okin argues that while women can be heads of families, this arrangement is still considered to be a variation on the norm.

28. For example, in "The Basic Structure as Subject," *The American Philosophical Quarterly* 14, no. 2 (1977): 159.

of his theory of justice. On the other hand, he needs to reject the idea that the participants in the original position know they are heads of families for other reasons, such as the bar on participants knowing their sex. There seems to be no way out of this problem, given the characteristics of the image, especially the veil of ignorance.

There are other problems with the assumption that individual heads of families are able to represent their families' interests, which Okin does not discuss. First, this assumption implies that there is no disagreement within families about questions of justice, or even of interests, as if spouses always have the same interests or that both parents have the same interests as children. It is not out of the question for there to be conflicts of interests between parents and children. There is also the possibility that a parent could put the children's interests ahead of their own, if their interests are different. That these kinds of possibilities are overlooked is a consequence of using an image which incorporates a view of the family as a homogenous unit that can be represented by its head. The family is one of the structures hidden behind the abstract individual of the social contract myth. Rawls's decision to put the family in the category of private arrangements shows the difficulties the image creates for understanding the family.

It is not surprising that these kinds of tensions and problems emerge once women's position in relation to any social contract is considered. The exclusion of questions about marriage and justice in the family is made possible by the image of a contract involving a group of individuals who do not know their position in society. The original position, combined with the image of the veil of ignorance, functions to reconcile people to the notion of the abstract individual, without close ties to others, and of indeterminate sex. Thus, women's interests can be excluded, and women treated as if not part of the contract.

In his more recent work, Rawls tries to overcome the problems that arise from making the parties in the original position heads of families, by calling them "rationally autonomous representatives of citizens in society."[29] This is, however, no great improvement. While it makes Rawls's position more consistent, in that we do not know what position in the family the parties occupy, there seems little point in making them represent citizens. If they cannot represent citizens' interests, social positions or conceptions of the good, then they must be simply abstract individuals, again sharing the same basic characteristics, and only one such individual is necessary.[30] Within the structure of the image, there can be no genuine pluralism, because no differences, sexual or cultural, are considered morally relevant.

29. Rawls, *Political Liberalism*, p. 305.
30. I will discuss the view that only one participant is necessary in the original position in more detail further on.

The distinction between essential and contingent characteristics of persons is assumed and expressed in concrete form by the image of the veil of ignorance. The characteristics that Rawls believes to be essential, like self-interestedness and instrumental rationality, become part of political organization through the myth, while others are excluded as morally irrelevant. As long as our sex is treated as a contingent characteristic, it cannot make sense to argue for a political organization that accepts sexual difference. This would also apply to cultural differences, and would often mean blindness to certain kinds of discrimination against particular ethnic groups, as well as encouraging assimilationist, rather than multi-cultural policies. Rather than being neutral, the myth of the original position makes a series of important assumptions about, and conceals a number of tensions concerning, the proper participants in decision-making. These aspects of the image can be seen clearly in the consequences of using it to try to address questions related to sexual difference.

Consequences of the Original Position

Okin's attempt to transform the myth of the original position for feminist purposes illustrates its power. Although Okin believes that there are several problems with Rawls's image of the original contract, she argues that a feminist political theory based on this image is possible if it is taken to apply to the family as an institution. But does the framework of the original position and the contract image itself make this impossible? Okin's view is that the original position is a brilliant tool for the critique of institutionalized sexism. She believes that if we want to examine the family, we should imagine ourselves as not knowing which position we would have in the family, then deciding on just arrangements. This application of the veil of ignorance is only relevant to adults. Okin is not concerned about the position of children in the family, because she believes that Rawls "makes a convincing argument from paternalism for their temporary inequality."[31]

However, Okin notes that Rawls's argument for unanimous agreement in the original position relies on an assumption "that all the parties have similar motivations and psychologies."[32] She wishes to question the assumption that sex is a morally irrelevant and contingent characteristic. Part of this questioning involves taking into account what she sees as conclusive evidence that women have a quite different moral standpoint and psychology to men—for example, the work by Nancy Chodorow and Carol

31. Okin, p. 185.
32. Ibid., p. 193.

Gilligan.[33] Okin considers various theories about the reasons for these differences: the gender structure (institutionalized sexism), the fact that both sexes are primarily reared by women, and "the experience of *being* primary nurturers."[34] If it is true that men and women differ in "basic psychologies, conceptions of the self in relation to others, and experiences of moral development,"[35] these differences would make it difficult to reach agreement in the original position, because parties in the original position would be reasoning differently.

This problem might suggest that the original position is an inappropriate image to be used in addressing questions of justice in the family. However, Okin thinks otherwise. She argues that the origin of the differences in moral standpoint and reasoning between women and men is simply the differing assignments of duties within the family. She says that women have been responsible for housework and child rearing, so have developed different moral concerns from men. If men were to participate much more fully in these activities, then they would come to share women's moral concerns. Correspondingly, Okin argues that with women's greater participation in what have been considered male preserves, women would take on some of the characteristics of male psychological and moral development. The result would be a gender-free society (a society without institutionalized sexism) with "conceptions of relations between self and others that . . . would . . . be more or less evenly shared by members of both sexes."[36]

Her main argument is that women and men should share roles in society, which would make everyone essentially the same in psychology and moral reasoning, and that, as a result, social arrangements would be fairer. Women would then be able to contract in the original position. She suggests that "[I]f principles of justice are to be adopted by representative human beings ignorant of their particular characteristics and positions in society, they must be persons whose psychological and moral development is in all essentials identical. This means that the social factors influencing the differences presently found between the sexes—from female parenting to all the manifestations of female subordination and dependence—would have to be replaced by genderless institutions and customs."[37] The move is from the need for representative human beings to determine principles of justice to the need to eliminate what she calls gender. People must change to fit into the

33. Okin cites Nancy Chodorow's *The Reproduction of Mothering* (Berkeley: University of California Press, 1978) and Carol Gilligan's *In a Different Voice* (Cambridge: Harvard University Press, 1982), as well as a number of other works.

34. Ibid., p. 194. These theories do not exhaust the possibilities. For example, given that not all women are primary nurturers, it might be important to consider women's capacity to bear children.

35. Ibid., p. 194.

36. Ibid., p. 195.

37. Ibid., p. 195.

original position, rather than the other way round. A consequence of holding onto the original position in this way is that it would not be genuinely relevant to political theorizing until after there had been massive social change. If it is taken to be applicable now, any differences between the sexes would have to be ignored, and the reasoner must be a fantasized amalgam of current masculine and feminine stereotypes.

The structure of Okin's argument gives us a very striking example of how the assumptions of the original position can affect the work of a feminist political philosopher—the analysis of oppression, the view of women's psychology, and the ideas for change. All these are subordinated to the notion of abstract individuals who reason identically and agree absolutely on principles of justice. While Okin notes that Rawls's original position is only a contract in an "odd and metaphoric sense,"[38] the contract image, in this peculiar form, still has the power to affect the reasoning she uses.

In accepting the original position as a way of determining principles of justice, she also accepts that the reasoners must be identical in essential respects. Thus she is forced to conclude that women and men must become alike in moral and psychological development. The original position, she argues, requires a gender-free world. In this case, it would not matter if one man alone decided on the principles of justice, because he could represent women's views and these views should be more or less the same as his own. Any feminist theory that is based on Rawls's original position has to deal with the problematic implication that social justice can only be achieved through a radical program of eliminating differences between women and men. Marion Tapper argues that liberalism has unfortunate implications for any feminist relying on the theory.[39] We can see these implications in Okin's work. However, what is most interesting here is the way the original position motivates Okin's argument and prevents her from seeing what her own questioning of Rawls's work suggests.

The main point for us is that the image of the original position determines the structure of Okin's argument. This reading of Okin shows that the image of the original position does more than simply clarify and dramatize views and commitments, as is claimed by some liberal commentators. It leads inexorably to the view that the structure of society can be determined by one impartial reasoner. Rawls unwittingly implied the force of his image when he wrote that the original position is "an intuitive notion that suggests its own elaboration, so that led on by it we are drawn to define more clearly the standpoint from which we can best interpret moral relationships."[40] The effect on

38. Okin, *Justice, Gender, and the Family* (New York: Basic Books, 1989), p. 90.

39. Marion Tapper, "Can a Feminist Be a Liberal?" in *Australasian Journal of Philosophy* 64 (supp.) (1986): 37–47.

40. Rawls, *A Theory of Justice*, pp. 21–22.

Okin's argument of using the original position image suggests that we need to be extremely sensitive to images when we attempt to subvert or transform them for other purposes: the analytic imaginary is not transformed so easily. The blindness created by the veil of ignorance can prevent theoretical awareness of a number of types of injustice.

Blinded by Ignorance

The images of the original position and the veil of ignorance provide a framework for the two principles of justice. Rawls's characterization of his social contract as one aimed at determining moral principles, rather than a design of government or society, seems to eliminate the dubious philosophical step of making the contract an exchange of obedience for protection or freedom for security. However, Rawls's particular contract image can be interpreted as mirroring this step. Although Nagel argues that Rawls exhibits a prejudice in favor of equality, it could also be argued that the prejudice goes the other way, because it legitimizes institutionalized inequality. The veil of ignorance in the original position can help to persuade people to accept inequalities, based on the questionable speculation that everyone would be worse off without them. There is a problem of interpretation or application of the original position and the principles. It might seem that the original position can be put to either extreme of conservative or progressive ends. Rawls claims in *A Theory of Justice* that his theory is applicable to a wide range of societies, including socialist ones.[41] However, due to the assumption about individuals competing with each other for scarce resources which is involved in the original position, the possible application of his theory is confined to the range between libertarian and liberal progressive. Rawls admits in the more recent *Political Liberalism* that the original position is in fact only useful to certain liberal societies.

Another important assumption incorporated into the original position, devastating for anyone who belongs to a group spanning more than one social or economic level of society, is the assumption that justice consists of nothing more than a fair distribution of social and economic goods between the levels. Injustices in the lives of oppressed groups spread across various socio-economic levels cannot be either perceived or eliminated from behind the veil of ignorance, and they are not subject to the principles of distributive justice. For example, many injustices against women could not be perceived through the veil of ignorance, because women belong to all the different groups in society, the worst-off, the best-off, and the in-between. Therefore,

41. Ibid., pp. 273–274.

women can be subject to systematic injustice from institutions or individual men without this being accounted for by the original position, because women are seen as having the appropriate share of social advantages for whichever stratum we happen to belong to.

This point is made explicitly by another feminist writer influenced by Rawls, Janet Radcliffe Richards, who writes: "It is *possible* that making women's average position *worse* in comparison with men's average position could increase the well-being of the worst-off group of all, and so achieve greater social justice."[42] The worst-off group may be manual workers, for example. However, she decides to ignore this point for the sake of simplicity, and uses the difference principle as a criterion of justice for women. Rawls himself says that women's inequality to men could be justified if women were better off than they would be by being equal.[43] The veil of ignorance ensures blindness to the oppression of any groups which are not just economically oppressed.

In *Political Liberalism,* Rawls says that we must abstract from cumulative social, historical or natural tendencies in order to eliminate any bargaining advantages. But what about bargaining disadvantages? For example, the indigenous people of a colonized country who have lost their land and had their language and culture devastated due to "historical tendencies" cannot claim adequate redress or compensation for what has happened in the past under such a system. The liberal individual who is modeled in the original position cannot use claims about belonging to a particular culture, speaking a particular language, and following particular customs as necessary social goods, because these are not goods for all and because Rawls's original position can only adequately help to conceptualize material loss. Although Rawls sees self-respect as important, he thinks only "what is necessary is that there should be for each person at least one community of shared interests to which he belongs and where he finds his endeavors confirmed by his associates."[44] However, the community of shared interests is too general a notion to cover the complexities of group identity, say, where a person belongs to a number of conflicting groups, or where the person's original community has been all but destroyed. The condition could be met without a significant alleviation of oppression. Cultural and group rights and such issues as self-determination for indigenous peoples are excluded by the contract framework.

Rawls is against religious intolerance and racial discrimination, and this is laudable as far as it goes.[45] However, a careful consideration of the problems left unaddressed by such a stance makes it clear that this is not enough.

42. Janet Radcliffe Richards, *The Sceptical Feminist* (Harmondsworth: Penguin, 1982), p. 355.
43. Rawls, *A Theory of Justice,* p. 99.
44. Ibid., p. 442.
45. Ibid., p. 19.

Some upholders of the contract myth have tried to remedy some of these difficulties. For example, Will Kymlicka attempts to accommodate group rights within a liberal framework.[46] However, in doing so he appears to move towards a communitarian position, because he uses concepts of personal identity dependent on belonging to a particular culture or ethnic group, concepts that are excluded by the original position.

Once the ideal of justice is set up through the original position, other possible critiques of an unjust system can be excluded. Justice as fairness, embodied by the veil of ignorance, can allow systematic injustice, and loss of autonomy. From behind the veil of ignorance only tangible benefits or kinds of property can be seen, and this means that other goods are overlooked. Another problem is the ideal of reason that is embraced through the myth of the original position.

Utopian Reason: My Shoes or Yours?

One of the major criticisms of social contract theorists who use the image of the state of nature is that it contains many problematic assumptions about human psychology. Rawls tries to avoid this by only assuming that the participants in the original position are rational, as well as some basic notions about how human beings will reason. Yet the ideas incorporated into the contractarian myths undermine the very notion of a contract. A number of philosophers have argued that because of Rawls's suppositions about the people in the original position there only really needs to be one moral reasoner who makes decisions for everyone.[47]

There are a number of different reasons for thinking this is true. If, as Rawls specifies, all parties are self-interested, rational, and, most importantly, behind the veil of ignorance, there is only one process of reasoning to be followed. The need for only one original participant is strongly implied by the idea that it is not actually necessary for the reasoners to discuss issues in order to reach agreement, and that a referee can negotiate between them. Finally, Rawls says that we could pick any one of the parties in the original position at random to find what has been unanimously agreed upon.[48] The surprising fact that there need only be one moral reasoner in the original position shows very clearly that it is no kind of contract, social or otherwise. There is no exchange, discussion, or agreement, but just one liberal abstract

46. Will Kymlicka, *Liberalism, Community and Culture* (Oxford: Clarendon, 1991), pp. 182–205.

47. The fact that only one reasoner is necessary has been noted by a number of philosophers, including Iris Marion Young, Carole Pateman, Alan Brown, and Michael Sandel.

48. Rawls, *A Theory of Justice*, p. 139.

individual. The myth of the social contract serves to disguise this, by suggesting that outcomes are based on discussion, and at the same time promote the ideal of the liberal individual by using a conception of reason so narrow that no discussion is necessary. This implication is surely a problem for a philosopher who wishes to promote fairness—the image of one moral reasoner deciding the principles of justice has connotations of a dictatorship or at best of paternalism rather than a free society.

The sole reasoner problem also suggests a deeper problem with the social contract image itself: theories that use the contract myth have to postulate a uniform criterion of reason, usually one based on everyone being equally self-interested. It cannot accommodate different psychologies, different styles of reasoning, or different ethical concerns. For example, an ethics of care that took others' particular interests into account could not be incorporated into a theory based on an original position like Rawls's. The image of the original position makes a certain view of human psychology and politics seem inevitable, as we have seen in Okin's work.

There has been some debate over whether the ideal of impartiality plays a role like that of the ideal observer of classical utilitarian theory. The ideal observer is supposed to take everyone's interests into account, and we are to adopt the perspective of such a being when formulating moral rules. On the one hand, the two ideas seem quite different, because Rawls's impartial reasoner is ignorant of their own and other's interests and the ideal observer knows everyone's interests. On the other hand, they are both supposed to make a decision on behalf of everyone on the basis of the knowledge available to them. The difference is subtle. At a fundamental level, there is just one reasoner who is deciding moral principles for everyone, rather than discussion and negotiation from a particular position that can advance particular interests and values. Rawls would like to distance his idea of impartiality from that of the sympathetic or ideal observer,[49] but in a most important respect fails to do so.

Kymlicka argues that the ideal of impartiality involves imagining ourselves in other people's shoes, and that this is the point of contract devices. My view is that while this can be a useful test of some ideas, it can mask or even promote intolerance. Imagining ourselves in another's place does not necessarily help us identify *their* interests. It is just as likely to merely identify what *our* interests would be if we were in their position. There is no reason to think that these interests would be the same. This limitation on imagining was illustrated clearly by the problems in understanding abortion by imagining

49. Rawls, p. 190. The actual conclusions reached by the impartial reasoner and the ideal observer may be different because of the specific assumptions made about how they will reason.

oneself attached to the violinist of Thomson's analogy. Kymlicka admits that there is something odd about a theory that aims to achieve the good of others by seeing it as an aspect of our own good.[50] However, it is not merely odd, it can be deeply misleading. Another excellent example of the limitations of imagining oneself in another's shoes is provided by a male advertising executive who performs the following test to decide whether his advertisements are sexist or offensive to women: he imagines himself in the position of the woman in any given advertisement and thinks about how he would feel. Generally, he finds that he would not be offended, so he feels it is right to go ahead with the advertisement.[51] His test was designed to determine how women *should* respond to the advertisements, not how women actually would or do respond.

If we take this as an illustration of how impartiality works, then it is clear that it will often be inadequate as a political model. Putting oneself in other's shoes does not necessarily provide an insight into other's values or an understanding of their experience. This is not to suggest that the attempt to imagine oneself in another's place is never useful or that it should be discouraged. Rather, these examples show that there are limits to the efficacy and justice of this procedure and that the contract myth, which promotes its adoption as the paradigm for political organization, is inevitably limiting. While Rawls probably has the view (personally) that different conceptions of the good can flourish in a liberal society, we can see that the liberal perspective which is written into the myth of the original position can actually work against this possibility. Thus, the central theme of the analytic imaginary concerning the power of the individual imagination to understand the experience of others emerges again, as it does in relation to each of these influential images.

The Myth of the Social Contract

There are a number of further implications of the myth of the social contract. The image of a contract, which implies the freedom of the parties involved and voluntariness in entering the contract, masks actual social inequalities which exist both prior to the existence of the contract and in what occurs after the contract is made. For example, women are often in a less powerful position than men, yet are considered to be able to contract into marriage as equals. The social contract myth makes it difficult to claim that

---

50. Kymlicka, p. 194.
51. Bart Pavlovitch, "Advertising," interview by Geraldine Doogue, *Life Matters*, ABC Radio National, 6 October 1993.

women really do not enter such contracts voluntarily.[52] A society governed according to Rawls's principles of justice could contain systematic injustices that could not be addressed by appeal to these principles, and could even flourish under the aegis of these principles. These problems arise partly from the fact that genuine contracts are made at a historical moment, whereas Rawls's ahistorical original position does not allow an assessment of historical circumstances.

Carole Pateman argues that although the original contract is just a story, a political fiction, it is one with serious consequences for the way our society works, and for the ways people see themselves. Her suggestion is that we neutralize this myth by giving up stories of political origins.[53] She understands the desire to make sense of our lives by postulating a beginning, both for feminists and contractarians, but she argues that the myth of a state of nature (or in Rawls's case, the original position) masks inequalities and women's lack of freedom in other so-called contracts as well, such as marriage, prostitution, surrogacy and employment contracts, which she sees as analogous to the idea of the original social contract. Pateman argues that we need a different notion of freedom, and that we should give up the idea of the abstract individual. But freedom as autonomy cannot become part of ideals based on the myth of the social contract, because this myth is based on a concept of negative freedom. Her argument is that the notion of a contract made by individuals obscures sexual difference, because the notion of an individual is based on men, not women, and to participate, women must give up sexual specificity.[54] The implications of the myth of the social contract need to be explored further in relation to all kinds of smaller-scale "contracts."

The myth of the social contract is one that can also be used to justify the exclusion of certain groups from the benefits of society. On the one hand, it suggests that everyone has made a kind of pact with each other, which explains law and order and social cohesion. But, on the other hand, the declaration that a contract justifies political arrangements makes it possible to claim that certain groups of individuals are not party to the social contract, such as illegal immigrants, so can be treated differently, or that certain people do not have the necessary requirements, such as rationality, to be part of the social contract. The latter has been most likely to occur, and this has been a difficult problem for women, but the former should also be of concern as the state asserts its rights to reward and punish on the basis of this myth. The social contract can justify exclusion and institutionalized oppression, or simply blind us to the existence of these problems.

52. Pateman, *The Sexual Contract* (Stanford: Stanford University Press, 1988), pp. 54, 62.
53. Ibid., p. 219.
54. Ibid., p. 223.

Instead of being stated from the outset, assumptions about human nature are smuggled into the images that are used to arrive at principles of justice.[55] This makes critique more difficult than in the case of Hobbes, for example, who argues directly that human beings are rational egoists. Instead of arguing similarly, Rawls says that free, rational persons will agree with the assumptions in the original position. To disagree, we have to confess to a kind of irrationality, or devise a new understanding of human reason. Within the framework of the original position, it is impossible to construct an alternative view of women and men, or cultures within cultures, which could allow for different interests.

Rawls's position and, implicitly, his use of contract myths is seen as the paradigm of a political theory. Attempts to criticize contemporary myths of contract are often seen as a return to ideas that liberalism replaced, rather than progress towards a more complex theory. In this way, theories and ideas based on real conditions can be excluded from political philosophy.

Reconceptions

There are a number of alternatives to a political theory based on the social contract myth, including communitarianism. Here I will concentrate on an interesting way of reconceiving political theory described by Iris Marion Young: a theory that makes diverse voices heard and taken seriously, and which has self-determination for different groups as its aim. While she does not set up a myth of origins, believing as she does that political theorists should reflect on current conditions, she argues it is possible to work with norms and ideals. Young argues for a political theory that incorporates difference through a principle of group differentiation and group-differentiated policies.[56] She also provides a philosophical critique of Rawls's particular approach to justice. In *Justice and the Politics of Difference,* Young argues that Rawls's project is a utopian one.[57] Her analysis of Rawls is connected with a critique of the ideal of impartiality, which, she argues, is reinforced and

55. Jean Hampton argues that the only way to make a successful Kantian contractarian argument is to "understand and make precise the conception of the person, and particularly the conception of human worth, implicitly underlying the contract image. I regard this as a tough, lengthy and long-term project." Jean Hampton, "Feminist Contractarianism," in *A Mind of One's Own: Feminist Essays on Reason and Objectivity,* ed. Louise M. Antony and Charlotte Witt (Boulder: Westview, 1993), p. 242.

56. There may be times and places where, when all difference from a specified norm is perceived as inferiority, it is of great practical value to uphold and defend universal rights. See chapter 5 for my discussion of a compelling argument to this effect by Uma Narayan.

57. Young also argues that Thomas Nagel's "view from nowhere," which I discuss in chapter 5, is utopian.

justified by the use of the original position. Young is critical of both the as-sumptions about the reasoning of the participants in the original position and the view of political organization that is implied by these assumptions. For example, she is particularly concerned by the assumption that in work-ing out the principles of justice, the participants are not even supposed to discuss their differences.[58] Young makes a connection between utopian thinking and the work of political philosophers who, like Rawls, use the image of the social contract. She believes that the ideal of impartiality, upon which social contract theories are based, is utopian because no-one can "adopt a point of view that is completely impersonal and dispassionate, com-pletely separated from any particular context and commitments."[59] It is clear that the kind of reasoner required by Rawls's original position would be im-possible to find, so it is utopian or rather, mythological, in that sense.

Young argues that the central feature of the Rawlsian myth is the idea that people should delegate their authority to the state, which is supposed to look after the general interest.[60] The metaphor characterizing the state is that of an umpire or referee who decides impartially between different interest groups. She notes that what usually happens in practice is that the more pow-erful groups and individuals have their interests served, because they are in a better position to press their claims. In Rawls's society, those in the best-off groups would be able to decide what is to the advantage of the worst-off groups simply because they occupy positions of greater power. The ideo-logical function of the myth of the neutral state, Young says, is to promote an ideal of distributive justice, and to cover over questions about actual decision-making procedures. The importance of decision-making proce-dures within the liberal conception of the state has been insufficiently stressed in the past because they have been perceived as neutral and fair. Yet, as we saw, the images which incarnate these procedures actually support very specific, biased results. Young argues that because an ideal of impartiality is assumed, it is possible for certain specific ideas about human nature and moral psychology to "rush to fill the vacuum created by counterfactual ab-straction" and for these ideas to be treated as objective, and universalized.[61] Although Rawls explicitly states that he is not trying to devise a particular so-ciety or government, in fact a particular society is presupposed and follows obviously from his principles of justice.

Young's proposed alternative is to actually take the interests of oppressed groups into account. She is careful not to define groups in terms of essential

---

58. Young, *Justice and the Politics of Difference*, p. 112.
59. Ibid., p. 103.
60. Young, p. 112.
61. Ibid., p. 115.

natures or special interests, but rather in terms of affinities based on practices or way of life, which leads to differentiation from other groups.[62] Relations between groups are based on diversity rather than opposition: saying a collective is a group does not exclude similarities with other social groups. Such groups are not based on political goals or particular interests. For example, feminists do not form such a group, but women do. The main idea is that certain oppressed groups should receive different or special treatment. Her three main examples are pregnancy and birthing rights for women, bilingual-bicultural rights for people whose first language is different from an official language, and Native American rights.

Political theory based on group differences is committed to basic changes in institutions. Young writes: "These changes must include group representation in policymaking and an elimination of the hierarchy of rewards that forces everyone to compete for scarce positions at the top."[63] One fundamental aspect of Young's proposal for political organization is what she calls a dual system of rights, a general kind of right involving rights that are the same for everyone, and a specific kind of right involving rights and policies that apply to particular groups.[64] For example, everyone is entitled to equal pay for equal work, but not everyone is entitled to leave from work to have a child. Such considerations are ruled out by the myth of the original position, because it is based on ignoring all kinds of difference, including sexual difference. Furthermore, the rights taken into account by Young go beyond the economic well-being and general liberties considered relevant in the original position.

The other fundamental aspect of a politics of difference is group representation in decision-making. Young argues for three main principles of such representation: (1) Self-organization of group members, (2) "Group analysis and group generation of policy proposals in institutionalized contexts," and (3) "Group veto power regarding specific policies that affect a group directly, such as reproductive policy rights for women, or land use policy for Indian reservations."[65] Representation of this kind applies not only to parliament and government organizations, but also to organizations and institutions in general. Her idea of group representation only applies to oppressed groups, since non-oppressed groups are already sufficiently represented.

Defining oppressed groups, deciding which groups are entitled to such representation, determining the nature and adequacy of rights, and how Young's principles could be implemented, are all questions requiring further

62. Ibid., p. 186.
63. Ibid., p. 167.
64. Ibid., p. 174.
65. Ibid., p. 184.

discussion. Some of Young's specific ideas about the kind of rights that need to be recognized are thought out with the American legal, historical, and political context in mind. Political philosophy needs to be sensitive to differences between particular countries in relation to such factors. One cannot simply directly apply principles from one country to another, although models drawn from other countries may be useful in thinking specific issues through. Nancy Fraser, in a discussion of Young's book, argues that we need to differentiate between differences that we wish to abolish, because they are the result of oppression, differences that should be universalized because they are important, and differences that should be enjoyed as expressions of diversity.[66] Nevertheless, Young's work provides an example of how one can begin the process of formulating political theory that recognizes oppression and historical and social reasons for treating some groups differently.

Affirming differences between groups always carries the risk that differences will be regarded as signs of inferiority. Yet, given the way theories like Rawls's make use of myths which can perpetuate disadvantage for oppressed groups, it is necessary to articulate the positive aspects of differences, and to take them into account within political philosophy.

Conclusion

The contractarian myths used by Rawls promote his assumptions and entail a system that cannot allow genuine pluralism in political life. The social contract image is a fundamental part of our way of thinking about the workings of modern political democracies. It is of great importance to understand the way the contract myth colors our views of politics, human nature, and moral reasoning. Recent developments in feminist philosophy have caused us to question these ideals, and it is clear that the kind of important considerations that have emerged in feminist contexts cannot be accommodated within the framework of the image of the social contract. The notion of fairness built into the contract entails the elimination of differences. The original position and the veil of ignorance are powerful tools of legitimation and persuasion of this idea of fairness as well as the liberal conception of the individual presupposed by it.

As noted, in Rawls's original position there is only one genuinely distinct individual, and there is every reason to believe that this individual is a man. Okin's attempts to explain how the original position could be used to redress

66. Nancy Fraser, "Debate: Recognition or Redistribution? A Critical Reading of Iris Marion Young's *Justice and the Politics of Difference,*" *Journal of Political Philosophy* 3, no. 2 (1995): 180.

injustices in the family illustrates how the original position itself elicits the view that people are essentially undifferentiated individuals, and that if they are not, they should be made so.

The contract begins to fall apart once women are brought into the myth, because the facts of difference reveal anomalies and tensions in the image of the contract. As we have seen in previous chapters, the image works both for and against the author's argument, because it gives plausibility to many kinds of subordination, but when these subjections are "re-inserted," the contract itself looks absurd. For example, if the family is put back into the original position, the subordination of women and children in the family becomes apparent. Furthermore, it becomes clear that the veil of ignorance does not hide men's position from them. The myth of a contract masks the implausibility and unpalatability of Rawls's theory of justice, as well as providing a framework for that theory. As we have seen, contracts are supposed to be a kind of agreement, but Rawls's is not. Contracts occur at historical moments, but Rawls's does not. If his arguments were stated baldly, without the use of the contract image, which he says "accords with natural piety," they would be far less convincing.[67] Rawls's images, therefore, work both at the level of enframement and persuasiveness.

We have seen that the myths of origins of the social contract allow many assumptions to become part of our political philosophy. There is the assumption that impartiality is the best form of moral reasoning, which is connected to the view that it is always possible for an individual to imagine themselves in another's shoes. This is another form of the basic fantasy of the analytic imaginary—of the ease of putting oneself in another's place.

Another assumption is that the interests of individuals, rather than groups, should form the basis of political organization. The contract image creates a framework that justifies exclusions from the contract, or inclusion only under certain conditions. It also generates a myth about freedom or voluntariness: as long as it is perceived that entry into the contract is voluntary, any "rational" decision within the contract itself can be justified. The myth of the social contract makes it very difficult to challenge any of the assumptions of liberalism or to work out a way that we can change our society. What this suggests for those working in political philosophy is that if we reject, say, Rawls's principles of justice, we must also reject the myths of contract, or we will face the same difficulties in a different form, so powerful is this aspect of the analytic imaginary.

---

67. Rawls, *A Theory of Justice*, p. 16.

5

Metaphorical Knowledge

Visual and spatial metaphors are important in epistemology, generally, and they are given a fascinating inflection in the analytic imaginary. As we saw in the introduction and chapter 1, Michèle Le Dœuff and others have argued that no thought is possible without metaphor. However, it does not follow that every metaphor is equally constitutive of thought. For example, Genevieve Lloyd's view in "Maleness, Metaphor, and the 'Crisis' of Reason" is that Descartes's metaphors of the mind in motion are inseparable from his thought in a way that Francis Bacon's metaphors of nature are not.[1] To reiterate briefly, she says that the necessity or embeddedness of certain metaphors is evident in the very fact that, at first, we find it difficult to see them *as* metaphors.[2] Spatial metaphors, for example, are basic in that they do not even seem like metaphors, and it seems almost impossible to speak without using them. Other such basic metaphors include those drawn from the senses, and temporal metaphors.

---

1. Genevieve Lloyd, "Maleness, Metaphor, and the 'Crisis' of Reason," in *A Mind of One's Own: Feminist Essays on Reason and Objectivity*, ed. Louise Antony and Charlotte Witt (Boulder: Westview Press, 1993), p. 82.

2. Ibid., p. 78. Much of the debate about metaphor in analytic philosophy has concerned the question of whether they can be paraphrased into similes or literal statements. As I mentioned in the introduction, Lakoff and Johnson consider that certain metaphors, such as orientational metaphors, are deeply embedded in language and thought. Donald Davidson, in a much-discussed paper, argues that metaphors must be understood literally and that most of them are false. Donald Davidson, "What Metaphors Mean," *Critical Inquiry* 5, no. 1 (1978): 31–67. See Lynne Tirrell, "Reductive and Nonreductive Simile Theories of Metaphor," *Journal of Philosophy* 88, no. 7 (1991): 337–358.

Although all these metaphors may appear in a range of discussions, there is a special connection between visual metaphors and epistemology. The sense of sight and visual metaphors have played a privileged role in epistemology from the origins of Western philosophy. Plato uses sight to represent our knowledge of the good in the *Republic*. He says that the eye is most like the sun, which is like the form of the good, and that the mind's eye understands and knows objects.[3] In the *Metaphysics* Aristotle writes that, "we prefer sight to almost everything else. The reason is that this, most of all the senses, makes us know and brings to light many differences between things."[4] However, Descartes describes the gaining of knowledge and understanding in terms of mental vision. In the "Rules for the Direction of the Mind" he argues that "We can best learn how mental intuition is to be employed by comparing it with ordinary vision."[5] Descartes thinks that we can achieve certain knowledge by using this mental vision to see clearly and distinctly, like God.[6] The Cartesian view of epistemology and the traditional reliance on visual metaphors in this area has had a profound influence on analytic philosophy. Le Dœuff's idea that there is a dialectic or feedback relation between metaphors and concepts helps us to understand the workings of visual and spatial metaphors in relation to the concept of objectivity in epistemology.

In this chapter, the tensions that arise in the use of visual metaphors in Thomas Nagel's *The View from Nowhere* will be examined. His work is an interesting example of the particular functioning of these epistemological metaphors within the analytic imaginary. He attempts to describe an objective standpoint which, he argues, is an ideal epistemological view we should aim for in all areas of philosophy. In order to characterize the objective viewpoint, he makes use of a number of visual as well as spatial metaphors. The central, organizing metaphor is the view from nowhere. There are, as well, the metaphors of the centerless world, concentric spheres of reality, the contrast between perspectives from inside and outside, and a variety of metaphors of vision concerning seeing things from various views and perspectives. Nagel's epistemology is based on the idea that we must strive towards an objective view of the world that incorporates our subjective viewpoint, and he makes

3. Plato, *Republic*, in *The Collected Dialogues*, ed. Edith Hamilton and Huntington Cairns (Princeton: Bollingen, 1999), p. 763; 508a–c.

4. Aristotle, *Metaphysics*, in *The Complete Works of Aristotle*, ed. Jonathan Barnes, vol. 2 (Princeton: Princeton University Press, 1984), p. 1552; 980a25.

5. René Descartes, *The Philosophical Writings of Descartes*, trans. John Cottingham, Robert Stoothoff, and Dugald Murdoch, vol. 1 (Cambridge: Cambridge University Press, 1985), p. 33.

6. In the *Meditations*, Descartes argues that "the mere fact that God created me is a very strong basis for believing that I am somehow made in his image and likeness, and that I perceive that likeness, which includes the idea of God, by the same faculty which enables me to perceive myself." Ibid., vol. 2, p. 35.

extensive use of metaphors to describe, explain, and justify his episte-mology. In this chapter, the distinction between levels of embeddedness has to be kept in mind in order to determine to what extent Nagel's metaphors are inseparable from the theories he puts forward, or to any theory of knowl-edge. By reading Nagel's work closely through his use of visual and spatial metaphors, we can see how his metaphors are of the constitutive kind and demonstrate their significant role in his epistemology. Nagel's images there-fore work at the level of expressibility as well as enframement.

Some of the metaphors Nagel uses are commonplaces in any talk about knowledge—for example, the basic contrast between views from inside and those from outside, and expressions such as "perspectives" and "points of view." The visual and spatial metaphors used by Nagel sustain profound as-sumptions and implications concerning the nature of knowledge. As Le Dœuff argues, metaphors can often work to cover over a difficulty or ten-sion. Several of Nagel's metaphors work to cover a number of serious ten-sions in his epistemological ideals, particularly with regard to the notion of objectification and the subject of knowledge. These metaphors include an updated visual metaphor, based on photography, metaphors of the center-less view and concentric spheres, and the common metaphor of points of view. As is the case with contractarian myths, feminist epistemologists who retain visual metaphors and the notion of objectivity have consequently re-peated the motifs of the analytic imaginary. Finally, I will consider ways of reconceptualizing our use and understanding of sensory metaphors in epistemology.

The View from Nowhere

Visual metaphors are generally paired with spatial ones. This pairing has its origin in an understanding of sight as a distinctively spatial sense, which can survey a field in one instant. The contrast with the other senses is most clear with hearing, as hearing something is always experienced through time.[7] Thus, it is not surprising that Nagel connects visual and spatial metaphors throughout his epistemology. Spatial metaphors often ensue from visual metaphors, but they can also exist in uneasy tension with them, as we shall see. The metaphor of the view from nowhere structures Nagel's thought and is closely tied to the other metaphors he uses. In *The View from Nowhere*, Nagel

7. See Evelyn Fox Keller and Christine R. Grontkowski, "The Mind's Eye," in *Discovering Real-ity: Feminist Perspectives on Epistemology, Metaphysics, Methodology, and Philosophy of Science,* ed. Sandra Harding and Merrill B. Hintikka (Dordrecht: D. Reidel, 1983), p. 219, for a discussion of the ap-parent atemporality of sight.

argues that we must "get outside of ourselves, and view the world from nowhere within it."[8] He acknowledges that this makes no sense if we take it to mean that we lose our point of view entirely. Accordingly, we need to understand his metaphor differently. This particular metaphor is supposed to convey the idea of a perspective from which we can see the world with ourselves in it and give an account of the world, ourselves, and an explanation of how we experience the world. This metaphor is both visual and spatial at once. The view is a visual image, like perspective, and *nowhere* is the space or place that the viewer must, paradoxically, occupy.

The metaphor is chosen to convey Nagel's notion of objectivity.[9] He states that objectivity is a method of understanding, and that it is beliefs and attitudes that are objective. However, as we will soon see, he also says that some philosophical positions and some things or facts are more objective than others. To become more objective about something, "we step back from our initial view of it and form a new conception which has that view and its relation to the world as its object."[10] The notion of needing to be distanced or to step back from something in order to understand it better, implied by the view from nowhere metaphor, is quite common. John Rawls also says that we need to view questions of justice from afar.[11] In Nagel's terms, our own viewpoint is the subjective viewpoint, and the view from nowhere is one that does not give our view a central or even special place. The view from nowhere is supposed to be a more objective viewpoint. For example, in the chapter, "Birth, Death, and the Meaning of Life" Nagel says that we will realize, from the objective viewpoint, that we are rather insignificant in the scheme of things. Yet although the view from nowhere does not give our view a special place, as the metaphor suggests, it is arguably still subjective because it is a view.

This supposedly objective view is a metaphor for Nagel's notion of objectivity—an impersonal, ahistorical, neutral perspective. He wants to *raise* our understanding so that we can "transcend our particular viewpoint and develop an expanded consciousness."[12] It is meant to be an impersonal standpoint, which abstracts from particular perspectives, or even the human perspective. Nagel thinks that the more objective our view is, and the less

---

8. Thomas Nagel, *The View from Nowhere* (Oxford: Oxford University Press, 1986), p. 67.

9. One of the reasons he thinks we must aim at objectivity is to try to avoid the dangers of skepticism. Nagel is particularly concerned about skepticism because he is a realist and he believes that a skeptical position is likely to develop from a realist position. See ibid., p. 71.

10. Ibid., p. 4.

11. John Rawls, *A Theory of Justice* (Cambridge: Harvard University Press, 1971), p. 22. The original position is meant to enable him to do this. It is worth noting that Nagel's views on political philosophy also involve a Rawlsian concern for impartiality. See Thomas Nagel, *Equality and Partiality* (Oxford: Oxford University Press, 1991), pp. 166–167.

12. Nagel, *The View from Nowhere*, p. 5.

personal it is, the less likely we are to be subject to error. This emphasis on the impersonal viewpoint does not mean he thinks that consciousness or subjectivity is not part of reality—he believes that it has a place in the philosophy of mind, and indeed, any world view. Although objectivity may not be achievable, Nagel argues that it is an ideal we must and cannot avoid aiming for. The view from nowhere metaphor is similar to the God's-eye view, or what Donna Haraway calls "the god trick,"[13] and suggests a desire to be God, all-seeing, all-knowing and in no particular place.[14] Nagel argues that we should strive to attain the reconciliation of subjective and objective points of view and that it is not fruitless to do so. The paradox of Nagel's position is reflected in the metaphor, which at the same time is an attempt to articulate the possibility and desirability of such a view.

The view from nowhere metaphor suggests a view from outside ourselves. Nagel does not think that we can really get outside ourselves, but he believes that the next best thing "is to form a detached idea of the world that includes us, and includes our possession of that conception as part of what it enables us to understand about ourselves."[15] The metaphor includes the idea of getting outside ourselves and becoming detached from our particular standpoint. The inside view is our subjective view and the outside the objective view. The objective stance of the view from nowhere is intended to apply to a range of areas and questions, and is used to judge views as more or less objective. Nagel considers questions about mind and body, personal identity, freedom, ethics, and the meaning of life, as well as issues about knowledge and reality in terms of his basic metaphor of the view from nowhere.

Three senses of objectivity emerge from this characterization of the view from nowhere:

(1) As a type of method; a method is more objective if it is more impersonal and detached.

(2) As a description of theories; some theories are more objective, because they are arrived at through the objective method.

(3) As a description of reality; the physical is more objective than the mental, which is subjective.

13. Donna Haraway, "Situated Knowledges: The Science Question in Feminism and the Privilege of Partial Perspective," *Feminist Studies* 14, no. 3 (1988): 581.

14. One commentator on Nagel, Kathleen Wider, has commented on this. "The view from nowhere is an objective, centerless, rational, disembodied view . . . and although it is a view we cannot achieve as finite, bodily creatures, it is one we strive to obtain, according to Nagel." She also notes the similarity with Sartre's epistemology. In Sartrean terms, the desire for a view from nowhere is the desire to be in-itself and for-itself at the same time: in other words, God. Kathleen Wider, "The Desire to Be God: Subjective and Objective in Nagel's *The View from Nowhere* and Sartre's *Being and Nothingness*," *Journal of Philosophical Research* 17 (1992): 460.

15. Nagel, pp. 69–70.

All three senses of objectivity are implied by the view from nowhere, and are reinforced, though somewhat ambiguously, by other metaphors Nagel uses, such as photography.

Photography

In the chapter on knowledge, Nagel uses a special type of visual metaphor based on photography to convey what is aimed at in the view from nowhere and how it is, paradoxically, impossible to achieve. The photographic metaphor screens an important tension in his understanding of objectification. This modern version of a visual metaphor increases the distance between viewer and the object looked at as well as placing a barrier between them. Nagel uses the photographic metaphor to try to convey the difficulties in the process of objectification. He says that, "However often we may try to step outside of ourselves, something will have to stay behind the lens, something in us will determine the resulting picture, and this will give grounds for doubt that we are really getting any closer to reality."[16] It is not very clear how we should understand this photographic metaphor. Perhaps the idea is to take a long-distance photograph without ourselves influencing the photograph in any way. Or could it be that the idea is to take the photograph without being behind the lens, as in the delayed shot where the photographer runs out and joins the group in the picture?

The difficulty in spelling out the details of the metaphor can be explained through the tension concealed by it. In his review of Nagel's book, "Contemplating One's Nagel," Jonathan Dancy argues that Nagel confuses two forms of objectification in this photographic metaphor: Hegelian objectification and absolute objectification. The Hegelian conception of objectivity suggests that views can be made more objective by an act of reflection, by focusing on the original view as object. Hegelian objectification does not transcend the subjective view; rather it incorporates it. The absolute conception of objectivity is where each successive, more objective view transcends the earlier, more subjective view as mere appearance. It is related to a generalizing or neutralizing tendency, reducing our view "to that which can be affirmed from any perspective whatever."[17] Dancy says that it does not follow from the fact that something stays behind the lens, which is true in Hegelian objectification, that the picture will be determined by it. It is only true that something in us determines the picture in terms of absolute objectification, which is the attempt to extinguish this subjective influence.[18] A more accurate

16. Ibid., p. 68.
17. Jonathan Dancy, "Contemplating One's Nagel," *Philosophical Books* 29, no. 1 (1988): 4.
18. Ibid., pp. 9–10.

metaphor for Hegelian objectification is the reflective process of taking a photograph of the photograph-taking. Thus, Nagel's photographic metaphor does not show the nature of his epistemic goal of combining subjective and objective.

Nagel's conflation of Hegelian objectification with absolute objectification can be seen in the metaphors he uses, both in the photographic metaphor discussed above and in the metaphor of concentric circles which is discussed further on. The tension, in this case, could be caused by Nagel's desire to retain elements of both forms of objectification. He himself accepts that there is a tension between the subjective and objective views, but this other tension might be more serious in that if he wishes to retain the notion of absolute objectification, he has to sacrifice the subjective. The metaphors can be understood as an attempt to cover this tension because they at first seem to convey Nagel's position in a coherent image. However, they also allow us to uncover it, because we find that the image itself does not make sense when we spell out its details.

Nagel believes that it is a problem for epistemology and metaphysics if our perspective affects our understanding of reality in any way, but he assumes this without argument. For him, the ideal would be if our particular, individual viewpoint did not affect the picture (of reality), or even better, if our human perspective did not affect the picture. Nagel's photographic metaphor, by imposing the camera between us and reality, also conveys and persuades us of his idea that our perspective prevents us from getting close to or understanding reality, and so must be eliminated.

The Centerless View

Another serious tension, concerning notions of the self, emerges through the metaphor of the centerless view. The centerless view, according to Nagel, is the view of the world seen from the view from nowhere. Yet this view still has to be seen by someone (some self). The notion of the self put forward by Nagel is one which has to incorporate the idea of a world out there not viewed from any perspective and the fact that we are individuals with perspectives. He tries to do this by speaking of everyone having an objective self whose ideal is to develop an objective universal view from its own perspective, but without according that perspective any special place.[19] In striving for objectivity, Nagel thinks we should aim to get beyond the particular moment in history and beyond the human to see the world as different beings might see it. The viewer from nowhere will see a centerless view.

19. Nagel, pp. 63–64.

Thus the image of the viewer represents the knower. Nagel's knower is a viewer trying to escape their own viewpoint. This viewer is the objective self which is located in an individual, but transcends the perspective of that individual. The viewing self is detached and "functions independently enough to have a life of its own."[20] This idea of an objective self is a very strange one. While at times Nagel talks of objectivity being one aspect of the self, along with the subjective self, at others he speaks as if it is a separate or even a core self, more significant than the subjective or empirical self. Because Nagel sees consciousness primarily as a viewpoint, he identifies the subjective self, or viewer, with consciousness.[21] However, the objective self is also a viewer.

Subjective and objective selves are two viewers, one which sees from a particular perspective, and the other which only uses that perspective to see an objective view, the centerless world.[22] It is a self inside each person, which views the world from the perspective of that objective self. Nagel argues that we should strive to attain this goal, even though it is an apparent contradiction. Yet the contradiction is even deeper and more serious than Nagel acknowledges, as the implications of the metaphor of the centerless view in relation to the self make clear. In his discussion of the self, Nagel refers to the empirical, subjective self, distinct from the objective self, as T.N. (in other words, Thomas Nagel, abbreviated as TN below). Norman Malcolm notes a number of images which Nagel makes use of to refer to the objective self. He writes:

> Here Nagel wants the word 'I' to refer to something that is not the person TN, but is 'the seat' of TN's experiences and capacities. Nagel employs different images to characterize the I that must be distinguished from the visible and tangible TN. The I 'underlies' TN's psychological continuities; it is 'the seat' of TN's experiences; it is 'beneath' the contents of TN's consciousness; in itself it has no point of view, but when its locus is TN it uses 'the eyes, the person, the daily life of TN as a kind of window' through which it views the world; it is 'a self that views the world through the perspective of TN.'[23]

---

20. Ibid., p. 65.
21. This alliance of the subjective self and consciousness, combined with his view that we should retain the subjective viewpoint, supports his anti-materialist, anti-reductionist views.
22. Norman Malcolm argues that the objective self is quite similar to the Cartesian ego, in that it is a self that is separate from any experiences an individual has. Malcolm, "Subjectivity," *Philosophy* 63, no. 244 (1988): 154.
23. Ibid., 157. And Nagel, p. 65. The objective self sounds like the photographer peering through the lens of the empirical self.

Thus, the objective self does not include the contingent characteristics of the person, but looks out from the person. In this respect it is even more extreme than Descartes's conception of the "I." Descartes clarifies that the essential self, or the mind, does not just *reside* in the contingent self, or the body, when he says: "I am not merely present in my body as a sailor is present in a ship."[24] Malcolm argues that there is one way in which Nagel's objective self is different from Descartes's I: Descartes's I is a thinking thing and will be wherever it is. However, Nagel's I, if it is nowhere, has no perspective, so it can have no consciousness. Nagel's I is dependent on location in a historical body, because he believes that consciousness and mind need a point of view.

Malcolm summarizes: "If the *I*, in its pursuit of objectivity, could really step away from every point of view, then it would become a mindless thing—which would appear to be a self-defeating achievement."[25] Consequently, Nagel's goal of aiming for objectivity, which he describes as a difficult but necessary one, is impossible. Its perfect attainment would also seem undesirable, from Nagel's own point of view, because the I needs to be located in a historical person to be conscious. Nagel's I needs to look out from the self, so could never really have a view from nowhere. The centerless view needs a center in order to be a view. Thus it is clear that this metaphor contains and covers a profound tension in the form of a contradiction that it seems pointless to try to overcome.

Concentric Spheres

A third set of unforeseen tensions arises in relation to another metaphor Nagel uses: the spatial metaphor of concentric spheres. These tensions concern the concepts of objectivity and objectification. This spatial metaphor does not mesh well with the visual metaphors of views and perspectives. Using this metaphor also leads to a number of important consequences. Nagel describes the process of objectification as a set of concentric spheres, each one more objective than the next.[26] In his terms, private life is one of the small, inner spheres, morality is a larger one, and physics a very large, outer one. The concentric spheres metaphor is a strange one, because physics is not a more objective view than morality, but simply a different view, a different subject or sphere. They are so different that they cannot be compared in this way.[27]

24. Descartes, vol. 1, p. 56.
25. Malcolm, p. 158.
26. Nagel, p. 5.
27. It is also unclear how morality can be separated from private life.

What is the difficulty or tension that is being covered here? Dancy argues that again it is Nagel's confusion about the two types of objectification. He claims that Nagel's image of concentric spheres suits Hegelian objectification, the view that greater objectivity can be achieved by reflecting on the original view as object, though the examples Nagel uses do not suit Hegelian objectification.[28] Dancy also claims that, alternatively, the metaphor does not fit absolute objectification, the view that greater objectivity can be achieved by transcending subjective views, because through the process of absolute objectification we would reject each earlier stage as mere appearance.[29] However, perhaps the image is more closely related to Nagel's overall project of showing the importance of objectivity at the same time as not wishing to reject subjectivity or the subjective point of view entirely. This interpretation of the metaphor would suggest that Nagel is interested in Hegelian objectivity, but has chosen rather bad examples. Yet Nagel also talks about seeing the interior perspectives as appearances. Consequently, the tension remains. In my judgment, the differences between private life, morality, and physics are better characterized as different areas of interest, rather than a series of more objective views. This way of conceiving these areas cannot be represented by the concentric spheres image. Nagel seems to be committed to absolute objectification, particularly because of his concern with generalizing over different points of view, an interpretation reinforced by the image of concentric spheres, probably in a way Nagel does not intend.

A further implication of the concentric spheres metaphor is that the self is an inner sphere surrounded by body which is surrounded by world. The empirical self is concerned with private life, the life of consciousness, and subject to the concerns of morality. Outside this inner self is the physical or material body, constrained by physics itself, but also part of a wider domain which physics alone can understand. Such an understanding of the self is reinforced by Nagel's other metaphors. Connecting the spheres metaphor with the previous discussion of the centerless view, it seems that the objective self is a sphere inside the empirical self.

The spatial and visual metaphors do not fit neatly together. Nagel thinks that consciousness is subjective, not only because it involves a specific point of view, but also because it cannot be explained by physicalist criteria. This implies that the physical is objective and the mental subjective. Describing reality in terms of concentric spheres emphasizes this split by putting those facts which are related to mental experiences at the center and putting those which are related to physical phenomenon in the outer, most objective, sphere. Another critic of Nagel, Colin McGinn, argues that in his discussion

28. Tuan Nuyen has pointed out to me that a spiral that loops back onto itself is a more appropriate image for Hegelian objectification.

29. Dancy, p. 4.

of the concentric spheres metaphor, Nagel belies his initial stipulation that only beliefs and attitudes can be objective. McGinn points out that by referring to concentric spheres of reality, Nagel suggests that some facts or things are more objective than others. It is clear that this is an implication of the use of the metaphor. While McGinn accepts that it is quite legitimate to say that some facts are objective and some subjective, he claims that the distinction is not a matter of degree, as is implied by the metaphor. Furthermore, he believes that Nagel is confusing the notions of the objective viewpoint and objective facts, and not making it clear which he is referring to.[30]

The concentric spheres metaphor has other important metaphysical implications. Nagel thinks we should accept a dual aspect theory—one that assumes we are one thing that has "mutually irreducible" physical and mental properties. Yet, as we have seen, because of the metaphorical structure of concentric spheres, subjective becomes aligned with mind, and objective with body. This particular metaphorical structure forces mind and body further apart, so that Nagel often sounds more like a substance dualist, despite his protestations to the contrary. The concentric spheres metaphor separates the inner, private, mental world from the outer, public, physical world. A central feature of Nagel's epistemology is its rationalist base. He believes that *a priori* formulations and hypotheses are the basis of most knowledge. The view from nowhere would be that of the rational consciousness which can step back from its own viewpoint, if that were possible.

There are links between the metaphor of concentric spheres and the Kantian metaphor of claiming territory through pure reason, which I discussed in chapter 1 with reference to Le Dœuff's reading of Kant. Nagel expands the concentric spheres metaphor in colonizing terms: "Each of us is a microcosm, and in detaching progressively from our point of view and forming a succession of higher views of ourselves in the world, we are occupying a territory that already exists: taking possession of a latent objective realm, so to speak."[31] The realm or territory which we come to know and possess is a physical one. The mental, however, that gains this knowledge, is not objectively known by us. Thus the colonizing of the outer sphere must be done by an aspect of ourselves we do not understand. Nagel's metaphor differs from Kant's in an important respect. Kant exhorts us to stake out our territory and be satisfied with what we have, whereas Nagel aims to convince us that "the truth is out there" and we should claim it. In order to find this knowledge, we must detach ourselves from our experience. The impossibility and undesirability of this project is highlighted by the difficulties that arise in trying to understand the concentric spheres metaphor.

30. Colin McGinn, Critical Notice of *The View from Nowhere* by Thomas Nagel, *Mind* 96, no. 382 (1987): 264–265.

31. Nagel, pp. 82–83.

The Inner Core

An important aspect of the concentric spheres metaphor is the image of the inner core. One way we can understand the stepping back of the view from nowhere is to consider Nagel's view of subjectivity in terms of the inner core metaphor. This metaphor exacerbates splits between the physical and the mental, and the senses and reason. Nagel sometimes conflates subjectivity with consciousness, but he also means it to be subjective experience. His concentric spheres metaphor relies on the idea that there is an inner core of experience that is subjective. In our own case, we have access to this inner core, and our main problem is moving away from it to greater objectivity. In the case of our relations with other people, and especially with bats and spiders, our problem is supposed to be in moving from the outer objective sphere to the inner subjective core—which, in Nagel's view, is impossible. In an earlier and very famous paper, "What is it Like to be a Bat?" Nagel tries to imagine what it would be like to be a bat in order to give some sense of the subjective character of experience. He chooses bats because in his view they have experience, but have very different sensory organs from human beings. However, he argues, we cannot imagine what it would be like to be a bat, but only what it would be like to act like a bat. He concludes that there is something that it is like to be a bat we do not have access to, something that cannot be described in physical terms.[32]

In *The View from Nowhere,* Nagel tells a wonderful story about his attempts to understand the desires of a spider trapped in the philosophy department's urinal, a habitat he believes the spider does not like. After months of watching what he takes to be the spider's attempts to escape, and trying to decide whether to rescue it from the urinal's flush, Nagel lifts it out and places it on the floor.[33] In a day, the spider is dead. Reflecting on his assumption that the spider did not like being constantly drenched in a urinal, that its life was "miserable and exhausting," an assumption he felt was proved incorrect by the death of the spider, he comments: "It illustrates the hazards of combining perspectives that are radically distinct."[34]

In my view we can draw quite a different moral from this story. The analogy between our inability to understand other people and our inability to understand animals is inappropriate. We cannot understand what a spider or a bat enjoys, precisely because we cannot communicate with spiders in the way that we can communicate with other people. The metaphor of a single sphere of experiences outside our own perspective is misleading, because

32. Thomas Nagel, "What Is It Like to Be a Bat?," *Philosophical Review* 73, no. 1 (1974).
33. It is surprising that Nagel's observations of the spider take place over months, rather than days.
34. Nagel, *The View from Nowhere,* p. 209.

it does not differentiate between cases where others can put forward their point of view, even though we may not fully understand it, and those cases, like that of the bat, where the experience is completely inaccessible.

There are other implications of the inner core aspect of the concentric spheres metaphor. Raymond Tallis notes that the subjective core is treated by Nagel as a special kind of fact that we do not have access to in the case of others. Tallis argues that subjectivity is not a fact, but rather, a pre-condition of knowledge. We cannot know anything without the senses or subjective experience, which raises a question about Nagel's identification of subjectivity with consciousness, because subjectivity seems more accurately represented as the capacity to experience. In Tallis's view, Nagel makes the same mistake as the physicalists in thinking that all knowledge is factual. The difference between Nagel and the physicalists is that Nagel believes that subjective experience is a fact or special kind of knowledge but the physicalist argues that subjectivity is not a fact or factual, so cannot be an object of knowledge. However, Tallis argues, objective knowledge can emerge "only against the background, and out of, necessarily pre-existing sense-experience."[35] Accordingly, the subjective quality of experience is not a supplement or additional extra to knowledge: "The idea of the subjective quality of experience either as something that at present lies beyond objective knowledge or as something that can be captured in it is totally misleading."[36]

Nagel's spatial metaphors establish and reinforce the confusion about the status of subjectivity. In terms of his images, the subjective is the inner core which objectivity transcends, or it is the photographer who is left behind the camera; the subjective is a realm of knowledge which either we are more or less trapped in (in our own case) or are unable to get access to (in the case of others, or of bats and spiders). Tallis argues that Nagel's use of bat experience also reinforces the idea that subjective experience is something beyond factual knowledge, because the bat's subjective experience is supposed to be what is left over after an objective description. In his view the fundamental error is to believe that objective factual knowledge "encloses" subjective experience when the reverse is true.[37]

We may not agree with Tallis that subjective knowledge *encloses* objective knowledge, or enclosing may be a misleading way to express the point. Nevertheless, the idea that subjective knowledge is a pre-condition or co-condition

35. Raymond Tallis, "Tye on 'The Subjective Qualities of Experience': A Critique," *Philosophical Investigations* 12, no. 3 (1989): 220.

36. Ibid., p. 221. It should be noted that the points made by Tallis are Kantian ones. An important trend in contemporary analytic philosophy is its pre-critical turn, and Nagel's epistemology certainly exemplifies this trend.

37. Ibid., p. 222.

for knowledge is a useful reminder and helps us to see how Nagel's metaphors have reinforced fundamental confusions by reinforcing splits between physical and mental and between the senses and reason. As we have seen, the role of the senses is minimized by Nagel. He thinks that we would be more like the objective self if we were deprived of all sensory input and ignores Kant's point that we need sensory perception to have understanding or judgment.[38] These splits are emphasized by the metaphorization of the subjective as the view from inside and the objective as the view from outside. The role played by these metaphors reveals another interesting facet of the analytic imaginary.

Double Vision

Nagel uses the metaphor of double vision to suggest how we can live with objective and subjective viewpoints. He writes: "Double vision is the fate of creatures with a glimpse of the view *sub specie aeternitatis.*"[39] As mentioned earlier, his view of the self involves two main aspects: that there is something irreducibly subjective about the conscious self, and that there is an objective self with a life of its own in each one of us.[40] These aspects posit a self radically separate from the world, from body and from others. Nagel, like the personal identity theorists of chapter 3, underestimates the importance of contingent, historical features of the self, particularly in relation to epistemology. This underestimation is both reflected in, and reinforced by the series of metaphors he uses. Recent work in epistemology has shown problems with this kind of notion of the self. Breaking down the division between subject and object, positing a relational self, and taking seriously the empirical self can all lead to a more integrated epistemology.

The opposition between the knower and the known, perpetuated by the view from nowhere, is related to these questions about the self. Nagel's idea is that we will turn the gaze back upon ourselves as object, applying the distinction between knower and known to ourselves. The need to reinforce links between the knower and the object of study is most obviously relevant in the social and human sciences because of these sciences' concern

38. Nagel, p. 62.

39. Ibid., p. 88. Rawls describes the original position in similar terms: "Thus to see our place in society from the perspective of this position is to see it *sub specie aeternitatis:* it is to regard the human situation not only from all social but also from all temporal points of view." Rawls, *A Theory of Justice*, p. 587.

40. Nagel also argues, in a section on personal identity, that we are essentially our brains. Nagel, pp. 37–43.

with people, but we can extend what we learn in these areas to philosophical epistemology, generally. Nagel's reliance on the objective knower masks differences between knowers and the kind of questions different knowers might want to ask and answer. Nagel's writing is a good illustration of this, because he assumes that questions about personal identity, primary and secondary qualities, theories of absolute versus relativistic space-time, and the search for agent-neutral values are of the most philosophical interest.[41] For him, it is the outer spheres that are of philosophical importance and thus those that will become the stock in trade of the analytic imaginary.

Nagel's metaphors promote a move away from subjectivity, as well as away from recognition of the importance of understanding and accepting the experiences of others. Although he argues that we need to bring subjective and objective views together, much of the point of his metaphors involves transcending the subjective, and more importantly, the particular. The image of getting outside ourselves in order to understand the world seems to be a rejection of our human limitations and capacities. The other aspect of this metaphor—of starting from ourselves and moving outwards—fails to acknowledge the way we find ourselves in a world peopled with others. It can even lean towards solipsism, because it relies on imagining ourselves in the place of others, a feat of imagination which Nagel admits is extremely difficult, even impossible.[42] It is interesting that while Nagel acknowledges the difficulty of imagining oneself in the place of others, the idea of striving for an objective viewpoint relies on the possibility of being able to do so. Although Nagel accepts that we may not understand the subjective experience of bats and spiders, the metaphor of a view from nowhere conveys the assumption that we can know the objective and therefore more important facts about what it is to be like anything at all—without actually having those experiences. This assumption connects closely to Nagel's use of the commonplace epistemological metaphors of points of view and perspectives.

Points of view

There is a deep ambiguity in Nagel's use of the images of "point of view" and "perspective," which are often used interchangeably to mean opinion, attitude, or outlook on life, as well as the particular way of experiencing the world which is necessarily unique to each individual. Nagel seems to play on

41. Ibid., p. 77.
42. Kathleen Wider discusses this problem in detail in her "Overtones of Solipsism in Thomas Nagel's 'What Is It Like to Be a Bat?' and *The View from Nowhere*," *Philosophy and Phenomenological Research* 50, no. 3 (1990): 481–499.

this ambiguity by implying that the subjective point of view is necessarily a biased one, which cannot be shared by anyone else. Yet as Malcolm, David Pugmire, and a number of other philosophers point out, we often have the same point of view, in the sense of attitude, outlook, or even experience.[43] This fact could be seen as a useful one for Nagel, if it is thought that the more people share points of view, the easier it is to move towards an objective self. However, as we saw in the discussion of utopian reason in the previous chapter, certain people may share points of view or a point of view within a certain group. Furthermore, they may take that view or perspective to be either characteristically human or the only rational view. As in the case of the social contract myths, Nagel's perspectival metaphors gloss over the way knowledge is conditioned by being part of a group—for example by sex, class, ethnic group, commitments and projects. The metaphor of the point of view from nowhere relies on the assumption that we can strip off our personal characteristics and thus reach a supra-human perspective.

If we believe that people have incommensurable points of view, that is a problem for any ethics and any epistemology. However, it is a far more serious problem for an epistemological position that relies on abstracting from particular points of view. One result of Nagel's reliance on absolute objectification and its generalizing tendency embodied in the view from nowhere is the idea that ethics should aim at arriving at principles upon which everyone would agree. Such an ethics concerns itself with the avoidance of conflict at all cost. One way to eliminate conflict is to abstract from a situation all those features which could potentially bring about conflict. But we need to ask ourselves whether it is the best way, and furthermore, whether we want to eliminate conflict. Points of view do not necessarily fit together to make up a picture.

The view from nowhere metaphor, like visual metaphors in general, suggests not only a non-place, but also a non-place outside time. Thus, the perspective is an atemporal or ahistorical one. This ahistoricism makes the problem of avoidance of conflict more serious, because the metaphor does not accommodate the way in which our historical perspective can affect our judgments, particularly our ethical ones. The notion of neutrality, which emerges strongly in Nagel's discussion of ethics, shows how the view from nowhere also has the implication of neutrality. In terms of such an understanding, if I am nowhere, I am on no side, and therefore can judge fairly. The attempt to incorporate all perspectives into one overarching perspective connects closely with the ethical ideal of choosing for the common good, rather than taking into account the actual interests of people. Nagel's metaphor of the

43. David Pugmire, "Bat or Batman?" *Philosophy* 64, no. 248 (1989): 207–217.

view from nowhere can thus be linked with John Rawls's original position and the veil of ignorance. Iris Marion Young argues that the view from nowhere, like the original position, is a kind of impartiality, which is utopian, because it is impossible to achieve.[44] The metaphor and the myth might appear very different, as one is used in epistemology and the other in political philosophy, yet the moral and political implications of Nagel's metaphors show that there are important connections between them.

Many feminist epistemologists are extremely critical of the notion of objectivity, because it often masks systematic bias against women and femininity.[45] They also argue against a reliance on visual metaphors in epistemology because these metaphors reinforce a separation from and domination of the perceived object of knowledge, most notably women and nature. Evelyn Fox Keller and Christine Grontkowski argue that sexual bias can be found in "The emphasis on the 'objectifying' function of vision and the corresponding relegation of its communicative—one might even say erotic—function."[46] The epistemological metaphors of Jean-Paul Sartre discussed in chapter 1 provide probably the most striking example of this phenomenon. Sartre writes: "What is seen is possessed; to see is to *deflower*," and the object of investigation is "like a woman whom a passerby catches unaware at her bath."[47] In these particular metaphors the erotic is subsumed under the objectifying function. What could be an experience of closeness is made into an objectifying one.

However, not all feminist philosophers reject visual metaphors and the notion of objectivity in epistemology. For example, Donna Haraway and Sandra Harding argue that feminists should maintain the goal of objectivity. It is worthwhile to discuss these two feminist alternatives to Nagel's epistemology which accept the empirical self, the limitations on imagining other's point of view, and try to take account of different, clashing perspectives. Haraway and Harding accept the aim of objectivity, and in one case, Haraway's, the reliance on visual metaphors. Yet they have unwittingly accepted some of the assumptions and implications involved in the view from

44. Young, *Justice and the Politics of Difference* (Princeton: Princeton University Press, 1990), p. 103. It is interesting that the word utopia itself literally translates as "nowhere" or "no place," and that the utopian theme of the philosophical imaginary discussed by Le Dœuff emerges here.

45. For example, Naomi Scheman, "Though This Be Method, Yet There Is Madness in It: Paranoia and Liberal Epistemology," in *A Mind of One's Own*.

46. Keller and Grontkowski, p. 220.

47. Jean-Paul Sartre, *Being and Nothingness*, trans. Hazel E. Barnes (New York: Pocket Books, 1956), p. 738. Martin Jay in *Downcast Eyes: The Denigration of Vision in Twentieth Century French Thought* (Berkeley: University of California Press, 1993) argues that Sartre is hostile to vision in general, based on his use of the look, but does not consider the role vision plays in Sartre's epistemology.

nowhere, and this will be evident in the metaphors and concepts that emerge in their work. These assumptions and implications affect any attempt to reclaim objectivity and visual and spatial metaphors. My reading shows the way these metaphors are deeply embedded in much epistemological thought. First I will discuss Haraway's work.

Situated Knowledges

Haraway argues that we need to emphasize objectivity through situated knowledges, a term that she uses to suggest knowledge theorized from a particular situation, rather than abstracted or detached from the world. In addition, she wants these views from somewhere to reclaim visual metaphors for feminist purposes. For Haraway, the problem is "how to have *simultaneously* an account of radical historical contingency for all knowledge claims and knowing subjects . . . *and* a no-nonsense commitment to faithful accounts of a 'real' world."[48] Part of gaining such faithful accounts is to take seriously the experiences of the marginalized. She expresses the value of marginalized experience thus: "there is good reason to believe vision is better from below the brilliant space platforms of the powerful."[49] The idea is that oppressed peoples can see things that non-oppressed peoples are unable to.

Haraway is aware of important feminist objections to the use of visual metaphors in epistemology. In her view the problem is not with visual metaphors as such, but with metaphors of disembodied vision which emphasize transcendence and the distance between subject and object. Nagel's view from nowhere is an excellent example of what Haraway calls the god trick: seeing everything from nowhere, which is really more like seeing nothing from everywhere. Her approach seems promising, given our apparent reliance on visual metaphors for understanding knowledge and given our difficulty in thinking them away. For Haraway, objectivity or seeing things properly is concerned with specific and particular embodiment. She says that only partial perspective, or seeing through particular perspectives, promises objective vision. However, difficulties arise in her attempt to reclaim objectivity and visual metaphors of knowledge.

First, interesting parallels emerge in relation to Nagel's concern with nonhuman sense experience. Haraway says that she has learned about partial perspective by "walking with my dogs and wondering how the world looks without a fovea and very few retinal cells for color vision but with a huge neu-

48. Haraway, p. 579.
49. Ibid., p. 583.

ral processing and sensory area for smells."[50] In her account, objectivity can be achieved by learning how visual systems work, for example, the eyes of an insect, or the camera eyes of a spy satellite and a space probe. She says that all views are mediated, and so people should take care to "see faithfully from another's point of view."[51] This conception of what it is to take account of others' experience again leads to a reliance on imagination, rather than actually learning or accepting what marginalized groups know. It may be a view from a body, but it still implies looking out from that view and using one's powers of imaginative insight to understand others. Haraway is aware of the dangers of romanticization and appropriation of the views of people who are oppressed. However, she seems unaware that thinking about epistemology in terms of visual metaphors may increase these dangers, particularly of appropriation, because she takes "seeing from below" as something that can be learned. Furthermore, on her view, the oppressed may not even be as good at this as others: "One cannot 'be' either a cell or molecule—or a woman, colonized person, laborer, and so on—if one intends to see and see from these positions critically."[52] Thus, this approach does not overcome the problem of thinking that we can see from other's viewpoints because this "seeing" is conceptualized as a skill that can be developed.

Haraway wants to emphasize the activity of vision, but the activity of visual metaphors is perhaps one of their greatest flaws, because, as we have seen, looking is so often equated with possession and domination. Generally, visual metaphors are *too* active, as in the equation of seeing with possession and domination put most forcefully by Sartre. Keller and Grontkowski argue that although vision itself is considered to be passive, mental vision or vision as metaphorically connected with knowledge is treated as active.[53] Haraway says that "*how* to see from below is a problem requiring at least as much skill with bodies and language, with the mediations of vision, as the 'highest' technoscientific visualizations."[54] In addition to the issue of understanding knowledge through the metaphor of seeing as a skill, the visual metaphor lends itself to an ideal of completion. Haraway argues that situated knowledges can be brought together, saying that the images of objectivity are "the joining of partial views and halting voices into a collective subject position."[55] In my view, it is not a question of skills, although we should try to develop these, but of devising ways to ensure diverse voices are heard, and respecting the knowledge of others. This is where metaphors of listening, as in Haraway's

50. Ibid.
51. Ibid.
52. Ibid., p. 585.
53. Keller and Grontkowski, p. 215.
54. Ibid., p. 584.
55. Ibid., p. 590.

ideas of a shared conversation and a web of knowledges, could be more useful.[56] Hearing and listening suggest a recognition of the distinctiveness of the experience of others and some acceptance of their claims. These ways of listening are of a different order from trying to see things from the perspective of others, because they do not involve taking over or replacing the experience and skills of others. Listening and hearing metaphors will feature at the end of the chapter, but first Sandra Harding's standpoint epistemology should be discussed.

Standpoint Epistemology

Sandra Harding also wants to retain the concept of objectivity, albeit in a revised form, in the context of standpoint epistemology. Standpoint epistemology is premised on the idea that members of socially marginalized groups have a critical vantage point from which to view social organization, and by implication, what is presented as knowledge by the more powerful.[57] In a recent paper, "Rethinking Standpoint Epistemology: What is 'Strong Objectivity'?," Harding argues that we should accept a revised notion of objectivity, more rigorous and objectifying than traditional notions of objectivity, with the commitment to neutrality removed. She calls traditional notions of objectivity "objectivism." By objectivism she means the striving for an epistemological viewpoint which abstracts from any particular point of view. In her view, work carried out under the aegis of value-neutrality is commonly found to have, for example, sexist bias. She argues that a major problem with aiming for neutrality is the way social interests and values which are shared by, say, the scientific community, can go unobserved.[58] Her answer to the problem lies in recognizing these interests and values, rather than, as suggested by the picture of a "view from nowhere," transcending, or abstracting from them.

To distinguish her position from one like Nagel's, Harding speaks of strong objectivity, based on a standpoint epistemology. By "strong objectivity" she means knowledge that actually takes into account the experiences of oppressed groups. Standpoint epistemology begins from marginalized lives and is sexually, ethnically, and historically situated. According to Harding's ver-

56. Ibid., p. 584.

57. See Nancy Hartsock, "The Feminist Standpoint: Developing the Ground for a Specifically Feminist Historical Materialism," in *Feminism and Methodology: Social Science Issues*, ed. Sandra Harding (Bloomington: Indiana University Press, 1987), pp. 157–180.

58. Sandra Harding, "Rethinking Standpoint Epistemology: What Is 'Strong Objectivity'?" in *Feminist Epistemologies*, ed. Linda Alcoff and Elizabeth Potter (New York: Routledge, 1993), p. 57.

sion of this view, oppressed peoples have a valuable contribution to make to knowledge because their view can often reveal aspects of the world oppressors are unaware of. Harding says that objectivism, unlike her "strong objectivity," leaves out the experiences of oppressed people and presents the experiences and ways of thinking of dominant groups as the standard for all.

Unlike Haraway, Harding is critical of visual metaphors of thinking from the perspective of women's lives, because she says that misunderstandings may arise from them. She suggests instead that we should use an image of knowledge-seeking as a journey in which one sets out from women's lives.[59] The metaphor of a journey is a kind of spatial metaphor, yet the movement involved in journeying implies the temporal, historical dimension of understanding, and does not suggest a hierarchy of perspectives. One practical example she gives is of starting off questions about the state and social institutions from women's experiences of caring for others.

However, in spite of her commitment to journeying images, a hierarchical system of visual and spatial metaphors is evident in her work.[60] Harding's solution to the problems of "weak" objectivity is to take into account the *viewpoints* of others at the stage of formulating questions and paradigms, though she thinks that the answers may be found in "the beliefs and activities of the people at the *center*." She says, "some people at the *center* must be intimate enough with the lives of the marginalized to be able to think how social life works from the *perspective* of their lives."[61] Although it is not inevitable, spatial metaphors often set up a hierarchical structure, in terms of center over periphery, or top over bottom. These spatial metaphors are particularly disturbing, as they suggest that there is a group of central people (white, middle class) who will make use of the experiences of the marginalized. It certainly does not seem to be the marginalized who are going to benefit or to produce knowledge.

Another metaphorical contrast of spatial location and corresponding vision emerges. Harding writes, "the activities of those at the bottom of such social hierarchies can provide starting points for thought—for *everyone's* research and scholarship—from which humans' relations with each other and the natural world *can become visible*."[62] The metaphor of "becoming visible to" may suggest that those at the top need to have or to know what it is like to have the same experiences as those at the bottom. That is sometimes precisely what cannot happen, given certain differences in social location.

59. Ibid., p. 78. She cites Nancy Hartsock and Dorothy Smith as authors who use the journey metaphor.
60. She mentions "learning to listen attentively" as important at one point. Harding, p. 68.
61. Ibid., pp. 54, 79. My italics.
62. Ibid., p. 54. My italics.

Those "at the top" may not be able to see what the important questions are which arise from different experiences.

The flow from the concept of objectivity to particular kinds of visual and spatial metaphors leads to the interesting idea: if metaphors and concepts are of a piece or in dialectical relation, then both will necessarily introduce or reintroduce the other. Thus, when Harding says we should have objectivity without the spatial and visual metaphors and their implications, she has set herself a difficult task. These visual and spatial metaphors work at the level of expressibility, in being deeply embedded in ways of thinking about knowing and in being inextricably connected to the concept of objectivity.

At times, Harding seems to be aiming for a kind of completeness by using as many different perspectives as possible and by suggesting that those in the dominant groups should take up the perspective of those in oppressed groups. For example, she writes: "Men, too, must contribute distinctive forms of specifically feminist knowledge from their particular social situation."[63] Elsewhere, division within the self is supported, like the "double vision" Nagel advocates: "the subject/agent of feminist knowledge . . . is the thinker whose consciousness is bifurcated, the outsider within, the marginal person now located at the center."[64] It seems that the refusal to give up objectivity and a perhaps unwitting use of spatial and visual metaphors means that this version of standpoint epistemology retains some of the assumptions of what Harding would call a weak objectivist, like Nagel. Harding says that we have to avoid "partial and distorted beliefs" and that feminist thought "criticizes all gender loyalties as capable of producing only partial and distorted results of research."[65] These comments show how visual metaphors interact with the assumption of weak objectivity that individual and group perspectives distort and lead us into error. The metaphors lead back to a certain conception of knowers and knowledge, including the assumption that error attends certain perspectives, simply because they are perspectives or "partial and distorted," and that we can somehow escape this by generalizing to incorporate all perspectives.

Both Harding's and Haraway's views are aiming at a view from somewhere, but at this stage still sound rather like god tricks.[66] Although they avoid the abstracting and transcendent nature of Nagel's view from nowhere, a con-

63. Ibid., p. 67.
64. Ibid., p. 65.
65. Ibid., pp. 71, 59.
66. Susan Bordo argues that Haraway's work exemplifies "a dream of being *everywhere*," in "Feminism, Postmodernism, and Gender-Scepticism," in *Feminism/Postmodernism*, ed. Linda J. Nicholson (New York: Routledge, 1990), p. 143.

sequence of their adherence to objectivity and the implicit and explicit reliance on visual and spatial metaphors of knowledge leads to the goal of incorporating other perspectives into one's own in order to achieve completeness of vision. The term standpoint epistemology is yet another example of a spatial metaphor and may suggest a reversal of traditional objectivist views which still shares the same framework. The flow in both directions between concepts and metaphors recognized by Le Dœuff needs to be understood. Nothing but the task of exploring alternative concepts and metaphors and ways of using them could avoid the problems pointed out here and transform the imaginary.

Reconceptions

A range of ways of taking into account the epistemological differences between contingent, empirical selves are excluded by a reliance on the particular metaphors Nagel uses. It follows from my discussion of Nagel, Haraway, and Harding that some visual and spatial metaphors are extremely difficult to separate from epistemology—they are deeply embedded in ways of thinking about knowledge. Although some of the specific metaphors Nagel uses, such as the photographic metaphor, could be dispensed with, metaphors such as points of view, perspectives, centers and margins, and inside and outside seem endemic to epistemology. However, I do not think that metaphors of a view from nowhere (though this is essential to Nagel's thought), or a view from everywhere, and all that follows from them are inevitable. These particular metaphors are neither deeply embedded nor operative at the level of expressibility within any *possible* epistemological project; indeed, other sensory metaphors could play an important role. Epistemology as conceived in analytic philosophy excludes the possibility that what are considered contingent characteristics of a person could be relevant. Lorraine Code, for example, considers whether one's sex could be relevant and argues that it could only be relevant to a reconstructed epistemology, because the ideals of epistemology, such as objectivity, impartiality, and universality, are "androcentrically derived."[67] Epistemology shares with the other subject areas of analytic philosophy this exclusionary aspect: according to those within the field, if one is doing feminist epistemology, then one is not doing epistemology. The visual and spatial metaphors discussed here are fully complicit in this

---

67. Lorraine Code, *What Can She Know? Feminist Theory and the Construction of Knowledge* (Ithaca: Cornell University Press, 1991), p. 314.

kind of exclusion, so experimentation with other metaphors may make epistemology a more pluralistic enterprise.

Uma Narayan, an Indian feminist, makes a number of important criticisms of epistemological projects that aim at incorporating different perspectives and valorizing the experience of oppressed groups. She points out that one problem which arises within overwhelmingly religious cultures, such as Hindu culture, is that women's experiences, for example, are valued highly as long as they remain within the traditional space allotted. Narayan argues that stressing individual rights can be necessary in a pragmatic sense when arguing for change within such a culture. At the same time, the need to be critical of the culture conflicts with the wish to affirm it in the face of more dominant cultures.

Furthermore, Narayan argues that it is possible to achieve some understanding of others whose experiences are very different from ours. Yet, she says "that it is *easier* and *more likely* for the oppressed to have critical insights into the conditions of their own oppression than it is for those who live outside these structures."[68] Even concerned people will often fail to notice more subtle forms of oppression. Of course, the development of empathy can have an ameliorating effect on this failure, as argued by Diana Meyers, for example, but cannot replace the insights peculiar to those with direct experience of oppression.[69]

With regard to the notion that oppressed people have an epistemic advantage over oppressors, Narayan argues that critical insight is not a necessary accompaniment of oppression. There are a number of possible risks in having insight into two modes of experience. One is that it will lead to compartmentalization, or having to assume a completely different role or stance depending on the context. A second risk is identifying wholly with either the dominant group or the oppressive situation. She points out that trying to maintain double vision can be uncomfortable and difficult, and seeing things from two places can leave one with no space to be at all.[70] Narayan warns against romanticizing the position of the oppressed, a romanticization which is likely to occur amongst those who do not actually suffer the oppression.

These are valuable reminders that it is not enough to try to see things from a point of view outside one's own, but that we must actually listen to the authoritative words others use to describe experiences we cannot fully understand. This does not mean simply expressing the attempt to put ourselves in

68. Uma Narayan, "The Project of Feminist Epistemology: Perspectives from a Nonwestern Feminist," in *Gender/Body/Knowledge: Feminist Reconstructions of Being and Knowing*, ed. Alison Jaggar and Susan Bordo (New Brunswick: Rutgers University Press, 1989), p. 264.

69. Diana Tietjens Meyers, *Subjection and Subjectivity: Psychoanalytic Feminism and Moral Philosophy* (New York: Routledge, 1994).

70. Narayan, p. 267.

others' shoes another way. What I am suggesting is that in listening or hearing, we do not assimilate the words of others to our own experience. What we hear may be partly unintelligible or inassimilable, but still we can accept what is said and take it seriously. Specific situations and experiences can give some people an authority that overrides our ability to share their experiences in actuality or imagination. The sense of hearing is not regarded as atemporal in the way that vision is, so it can also be used to suggest historically situated knowledge. A philosopher who expresses the proper ethical relation with the other in terms of metaphors of hearing and listening is Emmanuel Lévinas. He argues that the other is prior to self, and that proper ethical relations can only occur when we are ready to hear the call of the Other. Lévinas uses metaphors of hearing in connection with the metaphor of the face of the Other: "The Other becomes my neighbor precisely through the way the face summons me, calls for me, begs for me, and in so doing recalls my responsibility, and calls me into question."[71] These hearing and listening metaphors need to be developed in the context of epistemology.

Another possibility, which has been suggested by Luce Irigaray in relation to women's sensual experience, is the sense of touch and the notion of the caress.[72] In relation to epistemology, touch suggests interaction between knower and known. We sometimes use tactile metaphors to describe knowing, such as grasping or apprehending the truth. Metaphors of touching may also be useful in certain contexts, because of the way they bring together subject and object, and are localized in the sense of not implying that we can take in the whole object or scene at once, as visual metaphors do. We could also reconceptualize vision in less distancing and dominating ways.[73] Lorraine Code notes that both touch and listening, in contrast to vision, "are possible only for explicitly situated knowers."[74] She argues that touch is more detailed and stable than vision, and that both touch and listening are more intimate. Listening in the context of conversation or dialogue also implies that the "object" of knowledge can correct the "subject," if they are not listening properly or not really hearing what is being said. As Gemma Corradi Fiumara puts it "When concerned with listening one can repeatedly be wrong in a propensity to create a more enlightening relationship in which

---

71. Emmanuel Lévinas, *The Lévinas Reader*, ed. Seán Hand (Oxford: Blackwell, 1989), p. 83.

72. Luce Irigaray, *This Sex Which Is Not One*, trans. Catherine Porter with Carolyn Burke (Ithaca, New York: Cornell University Press, 1985), p. 26.

73. For example, Teresa Brennan, in "'The Contexts of Vision' from a Specific Standpoint," in *Vision in Context: Historical and Contemporary Perspectives on Sight*, ed. Teresa Brennan and Martin Jay (London: Routledge, 1996), argues that vision can be conceived as receptive, but is rarely experienced that way in contemporary life.

74. Code, p. 148–155.

even the object can teach and instruct."[75] Exploring these metaphors would be extremely useful to epistemology. The issue of sensual metaphors in epistemology is not to choose to replace the privileging of sight with the privileging of another sense, but rather we need to develop our understanding of the relevance of the neglected senses, to consider using different senses together, or different sensual metaphors where appropriate.

Conclusion

The metaphor of the view from nowhere works at the level of enframement, as a kind of framing device for Nagel's epistemology and is implicit in his discussions of all the issues he deals with.[76] It determines his construal of philosophical problems, and the kind of solutions to them considered possible. Although the metaphor of the view from nowhere is not used insistently throughout the text, derivative metaphors are—for example, the struggle to get outside myself, the inside-subjective/outside-objective opposition, and the centerless view. These metaphors maintain Nagel's epistemological stance by reinforcing the spatial contrasts which justify the need to aspire to the view from nowhere. Nagel's metaphors clearly work at the level of enframement. Certain spatial and visual metaphors work at a deeper level; for example, views and perspectives, the distinctions between outside and inside, and center and periphery. Without these metaphors Nagel could not even begin to describe his project. In this way some of Nagel's metaphors work at the level of expressibility. However, because a number of the central metaphors Nagel employs are frankly paradoxical, Nagel's imagery does not generally work at the level of persuasiveness, at least in a direct way. Nagel expresses his thought through metaphor, which thus provides some plausibility to his views and perhaps disarms objections, but he does not seek directly to persuade the reader of the truth of his theories through metaphor in the way Thomson uses analogy in relation to abortion.

Of course, metaphors also work in other ways. As we have seen, the metaphor of concentric spheres and the photographic metaphor serve to hide a confusion or tension between two different kinds of objectivity, Hegelian objectivity and absolute objectivity. The metaphor of concentric spheres is important for the characterization of subjectivity as a special sphere, which we must transcend. Together the concentric spheres and pho-

75. Gemma Corradi Fiumara, *The Other Side of Language: A Philosophy of Listening* (London: Routledge, 1990), p. 47.

76. The role it plays strikes one as similar to the foundational role of Descartes' tree and Kant's island in that it provides a framework and structure for his ideas.

tographic metaphors promote a separation of the objective from sense experience, as well as a dualistic separation of mind and body. There is a tension between the need to transcend the subjective, often allied with consciousness, and the belief that consciousness, stripped of the particular, is capable of understanding the non-human world. This tension is evident in Nagel's use of the metaphors of concentric spheres and the centerless world. Visual and spatial metaphors reinforce an atemporal, ahistorical view of the knower. Again, this use of images implies the view that we can imagine ourselves in the place of others, and we should try to do so, even though it may be difficult.

Visual and spatial metaphors also work at the level of expressibility. In the attempt to construct new epistemologies we can see the hold that visual and spatial metaphors have on our ways of thinking about knowing, and how recent attempts to reclaim visual metaphors have headed towards the view from nowhere. However, although these metaphors are deeply embedded, it is possible to think knowledge in other ways, such as through metaphors of hearing and listening. The analytic imaginary shares its privileging of the visual with other philosophical imaginaries, yet this is not a necessary feature of any philosophical imaginary. Visual and spatial metaphors may not be separable from Nagel's thought, but they may be separated from certain aspects of epistemology, combined with other metaphors, and reconceptualized.

6

Modeling Aesthetics

Although aesthetics is a relatively marginal area of analytic philosophy, an examination of the way imagery works in this area deepens our understanding of the analytic imaginary. The most prevalent use of imagery in analytic aesthetics is a full-scale model to represent and explain the arts. Although models are often thought to be similar to analogies, the model discussed here serves a very different purpose from the argument by analogy that we encountered in chapter 2. The most obvious difference is that while Thomson uses the violinist analogy to argue for a particular conclusion, the model here is used to *explain* artworks and our experience of them. However, the model shares a number of important functions with the other images (analogies, thought experiments, myths, and metaphors) discussed so far, and similar themes emerge. Models are an attempt to represent the fundamental structure of the phenomena they seek to explain. Models are used extensively in science to explain, for example, the movement of planets, the structure of DNA, and climatic patterns.[1] Models in aesthetics are supposed to represent the fundamental structure of artworks as well as our experience of them.

---

1. Useful discussions of the nature of models are given by Paul Ricoeur in *The Rule of Metaphor: Multi-disciplinary Studies of the Creation of Meaning in Language,* trans. Robert Czerny (Toronto: University of Toronto Press, 1977), and Max Black, *Models and Metaphors* (Ithaca: Cornell University Press, 1962). Black distinguishes between three "levels" of models: scale models, analogue models, and theoretical models. The sense of model I am using here best corresponds to the theoretical model which is based on (supposed) similarity of structure and is something more familiar than the thing it models.

A linguistic model of art has been popular within analytic aesthetics for a number of decades, its best-known proponent being Nelson Goodman in *Languages of Art: An Approach to a Theory of Symbols.*[2] As the title suggests, Goodman's project is to give a general theory of symbol systems, of which art is just one example. He believes that representation in art and elsewhere should be understood through the concepts of denotation, or referring, and exemplification, which occurs when an object both has and refers to a property, such as a paint sample.[3] So, for example, a painting may denote an object, such as a bottle, and exemplify a color, such as gray. The painting may also metaphorically exemplify a mood, such as sorrow. Aesthetic objects are distinguished from non-aesthetic ones by a range of "symptoms" related to the richness and density of the object in syntactic and semantic terms, and interpretation is a matter of making sense of the ways in which the symbols function.[4]

More recently, Kendall Walton, in a book entitled *Mimesis as Make-Believe: On the Foundations of the Representational Arts,* has introduced the idea that the arts can be modeled on games of make-believe. He criticizes the linguistic model for neglecting the way in which art is productive and creative, rather than referring to something already in existence. He says that, "Those who are set on using a linguistic model for representation will not find encouragement in the recognition of fictitious objects." Also, he says, "Nor is it obvious that linguistic predicates deserve . . . to be taken as models for understanding others, such as representations."[5]

Walton's "make-believe" model is highly influential among analytic philosophers interested in aesthetics. Judging by the reception of Walton's book, and the responses to articles he has been writing in this vein for over twenty years, the make-believe model is commonly regarded as *the* replacement for the linguistic model and the most fruitful model of art in recent analytic aesthetics. Malcolm Budd writes that "it is an outstanding work that will command its field for many years," and Colin Lyas says: "this is a work of very great importance that will set the agenda for discussions in aesthetics for a long time to come."[6] Walton's work is considered important because,

---

2. Nelson Goodman, *Languages of Art: An Approach to a Theory of Symbols* (Indianapolis: Hackett, 1976).

3. Ibid., pp. 52–56.

4. Ibid., pp. 252–255.

5. Kendall Walton, *Mimesis as Make-Believe: On the Foundations of the Representational Arts* (Cambridge: Harvard University Press, 1990), pp. 126, 129.

6. Malcolm Budd, review of *Mimesis as Make-Believe* by Kendall Walton, *Mind* 101, no. 401 (1992): 198. Colin Lyas, review of *Mimesis as Make-Believe* by Kendall Walton, *Philosophy* 66, no. 258 (1991): 529.

as Richard Wollheim puts it, "it presents a powerful, timely critique of the various linguistic, semi-linguistic, quasi-linguistic models of artistic content or meaning that are so much in favor today, all across the spectrum from Nelson Goodman to Jacques Derrida."[7] In addition to being seen as providing a critique of previous models, Walton's work is hailed because of its generality; Alan Goldman says that Walton has produced a theory that is very rich and has "enormous scope, covering representations of all sorts."[8] Thus, Walton's work is seen as significant because it offers a whole new way of understanding all kinds of art. I will argue in this chapter that the problems which arise in relation to Walton's view of art and aesthetic experience can be traced to the attempt to make art fit a single model, as well as the characteristics of the particular model used.

Walton uses the make-believe model to explain mimesis, representation, and fiction: "What all representations have in common is a role in *make-believe*."[9] His idea is that we can understand art better through the use of parallels with children's games involving make-believe, such as "playing house and school, cops and robbers, cowboys and Indians."[10] Although it is possible to think of Walton's use of children's games as analogical, it makes most sense to think of it as a model that attempts to explain the complexities of art and our experience of it. The "children's games" model introduces a number of important assumptions, covers tensions, and restricts the range of acceptable views of representation and the interpretation of art. The model works primarily on the level of providing a framework for the understanding of art and our responses to art, a framework into which aberrant examples and experiences are either forced to fit or rejected. I examine the ways in which Walton makes the shift from children's games of make-believe to works of fiction to demonstrate how using the model leads to oversimplified and implausible descriptions of art and our experience of art. However, matching artworks to the model also leads to some unnecessary complications. Walton's model is also made more diffuse by the use of two different types of children's games: those that involve toys specially designed to be played with in a certain way, and those that do not. His attempt to combine these two types of games leads to a number of serious tensions. Furthermore, the model serves to elide the differences between make-believe and imagination. The overriding theme of the analytic imaginary regarding imaginative self-projection arises in a stark and explicit form. In the final section, I discuss Italo Calvino's fascinating novel *If on a Winter's*

7. Richard Wollheim, "A Note on *Mimesis as Make-Believe*," *Philosophy and Phenomenological Research* 51, no. 2 (1991): 401.

8. Alan Goldman, "Representation and Make-Believe," *Inquiry* 36, no. 3 (1993): 335.

9. Walton, p. 4.

10. Ibid.

Night a Traveler to show how the make-believe model excludes more fruitful approaches to the interpretation of art.

The Model

The principal model of our experience of art that Walton uses is a children's game that I shall call "the stump-bear game"—the most important type of make-believe game, which contrasts with children's games involving toys, such as dolls or trucks. In his account of the stump-bear game, children playing in a forest designate tree stumps to count as bears. Any stump is a bear in the game, or in Walton's terminology, it is "fictional in the game" that there is a bear. Walton's story continues:

> Meanwhile, however, unbeknownst to anyone, there is an actual stump buried in a thicket not twenty feet behind Eric. Fictionally a bear is lurking in the thicket, although neither Eric nor Gregory realizes the danger. No one imagines a bear in the thicket; it is not fictional that a bear is there because someone imagines there is. But it is fictional. What makes it fictional? The stump. Thus does the stump generate a fictional truth. It is a prop. Props are generators of fictional truths, things which, by virtue of their nature or existence, make propositions fictional. A snow fort is a prop. It is responsible for the fictionality of the proposition that there is a (real) fort with turrets and a moat. A doll makes it fictional in a child's game that there is a blonde baby girl.[11]

This description of the stump-bear game contains the fundamentals of Walton's theory of art. An object, or a "prop," prescribes certain make-believe games. The prop, or the stump, stands in for something else—in this case a bear. It is odd that Walton outlines the stump-bear game in such detail, since he believes it is least like artworks because it only involves what he calls an *ad hoc* prop. Ad hoc props, such as the stump, do not generate any specific imaginings as they are not designed to be part of a game of make-believe. Walton argues that games involving toys are more like artworks because dolls prescribe specific make-believe games in the way that artworks do. What is important about the model is that it is not the characteristics of the prop as such, or the actual game that is played, that determines the nature of the experience, but a set of rules about how the game should be played. Among Walton's preferred examples of representational art are Dickens's *Tale of Two Cities,* Hitchcock's *North by Northwest,* Ibsen's *Hedda Gabler,* Mozart's *The Magic Flute,* Michelangelo's *David,* and Edgar

11. Ibid., pp. 37–38.

Allan Poe's *The Telltale Heart*.[12] In trying to link such artworks and children's games, he does not compare a particular artwork with a particular game but describes some aspect of a game, such as make-believe, and tries to show how it is involved in a range of artworks. He acknowledges that there are differences between children's games and art appreciation. For him, what is important for the success of the model is that those differences are ones of degree rather than kind.[13] Walton often states the modeling relation as if it is obvious; for example, he writes: "We should expect viewers of paintings and films, spectators of plays, readers of novels and stories to participate in the games in which these works are props much as children participate in games of cops and robbers, cowboys and Indians, dolls and mud pies. They do."[14] There is an important connection between this use of a model and foundationalism.

Foundations

The use of a model to explain our experience of art is closely linked to foundationalism in the sense that the make-believe model provides a structural basis for further understanding. As the title of his book suggests, Walton is attempting to give a foundational theory of art, "to construct a single comprehensive and unified theory, one with many applications."[15] He believes that all representational art can be understood in terms of the make-believe model. Make-believe is supposed to be "crucially involved" not only in art, but also in religious practices, sport, morality, "'theoretical entities' in science, and in other areas in which issues of metaphysical 'realism' are prominent."[16] Walton also argues that his theory can apply to non-representational arts—abstract painting, music, and architecture. However, as we shall see, the model constrains Walton to make his case for this by arguing that these arts are, in fact, representational. The other sense in which the use of a model makes his theory foundational is that it gives a developmental account of our experience of art, starting with children's games and building on them for more complex cases.

The specific foundations for Walton's theory are provided by children's games, including the stump-bear game already described, the doll which children make believe is a baby, and the mud pies that are "make-believedly" real pies. As a description of aesthetic experience, it fits *playing* with dolls,

12. Ibid., p. 1.
13. Ibid., pp. 224–229.
14. Ibid., p. 213.
15. Ibid., p. 8.
16. Ibid., p. 7.

and I show how such a model over-simplifies and distorts our experience of art. A number of authors have argued that the foundations of representational art cannot be explained in terms of make-believe, but I argue the stronger case that the attempt to provide a foundational theory or a single model of all art is itself misconceived.[17] In my judgment, the assumption that there must be one model for all the arts, or even for all the representational arts, is untenable. The single model pushes our understanding of art in two undesirable directions: towards over-simplification in some respects and unnecessary complications in others. We can understand the problem by looking at Walton's attempt to give a foundational theory through his model. As in relation to the other images, the model tells us more about the analytic imaginary than about the nature of the object of inquiry, art, as such.

The importance of foundations is intimately connected with an interest in metaphysics. Walton's aim is to answer both metaphysical questions about fictional entities and aesthetic questions about the nature of art and our experience of it. He gives two examples of aesthetic questions. One example is the question of what point there could be to having an institution that involves recognizing fictitious entities. Walton's rather sketchy answer is that engagement with artworks is beneficial in "helping us to clarify our thoughts and come to grips with our feelings about our position in life or whatever."[18] The other aesthetic question Walton is interested in is how to explain the nature of the experience of being emotionally involved in a fiction or artwork. Both questions are closely tied to metaphysical considerations as they take the central feature of art to be its non-reality and that it follows there is something puzzling about interest in non-real things. Using the model has a restrictive and over-simplifying effect on the kind of answers which can be given to these questions.

Games, Make-Believe, and Imagination

Walton's model oversimplifies aesthetic experience by obscuring the complexity of make-believe and imagination as well as the differences between them. To justify his use of the children's games model, he has to show a structural similarity between our experience of art and make-believing in the children's games. Walton acknowledges that the concept of make-believe is not

---

17. See, for example, David Novitz, Critical Discussion of *Mimesis as Make-Believe* by Kendall Walton, *Philosophy and Literature* 15, no. 1 (1991): 128.

18. Walton, p. 288.

distinctively aesthetic, and that works of art are just one example of representations.[19] His view is that representational works function as props in games of make-believe in the way dolls and teddy bears do in children's games—the only major difference in these experiences is that our response to art is more sophisticated.[20] The model is intended to be the simple form that can illuminate complex and subtle works and experiences.

Before outlining his theory of make-believe, Walton makes some remarks about imagining. There are two unusual features of Walton's account of imagining, which are both related to his attempt to show that "imaginers, like the stumps, are *props* as well as objects."[21] The first feature is Walton's claim that all imaginings involve imagining *de se* (imagining about the self).[22] Walton says that "*De se* imaginings in general are such that the imaginer cannot be unaware that his imagining is about himself."[23] This claim is puzzling. There seem to be many cases of imagining where we do not appear to be imagining about ourselves. We simply have to think of cases where we imagine an event, such as the first fleet arriving in Australia, without imagining ourselves seeing it or being there. The idea that all imagining is self-imagining is central to Walton's theory. It reinforces his view that our response to art always involves make-believing of some kind: for instance, make-believing that *we* are seeing things or make-believing that *we* feel emotions.

The second unusual feature, which exists in uneasy tension with the first, is that we can imagine ourselves being someone else. He says that in a case where we imagine that we are someone else, the self is a "bare Cartesian I."[24] But the problem with this idea is that such a self, stripped of all "contingent" features of identity, is an inadequate subject for imagining being another self. In such a case, both selves would be bare Cartesian selves, and there would be no content to the imagining.[25] Walton's view, like those views of the self which emerge in relation to the other images, is that contingent features of the self are irrelevant to identity, and so imagining oneself to be another is simply to entertain a proposition. He also believes that imagining oneself in

19. Ibid., pp. 7, 54. Walton thinks that anything used as a prop in a game of make-believe is a representation. For example, he says that the bread and wine used in communion may count as representations in his sense. However, he does not commit himself on this point.

20. Ibid., p. 11.

21. Ibid., p. 35.

22. Ibid., p. 29.

23. Ibid.

24. Ibid., p. 32.

25. See Bernard Williams, "Imagination and the Self," in *Problems of the Self: Philosophical Papers, 1956–1972* (Cambridge: Cambridge University Press, 1973), p. 44. Williams argues that the only way one could imagine being, for example, Napoleon, is "in fantasy, something like playing the rôle of Napoleon." See also Richard Wollheim, "Imagination and Identification," in *On Art and the Mind* (Cambridge: Harvard University Press, 1974).

an other's shoes is the principal way to learn about others and oneself.[26] This view connects with the feature of the analytic imaginary which has emerged in relation to each image I have examined, namely, the belief in the power of individuals' imaginative self-projection. The self-referentiality of Walton's account of imagining makes explicit the presupposition that imagining ourselves into the position of others must be a projection of the self.

Throughout his book, Walton writes as though imagining and make-believe can be substituted for each other at any point without altering the argument and relies on the richness of imagining in using the make-believe model. If the account was given exclusively in terms of make-believe, it would appear awkward and unconvincing. For example, when reading, we may imagine things *about* characters and events, but we do not necessarily make believe that we are being told a true story. Thus it is possible to agree that our experience of art involves imagining without being committed to the idea that it involves make-believe.[27]

By connecting his analysis of imagining and his description of the stump-bear game, Walton links imagining and make-believe in a way that may make us overlook the important differences between them. The make-believe model is supposed to be implicit in the use of the language of imagining. However, if the way imagining is used is examined, it is incompatible with the make-believe model. In order for Walton's model to work we must see psychological make-believe as a rule-bound game like the stump-bear one. He calls a variety of imaginative activities "imagining that," which maps onto "to believe that." By doing so he seeks to justify grouping imagination and make-believe together, but there is little justification for treating only propositional imagining, or "imagining that something is the case" as relevant to aesthetic experience. The model of the children's game masks the distinction between all the various types of imagining and propositional imagining, as particular examples are understood on the make-believe model. Make-believe involves taking an object to be something that it is not; for example, children may make believe that a stick is a horse. Trying to understand artworks through the make-believe model entails that we respond to artworks by make-believing something about them. For example, the model dictates that rather than simply seeing a painting and appreciating style, colors, shapes, or ideas and associations which may be evoked, we must make believe that the painting is really something else or make believe that something is in the work that is not.

26. Walton, p. 34.

27. Pettersson, for example, also argues that imagining does not presuppose make-believe. Anders Pettersson, "On Walton's and Currie's Analyses of Literary Fiction," *Philosophy and Literature* 17, no. 1 (1993): 88.

A good illustration of the distortion involved in reducing imagining to "make-believing that" is provided by Walton's discussion of Kasimir Malevich's *Supremacist Painting*. The painting contains a number of overlapping geometrical shapes, including a yellow rectangle overlapping a green line. Walton says that we "make believe" that the yellow rectangle is in front of a green line, whereas in fact (according to Walton) it is not in front of one green line, but bisects two green lines. Instead of accepting that we see shapes on a flat surface, he argues that we *make believe that* there is a three-dimensional arrangement. The experience of seeing the shapes is made to correspond with the model of make-believing that we see a bear rather than a stump.

Even combining the two types of games' models does not enable Walton to account for all the different ways of imagining or being imaginative, particularly in our experience of art. We imagine about, of, and in relation to works of art, and we also think about works of art. Not all, or even most, of our responses to works of art can be construed in terms of make-believe. Using the model of the stump-bear game works to cover over the complexities of imaginative response.

Games and Egocentricity

There is another, related way in which the children's games model simplifies Walton's characterization of our imaginative responses to art. In the tree stump game, Eric and Gregory make believe, or imagine of themselves, that they are afraid of a bear. Thus their imagining is a kind of self-imagining. The point is that regardless of the nature of the artwork, all our imaginings are about ourselves. Charlton notes that Walton's choice of children's games results in a theory that is "excessively egocentric": "Children playing pirates do fantasize about themselves; a charm of works of art is that they can make us forget ourselves . . . Walton describes us (chap. 9) as responding to 'verbal representations' by imagining ourselves hearing the author narrate and thereby learning what is fictionally true: we are at the center of our thoughts like children who make-believe that they are being menaced by bears."[28] The model provides the framework for taking all of our responses to art to be self-reflexive in this way. Furthermore, this assumption is made more plausible by the model of children's games, because in such cases it makes sense to say that children, for example, make believe that they feel fear or that they are a doctor.

Even if it is thought that we sometimes make believe things about ourselves in relation to artworks, it does not follow that this is an accurate or

28. William Charlton, review of *Mimesis as Make-Believe* by Kendall Walton, *British Journal of Aesthetics* 31, no. 4 (1991): 370.

proper description of our response to *all* artworks. Although some artworks may evoke the sense that we are spectators or voyeurs, as in the case of paintings of nudes who seem to be looking out at or seem to be aware of being looked at by the spectator, most artworks do not convey this sense. Thus, not all our responses to artworks involve self-imagining. Art can open us to new situations, outside our own experience, at least to a certain extent. Coming to appreciate art is one of the ways we can learn something about unfamiliar lives, not by using artworks for our own fantasies, but by reflecting on the diversity of ideas and experiences art offers us. Acquaintance with art cannot be a substitute for experience, nor overcome the limitations of our imaginations, but it can enrich our lives and prepare us to accept ideas we are not accustomed to. The children's games model cannot account for the potential enrichment of ourselves through our experience of art, because it reduces our responses to art to self-regarding ones. Yet, the model also generates unnecessary complexity in relation to some aesthetic questions.

Props and Worlds

One of the main aims of using a model is to make a complex phenomenon understandable in terms of a more simple structure. In many ways the children's games model is too simple, as we have seen. However, there are two ways in which the model also leads to an unnecessarily complicated structure. The first results from relating games to fictional worlds, and the second concerns the phenomenology of aesthetic experience.

While describing and explaining aesthetic experience, Walton wants to solve puzzles about the status of fictional entities and fictional truths. In order to do this he tries to show how artworks function in make-believe games like the ones children play. Walton introduces the idea of fictional truth by saying that "When it is 'true in a game of make-believe,' as we say, that Jules goes on a buffalo hunt, the proposition that he goes on a buffalo hunt is *fictional*, and the fact that it is fictional is a *fictional truth*."[29] In his words, whatever is true in what he calls fictional worlds is fictional. Walton defines a prop, such as the stump, as a generator of a fictional truth. A fictional truth "consists in there being a prescription or mandate in some context to imagine something. Fictional propositions are propositions that are *to be* imagined—whether or not they are imagined."[30] In his view, something

29. Walton, p. 35.
30. Ibid., p. 39. The theory seems to suggest that "it is fictional that" means it is "fictionally true," or "true in a fictional way that." However, Walton says he does not accept this. To say that something is fictional is to attribute fictionality to it, not a kind of truth, although certain things can be fictional and true.

is a prop whether or not anyone is imagining anything about it, or is even aware that it exists. We should not identify the fictional with the imagined, because we may imagine, for example, that there is a stump when there is not, and there may be a stump there that we are not aware of.[31] Walton argues that each artwork is a fictional world, and also that each make-believe game that is played with an artwork is a fictional world. In the terms of the model, paintings and novels are props too. The artwork as a whole is a prop and certain representational parts of it, such as a figure or a building, can also be props. Thus, Walton thinks that we play games of make-believe with artworks in the way that children play with stumps, dolls, and trucks.

Although Walton points out that he is using the language of fictional worlds, he does not really want to refer to such entities.[32] If one accepts this, it is still a cumbersome framework to use in discussing art objects—more cumbersome than simply referring to different interpretations. It becomes more elaborate through the use of games: since no game is identical to any other, there must be a different world for each game. Correspondingly, there is a different world for each artwork. The personal nature of the imagining—his view that every imagining must be a self-imagining—means, moreover, that each viewer of an art work creates another fictional world. This is also true because each viewer, according to Walton, plays a different game with the artwork. Thus a world corresponds to every part of every artwork in relation to each person at different times. The use of the model of children's games leads to a proliferation of fictional worlds around each artwork. The prop aspect of the model means a further proliferation of games and worlds, because different viewers may play different games with different props (parts) of artworks at different times. Yet these possibilities conflict with the notion that only certain imaginings are dictated or prescribed. The complexity of the language of games and worlds is matched by a similarly complicated phenomenology.

The Stump Is a Bear:
Phenomenology of Aesthetic Experience

The structure of the model is mirrored in Walton's analysis of aesthetic experience. Just as the stump stands in for a bear, so the artwork has to stand in for something else. Spelling out what various artworks stand in for often creates difficulties for the model, particularly in relation to our experience

31. Ibid., p. 37.
32. Ibid., pp. 67, 64. Walton says that we should not confuse fictional worlds with the theory of possible worlds, because fictional worlds differ from possible worlds in allowing impossible things and by being incomplete.

of art. There are two kinds of problems with the model from an experiential point of view.

First, Walton's claim that we make believe that we are seeing or experiencing a scene, say, rather than simply seeing or experiencing one, has the implication that there are two layers of experience. For example, he describes seeing Meindert Hobbema's painting *Wooded Landscape with a Water Mill* thus: "On observing Hobbema's canvas, one imagines one's observation to be of a mill."[33] One experience is that of seeing the artwork itself, while the other is the make-believe experience interposed between us and the artwork. Walton says that these two aspects are part of a single experience.

There are problems for Walton both in accepting and rejecting this phenomenology. On the one hand, it is not clear how two such different experiences could become one or be experienced as one experience.[34] However, if the "double layer" phenomenological account is rejected as implausible, there is no theoretical space left for make-believe, since if there is not a separate experience, then one will be seeing simply the original picture. It is difficult to understand what Walton could mean by make-believing that we see something except that we are visualizing it. Yet the problems with even a relatively simple representational example suggests that art will not fit the model. It seems both more accurate and straight-forward to say that we look at pictures of mills, people, rectangles, and so on; yet, Walton's model constrains us to complicate our experience.

The second problem with the model's attempt to describe the structure of aesthetic experience is that it does not seem to accord with many actual experiences of art. Walton claims that the confirmation of his theory is in its explanatory value.[35] But what his theory attempts to explain is our *experience* and to do that it must correspond with our experience. However, the make-believe games supposedly played with artworks are not games we are aware of playing, and it is characteristic of games of make-believe that they are played deliberately and consciously.[36] Therefore, the make-believe model is imposed on experience, rather than reflecting that experience.

33. Ibid., p. 294. See Rob Hopkins, review of *Mimesis as Make-Believe* by Kendall Walton, *Philosophical Books* 33, no. 2 (1992): 127. Hopkins believes Walton is probably committed to the idea of there being two layers of experience.

34. As Rob Hopkins says, "it is wholly unclear how visualizing and visual experience of a picture *could* be integrated into a single experience, when each has its own phenomenology." Ibid., p. 127. Malcolm Budd argues that Walton's claim that our make-believing and seeing in the case of pictorial experience are inseparable seems "to amount to nothing more than that my perception of the picture is the *object* of my imagining: I am imagining *of* my seeing the picture that it is my seeing the scene depicted." Budd, p. 197.

35. Walton, p. 214.

36. Pettersson points out that if Walton tried to avoid the problem by saying that in our response to art we play these games unconsciously, the theory becomes metaphorical, because we can only play unconscious games of make-believe in a metaphorical sense, p. 86.

Both these problems become particularly acute in regard to abstract art and music, as these art forms do not even seem to suggest that we would need to make believe the shapes and sounds. Abstract art is included under visual representation, because it is supposed to lead us to make believe that the shapes occupy space in a manner different from the way they actually do, as in the Malevich example above. The confines of the model also lead to a rather narrow analysis of music. Pieces of music purportedly lead us to make believe that the music is representational, describing a scene or narrating a story. However, given that narrative music is quite rare, Walton says that we usually make believe that we are feeling emotions or that the music represents emotions. Walton describes the experience thus: "In place of fictional perception of external objects we have fictional introspection or self-awareness. If I am right, this is likely to be true even of such stalwarts of musical purity as Bach's *Art of the Fugue;* and to whatever extent introspection is analogous to the 'external' sense, it will be reasonable to expand our understanding of 'depiction' to include them."[37] This description of our appreciation of music relates back to the egocentric aspect of the model in that the focus is on introspection. Such an analysis may apply to a small range of cases, if it was accepted that we make believe emotions in response to art. However, there are still many other cases where a different kind of experience is involved, based on appreciation of music as sequences of sounds. If the children's game model is accepted, where every prop is a stand-in for something else, an equivalent in the case of all art forms must be found. However, such an understanding of art makes it appear always to be a substitute for another thing, rather than works which are appreciated for themselves.

For similar reasons, the children's games model excludes our appreciation of formal elements in the visual and other arts. Walton therefore writes: "I disavow any implied commitment either to a picture theory of language (or 'symbols') or correspondence theory of truth, or to an imitation or resemblance theory of depiction."[38] However, disavowing a commitment does not mean that the model does not necessitate a reliance on an imitation theory of depiction. Particularly in his discussion of painting, Walton focuses only on what they depict, rather than surface features. He believes that a concern with the non-depictive characteristics of works is a special function of the art critic, rather than the ordinary appreciator of art.

One example of representational art, used by Walton, is Seurat's *Sunday on the Island of La Grande Jatte,* and his discussion is concerned primarily with the depicted people, objects, and events. We are supposed to make believe that when we see this picture we see a couple strolling in a park. Yet even

37. Walton, p. 336.
38. Ibid., p. 3.

this obviously representational example could involve other ways of seeing. It would not be improper for a viewer of this painting to be interested in the use of the pointillist technique and the play of colors and light in the painting, with little concern for the strolling couple. One could also have an interest in the thematic aspects of the painting that are related to the formal elements of the work. Linda Nochlin argues that the painting is an anti-utopian allegory and refers to composition and brushstrokes in support of her view. She writes: "It is through the pictorial construction of the work—its formal strategies—that the anti-utopian is allegorized in the *Grande Jatte*."[39] In other cases, our interest in non-representational aspects of artworks could be even stronger, as in action painting, minimalism, poetic writing, and so on. A concentration on representational aspects of works can lead to impoverished understanding of them and of the different ways we can experience art. The children's games model, where a toy or stump always represents something else, creates this limitation.

Make-Believe Emotion

Making artistic examples fit the make-believe model leads to a disregard for much of our ordinary aesthetic responses and interests in art. This problem is especially significant in relation to our emotional responses to art. In analytic aesthetics, one of the central questions about emotions is taken to be why we emotionally respond to characters and events in fiction, given that the characters do not exist and the events have not occurred. Colin Radford's famous paper on this question, "How Can We Be Moved by the Fate of Anna Karenina?," argues that emotions such as pity for Anna Karenina are irrational.[40] It has generated many answers over the decades, and Walton's answer is considered to be perhaps the most significant and influential, his argument being that the structure of our emotional responses can be explained in terms of games of make-believe. Although he admits that we may have genuine emotional responses to art, he says that they are not characteristic responses and we have them only in so far as we are thinking of something similar in life. In his view, the characteristic emotional response to art is make-believe emotion, or pseudo-emotion.

39. Linda Nochlin, *The Politics of Vision: Essays on Nineteenth-Century Art and Society* (New York: Harper and Row, 1989), p. 171.

40. Colin Radford, *Proceedings of the Aristotelian Society* 49 (supp.), (1975): 67–80. See also Peter Lamarque, "How Can We Fear and Pity Fictions?" *British Journal of Aesthetics* 21 (1981): 291–304, and Gregory Currie, *The Nature of Fiction* (Cambridge: Cambridge University Press, 1990).

Walton argues that we only make believe that we are having emotional responses, because we are reacting to representations, not real things. Not surprisingly, the primary example is a case of what he calls quasi-fear. This example, where "Charles" is frightened by green slime in a horror film, relates directly to the stump-bear game. Just as the children make believe that they are afraid of bears, Walton claims that Charles is not genuinely afraid but is imagining being afraid.[41] Walton compares Charles' fear to that of a child running from a make-believe monster, but asks us to think of an undemonstrative child, so his "proposal is to construe Charles on the model of this undemonstrative child."[42] He is not really in danger, but only make-believedly in danger. This understanding of our emotional experience of art is clearly modeled on the stump-bear game. As in Walton's descriptions of our perceptions of artworks, the model leads to a distortion, even a denial, of that experience. "Charles" may claim that he is afraid, but given this model, he is not really afraid. Rather, it is true in that fictional world that he is afraid. Just as in chapter 2, where the analogy leads to emotions being excluded from discussions of abortion, the model here promotes the idea that emotions should not be taken seriously, because they are just part of a game. Our experience is denied and reduced to quasi-experience by the model. The model also places limits on the possibilities of interpretation.

Games and Rules

The reliance on rules to describe what is involved in the interpretation of art, necessitated by Walton's model, limits the variety of interpretative possibilities. The list of rules that are supposed to govern the generation of fictional truths includes principles of generation, the acceptance rule, and the supplementation rule.[43] By a principle of generation, Walton means that there are explicit or implicit rules governing how props generate fictional truths. An important difference between children's games and works of art in relation to this point arises here. Children's games of make-believe are different in that their rules are usually explicit while the rules for interpreting art seem at best implicit, or perhaps even non-existent. Walton acknowledges

41. Walton, p. 247. It is interesting to note that at this point Walton does not use the expression "make-believe that," perhaps because it is so implausible.

42. Ibid., p. 244. This is an example where imagining *de se* is explicitly relied on; Walton says: "Charles does not merely imagine *that* he is afraid; he imagines *being* afraid." Ibid., p. 247.

43. Principles of generation are principles that govern what we are to imagine. The acceptance rule is the rule that "whatever is in fact imagined . . . is to be imagined." Ibid., p. 44. The supplementation rule is the rule that fictional propositions should be added to in ways that preserve coherence. Ibid., p. 46.

this: "Some [principles], including most involving works of art, are never explicitly agreed on or even formulated, and imaginers may be unaware of them, at least in the sense of being unable to spell them out."[44] Games, particularly the kind of games Walton describes, are dictatorial about what we make-believe or imagine in ways that artworks are not. This shows that there is a deep problem with trying to model artworks on rule-governed games. The games model breaks down, because games are governed by rules, whereas the interpretation of art is not.[45] Artworks have even less in common than games, making the search for a model which can explain all the media and genres of art inappropriate.

Walton argues that only some games of make-believe are authorized.[46] By "authorized" he means that the game is prescribed by the props within a certain context. The stump-bear game is different from other kinds of games because the make believing involved is not authorized—in such a game one can imagine that anything is anything—whereas authorized games are ones which use toys as they were designed to be used. In terms relevant to the interpretation of art, authorized games can be understood as accepted or standard interpretations of works of art. Although Walton himself does not intend to be overly restrictive on the range of possible interpretations of any given artwork, the model makes it particularly difficult to deal with works that are not straightforwardly representational, and to raise questions about differences between the subjects who experience art. These exclusions can be understood more clearly by looking at how the model constrains Walton to interpret a particular example and the other interpretations that are consequently overlooked.

If on a Winter's Night a Traveler

In order better to understand how the model of children's games affects Walton's analysis of artworks, one of his examples, Italo Calvino's novel, *If on a Winter's Night a Traveler*, will be discussed in some detail.[47] The story is

44. Ibid., p. 38.

45. Berys Gaut notes in relation to the appreciation of art: "We cannot state any rules, however complex, in many cases, and the mere existence of a right or wrong answer does not entail that a *principle* exists which explains why it is right or wrong. This suggests that appreciation ought not to be thought on the model of a game, but as a *practice*, which may be only partly rule-governed." Gaut, review of *Mimesis as Make-Believe* by Kendall Walton, *Journal of Value Inquiry* 26, no. 2 (1992): 299.

46. Walton, pp. 397–398.

47. Calvino's novel is a useful example because it is one of the few actual examples Walton refers to several times, and because it is almost the only work that feminists and others working in aesthetics also discuss. It also brings out a number of important points concerning the nature of our response to art.

about a male Reader who begins reading a novel only to discover that it breaks off. In his desire to continue the story he meets another reader and her sister, and gets a new copy of the book. However, inside the new copy is a different story, which again breaks off. This process is repeated throughout the novel. There is a meta-story of the Reader's hunt, and within this tale there are ten different beginnings with their unfinished narratives within an array of voices and styles. The meta-story concludes with the Reader marrying the Other Reader. Calvino makes extensive use of direct address to us, the readers. The first sentence of the novel is: "You are about to begin reading Italo Calvino's new novel, *If on a Winter's Night a Traveler*."[48] This reader— "you"— is in one sense the actual reader of the novel, in another the Reader character. At one point he directly addresses the Other Reader, a woman, and fantasizes about what her/your flat would look like. The Other Reader is also a character called Ludmilla with whom the Reader falls in love. She has a sister, Lotaria, who loves to dissect novels in every way imaginable.

Walton holds that when anyone reads a novel, they make believe that someone is telling them a story of actual events. Yet, within the terms of the model, he wants to account for cases where, as in Calvino's novel, this does not seem to be true. He says that sometimes artworks discourage participation in games of make-believe: "One obvious way in which works sometimes discourage participation is by prominently declaring or displaying their fictionality, betraying their own pretense. Calvino's *If on a Winter's Night a Traveler* does this especially blatantly."[49] Walton's idea is that we usually pretend to ourselves (make believe) that we are hearing a true story. However, if we are constantly reminded that it is not a true story, he thinks that this spoils the make-believe and we become less involved. "The fact that *If on a Winter's Night a Traveler* and *Vanity Fair* are mere fictions is certainly not news to the reader, but emphasizing it, compelling the reader to dwell on it, restrains his imagining otherwise."[50] Walton thinks that being reminded of reading the novel inhibits our game of make-believe.[51]

Walton's account of meta-fiction is reduced to a theory of meta-make-believe, or thinking about make-believe.[52] There are two broad possibilities as to what the character of one's meta-make-believings would be: they could either involve thinking about how oneself might make-believe about the novel, or about how others might make-believe about it. Walton would have to opt for the former, for otherwise the description would violate the rule that imagining necessarily involves self-imagining. The example does not sit

48. Italo Calvino, *If on a Winter's Night a Traveler* (London: Minerva, 1992), p. 3.
49. Walton, p. 275.
50. Ibid.
51. Ibid., p. 283.
52. Ibid., p. 288.

comfortably with the model, because even though Walton says the experience involves games of make-believe, it is not, even in his terms, a game of make-believe itself.

In a section on ornamentality,[53] Walton describes ornamental works of art, such as fabric designs and ornamental chairs, as those fictions that discourage participation in games of make-believe. One might presume that they are not representational and must be exceptions to Walton's theory. However, he argues that ornamental chairs, such as Chippendale chairs, are representational because they represent themselves. His explanation of our response to *Winter's Night* shows that he also considers it to be an ornamental work in this sense. By implication, there will be a great many works in this category of artworks which represent themselves, and the items which fall into it will be extremely disparate.

Another reference to the novel comes in a footnote to Walton's discussion on asides to the audience:

> Italo Calvino's *If on a Winter's Night a Traveler* is a long, extended aside; it is fictional in the reader's game that he is addressed constantly during his reading. But there still is little *interaction*. It is not often fictional that the reader and narrator respond very much to each other or that they converse together. Even when it is fictional that the reader speaks and the narrator replies, it is the words of the text, not what the reader actually says, that determine what fictionally he says. When Calvino writes: ' "I prefer novels," she adds, "that bring me immediately into a world where everything is precise, concrete, specific. . ." Do you agree? Then say so. "Ah, yes, that sort of book is really worthwhile" ' (p.30), he is putting words into the reader's mouth. Contrast children's games: It is because Gregory actually says, 'Watch out for the bear!' that fictionally he says this.[54]

Walton is pointing to a major difference here between art and children's games, which suggests that the purported structural similarities are severely strained. Furthermore, as we have seen, the reader is not just a person who the aside is addressed to—the Reader is a character in the overall story. This Reader is also discussed in the third person when the narrative is addressed to the female reader: "The Reader is looking for a comfortable place to sit and read."[55] Even when this Reader is being discussed, we know only what he knows, not what any of the other characters know. Walton's model cannot account for the complexities of the novel. For it is not one aside, but at the very least an aside with ten different asides within it.

53. Ibid., pp. 274–289.
54. Ibid., p. 235.
55. Calvino, p. 145.

A further reference by Walton to the novel appears in the context of considering whether artworks prescribe imagining for a particular person. The direct address to the reader raises questions about how one experiences that direct address. Note that in the previous quotation Walton uses the male pronoun to refer to the reader: "it is fictional in the reader's game that he is addressed constantly during his reading." In the context of arguing that artworks do not prescribe imagining for a particular person, he writes: "Compare 'you' used in novels such as Calvino's *If on a Winter's Night a Traveler*."[56] The point of the comparison seems to be that when Calvino writes "you" he is not referring to a particular person but to any person who happens to be reading the novel. This is not straightforward, however, because the "you" who is addressed is male, and it is only in one chapter that he addresses the female reader. Here Calvino writes: "What are you like, Other Reader? It is time for this book in the second person to address itself no longer to a general male you, perhaps brother and double of a hypocrite I, but directly to you who appeared already in the second chapter as the Third Person necessary for the novel to be a novel, for something to happen between that male Second Person and the female Third, for something to take form, develop, or deteriorate according to the phases of human events."[57] Walton does not address the question of what kind of effect on readers the use of second person address to a male reader is likely to have. The model promotes the view that artworks address a universal subject, and that there is a universal response, a variation on a familiar theme in this book. It could be argued that Walton is correct in that Calvino is addressing a universal subject, and that this subject, according to Calvino, is male. This important question cannot be addressed within the parameters of the model.

The novel poses a problem for the children's games model by exposing its limitations and weaknesses. The level of involvement of readers may differ, as it does in most cases. Walton has singled out one type of self-referential literature, yet even this one example creates difficulties for his model. Furthermore, there are a number of important questions about this work which the model prevents Walton from addressing.

Reconceptions

A number of alternative readings of *If on a Winter's Night a Traveler* raise questions Walton does not and perhaps cannot discuss, due to the limitations of the model of art he uses. One important question concerns the role of the

56. Walton, p. 136.
57. Calvino, p. 141.

author: whether the meta-fictional techniques free up the reader to interpret, or whether the author in fact manipulates the reader to experience
the novel in a certain way. This is an interesting question—do authors control more by their absence than by announcing their presence? One critic,
Madeleine Sorapure, argues that Calvino undermines his own authority
through a number of strategies. As we saw, one is by placing his name at the
beginning of the novel. The last line of the novel is "And you say, 'Just a moment, I've almost finished *If on a Winter's Night a Traveler* by Italo Calvino'."[58]

A second strategy is to place many substitutes for the author in the text: a
number of different characters describe writing a novel which sounds very like
Calvino's. Another is to invite the reader to take an active role in constructing
the text "by making his novel exceedingly fragmentary, with abundant and
wide gaps for the reader to fill."[59] A fourth reason Sorapure gives in support
of her view is that a number of different types of reading are portrayed in the
novel. The male reader doggedly pursues the continuation and resolution of
the story like a detective, but the female reader involves herself in the novels.
Sorapure's points imply that interaction with a text is not a matter of being
able to put words in, as Walton claims, but having freedom of interpretation.

By contrast, Melissa Watts argues that the reader in fact *loses* power in reading Calvino's novel. She says that the experience of reading the novel is one
of endless frustration, which is dictated by Calvino.[60] In her view, Calvino
manipulates our responses in a number of ways. One is by the use of second
person address, which restricts the range of possible responses. A second way
is through the relatively limited information we have about the Reader character. Using second person address in the novel's fragments means we are
reading as if *we* are the Reader. Watts argues that Calvino "does impede the
reader's free manipulation of this fiction, more effectively than the nine-
teenth century omniscient narrator."[61] If this is true, it implies that all readers must read as a male reader, and accept being called "you" because the
text is written to a male reader. This is true of many texts, including philosophical ones, and women may commonly need to adopt this reading strategy
if the address to a male reader is insistent.

The different views on this point emphasize that the interpretation Walton has been constrained to make obscures differences in experiencing art.
The novel does not just make us think about make-believe. And although
the novel is frustrating, it is still involving us to a surprising extent. There is

58. Ibid., p. 260.

59. Madeleine Sorapure, "Being in the Midst: Italo Calvino's *If on a Winter's Night a Traveler*,"
Modern Fiction Studies 31, no. 4 (1985): 705.

60. Melissa Watts, "Reinscribing a Dead Author in *If on a Winter's Night a Traveler*," *Modern
Fiction Studies* 37, no. 4 (1991): 711.

61. Ibid., p. 714.

freedom to read and interpret the novel in different ways. There are also a number of different ways we can interpret the meta-narratives. The techniques used in the novel may restrict the range of possible responses. However, it does not block response in general. We can be well aware that we are not being told a true story, but be involved nonetheless without any need for make-believe. We continue to be involved in *Winter's Night* after we realize that none of the stories will finish (in the conventional sense), and this is perhaps one of the most interesting aspects of the novel. The various uses of address in Calvino's novel do not prevent involvement in either the framing story or the shorter stories. Naturally, people's experiences will not all be the same, and there may be some kind of resistance to enjoying the novel, perhaps because of a feeling of being manipulated. One would expect different levels of involvement with all artworks.

The continued involvement of readers suggests that there is a different structure to aesthetic experience than one based on children's games of make-believe and that there are other interesting questions raised by Calvino's novel. The theories of reading, authorship, and interpretation pertinent to the novel cannot be properly discussed within the framework of the children's games model, and while it is possible to mention or to touch upon them, they raise problems for a view based on a single model. Given that there cannot be a general theory of the author's role, it is problematic that Walson's model allows only for general theories.

The particular form of address used in literature is just as important as it is in philosophy. I have already mentioned that for most of the novel, except for six pages, only a male reader is being addressed. Teresa de Lauretis puts it like this: "for six pages [Calvino] gives the Woman reader the honor of the second-person pronoun, of being addressed as "you"—of being, that is, the protagonist."[62] She argues that the male reader is compensated for the brief address to the female reader by the Reader character getting to have sex with the Other Reader character immediately afterwards. She notes that,

> By the end of the search of the apartment, the male Reader has become again the 'you': 'Don't believe that the book is losing sight of you, reader,' Calvino feels the need to reassure him, since the second-person discourse has shifted to the Woman for all of six pages. And, to reimburse him for his temporary loss of narrative status, the text gives him a bonus: when the Other Reader comes home, shortly after, he succeeds in getting her into bed.[63]

62. Teresa de Lauretis, "Calvino and the Amazons: Reading the (Post)Modern Text," in *Technologies of Gender: Essays on Theory, Film, and Fiction* (Bloomington: Indiana University Press, 1987), p. 78.
63. Ibid., p. 79.

De Lauretis's comments point to the need to take account of the way gender is inscribed in the various forms of address to the reader, a question that a discussion of asides and make-believe has nothing to say about.

The issue of gender is central to understanding the devices which are used in the text. The main character in all the short stories is also a male, often in love or desiring a female character. Here, the narration is usually in the first person. For example, "This morning I spoke for the first time with Miss Zwida," and "There was a definite intention in what I said: to propose to Makiko a meeting under the ginkgo that same night."[64] The use of these different forms of address must affect different readers differently. For most of the novel (for me, a female reader) there is a feeling of eavesdropping, and in the chapter where the female reader is addressed directly, I thought: "No that's not me." This response indicates that the experiences of male and female readers must be different, and perhaps Calvino is deliberately highlighting that fact. Focusing on that address is a useful way to begin thinking about the issue of different reading experiences. This example relates to the central theme of the analytic imaginary—the belief in individuals' power to imagine themselves in another's place. The use of different forms of address can invite or discourage readers to imagine themselves in other's places and can render problematic the move to imagining oneself in another's place. Furthermore, these forms of address can be directed to specified or unspecified audiences. We have come full circle to the violinist analogy of chapter 2, where Thomson uses the direct address to the reader in order to suggest that an abortion is something that can happen to anyone.

Calvino's address to the reader is different, because it addresses a reader of a particular sex, and this is precisely the point that a simple model for all art causes Walton to overlook. There are a number of different ways we can interpret Calvino's direct address to the reader. We could think that the novel is designed only for men and that women can only feel alienated or excluded when reading it. Alternatively, one could argue that the novel questions just such reader identifications by starkly exposing them. Another point about the male Reader and the male narrators of the different stories is that they are all heterosexual. A gay man might feel as alienated by the stories as a woman is likely to. Another way of highlighting this point is that one could respond to the question in analytic aesthetics of "Why do we feel pity for Anna Karenina?" by saying that we do not feel pity, but empathy, for example, depending on our sex, or our circumstances, or our interpretation of the novel. There are major differences in the kind of emotional responses

64. Calvino, pp. 59, 205. This fact may seem to conflict with the claim made by Watts that these stories use second person. However, these stories, written in first person, often refer to a second person reader.

possible, and they may be relevant to our evaluation and interpretation of artworks. Whether we are encouraged to imagine ourselves in the place of another or not will differ between artworks, and Walton's egocentric model of imagining does not allow us to be sensitive to these differences.

It might be said of Calvino's novel that it is an unusual one, so the kind of points which arise here are not relevant to most novels. Yet most narrative works tend to incorporate points of view in some way: in the use of first, second, and third person address, giving or withholding knowledge of certain characters' inner states; giving the same or lesser or greater amounts of knowledge; focusing on certain characters to the detriment of others; and making some characters more attractive than others.[65] Of course, not all works involve character and not all of those which do, ascribe gender to their characters. My point is simply that when artworks do involve these issues, we need to be sensitive to these differences, and we should be wary of any model of aesthetic experience that elides or denies them. I am not suggesting any intrinsic link between the sex of writers, characters and readers. We may identify with characters not of our sex, and writers may write from viewpoints they do not personally share, more or less successfully. However, these differences are relevant in many cases, and that is why they should be taken into account.

The point is not that we must agree with the particular readings given here, but that these readings make it possible to ask certain types of questions that cannot be properly asked or answered within the children's games model. Not all aesthetic questions are metaphysical, or necessarily connected to metaphysics. Any aesthetic theory must be wary of privileging a certain style, form, or type of art. It is useful to see what emerges from a discussion of just one form, one genre, one artwork, or to compare several. In such a discussion, differences between realist and formalist or abstract works can be accepted. Criticism that focuses on portrayal of difference in what something represents can show how it does so, and perhaps shed light on the very metaphysical questions which bother philosophers. A theory sensitive to differences between artworks makes more sense of that vexed question of why we have emotional responses to fiction. Walton's overriding concern with metaphysical questions, characteristic of the analytic imaginary, means that aesthetic questions of value and interpretation are rarely given the attention they deserve.

The most important point that emerges from comparing the reading of Calvino's text, as prescribed by the make-believe model, and other readings is that we need to take into account differences in responses and interpretations and to not try to formulate a universal theory based on a single model

---

65. Artworks can both increase our understanding of others and reveal the limitations of our understanding of cultural and gender differences, for example.

or an expectation of a universal response. If analytic aesthetics were more contextual and were to look at particular works and genres, readings which are sensitive to difference, like de Lauretis's feminist readings, could be included. In a philosophical aesthetics based on a single model, it is easy to work with an unacknowledged canon and to ignore questions about why some artworks are neglected.[66] Analytic aesthetics would benefit from taking seriously the differences between various forms, genres, and even particular artworks. There are three major ways in which philosophical aesthetics needs to acknowledge difference. They include differences in what we evaluate as art, differences in understanding and interpretation of works, and differences in responses to artworks. These differences cannot be subsumed under a single model of experience, whether it be the children's games model or some other.

Conclusion

The model of children's games works primarily on the level of enframement, although the model is clearly appealing and captivating in persuasive terms, and it provides the primary terms in which art is discussed. The model is partly persuasive— given that generality is desirable in the analytic imaginary— in that it is a model for all the arts. It structures the theory in two different ways: one, by leading to a simplification of art and aesthetic experience, two, by being in excess of our actual experiences. The model simplifies, because the reliance on the model of games of make-believe leads to and reinforces a focus on imagining about oneself. The stump-bear game supports Walton's views that all imagining is self-imagining because Eric and Gregory are supposed to imagine, of themselves, that they are afraid.

The variation on the model—games with specific toys, like dolls—facilitates the view that there are rules that must be followed and authorized games that must be played in our relation to art. On the other hand, the use of the stump-bear game, which is surprising at first, enables Walton to suggest a greater freedom that in certain respects is more like our response to artworks. This particular game also involves an emotion—fear—which is useful for his position that we make believe our emotions in response to art.

The model enables Walton to conflate make-believing and imagining by implying that we can generalize from the simple case of the game, where

66. In Walton's book, there are many examples, but only fragments of readings on any work, and very rare references to works by women. There are one or two sentences on Virginia Woolf's *Mrs. Dalloway,* a short paragraph on George Eliot's *Daniel Deronda,* and a discussion of a play about Emily Dickinson. Walton's main interest in these texts is in questions relating to whether an assertion can be attributed to the narrator or a character.

"imagining that" can be interchanged with "make-believing that" to other cases where such a substitution is at best awkward, at worst completely incorrect. His notion of make-believe relies on all the rich senses of imagining, but these are unspoken in his outline of the theory.

Reliance on the model image leads to an oversimplified account and results in awkward and contrived analyses of ornamental, abstract, and postmodern works. This became clear through an examination of his description of abstract and representational painting, and through the comparison of Walton's account of Calvino's novel, *If on a Winter's Night a Traveler,* to alternative accounts. The attempt to provide a foundational account of aesthetic response through the model also makes it difficult to talk about differences in those responses.

Alternatively, the model is in excess of what is needed for talking about both the viewing and interpretation of art and causes complications. First, the use of games, and the construal of each game as an entity, commits Walton to an unnecessarily, inaccurately complex way of talking about artworks, with a world for every work as well as a world for every game. Second, the dual phenomenology of all the games he mentions, the mud pies and real pies, the stumps and bears, the dolls and babies, forces Walton to misconstrue and complicate the phenomenology of our experience of artworks. For example, the model leads him to say that when we see a painting of a mill, we both see a picture of a mill and make believe that we are seeing an actual mill.

The idea that make-believe games are a universal foundation for the arts paves the way for the view that there is a universal aesthetic experience, and that all art should be regarded in the same way. Even if what he says about children's games is correct, it does not follow that they are a good model for theories of art, as demonstrated by the difficulties that arise from trying to make art fit the model. Walton's model of art as children's games is rather like the common claims about images which Le Dœuff points out, "the child in us coming to the surface" writ large. Art, as an example, can be explained away in terms of children's play.

Walton, like many analytic philosophers, has a deep concern with metaphysics, which on occasion seems to override or minimize his direct interest in art. He argues that he gives an integrated theory where aesthetic and metaphysical views reinforce each other. However, it seems that metaphysical considerations dominate over aesthetic ones. Walton's concern with metaphysics could motivate his desire to link his favorite examples to one foundation, which in turn is related to his view that children's games of make-believe are a universal cultural phenomenon. However, the difficulty of explaining all the disparate arts through one characteristic model is sharply illustrated by Walton's attempts to do so. It seems that any attempt to provide a single model for all the arts is likely to run into similar difficulties, both because of the disparate nature of art and the distorting effect of models. We can see that the model gains most of its initial plausibility through the combination of the *ad hoc* games with the other kinds, in the hope that combined it will cover the major features of art. Yet the attempt does not do justice to artworks or our experience of them. The model breaks down when we examine it carefully. If we accept children's games as our aesthetic model, we accept an over-simplified and distorted view of art and our response to it.

The model strengthens the idea, put explicitly by Walton, that we gain understanding of art by make-believing that we are in someone else's shoes, rather than just listening to what the other person has to say, or by taking in what the artwork has to say to us. Thus, this basic characteristic of the analytic imaginary is revealed again. The model serves to promote the view that there is a universal subject who experiences art, and that art is addressed to this subject.

Conclusion

The Images

The notion of a specific philosophical imaginary like the analytic imaginary is understood best by looking at the stock of images in contemporary analytic philosophy. The images I examined in this book are particularly influential in contemporary analytic philosophy and reveal important and pervasive characteristics of the analytic imaginary. Each of the types of images has a highly significant philosophical role to play in the particular area within which it is employed, as well as being part of the "core" of analytic philosophy. As we have seen, these images are used deliberately by the philosophers concerned, yet they involve assumptions and have implications of which these philosophers are often unaware.

In the Introduction, I argued that images work at three levels of embeddedness—the levels of expressibility, enframement, and persuasiveness—that need to be examined in order to understand the nature of the analytic imaginary. Expressibility is the deepest level in the sense that images that work at this level are as difficult to paraphrase as to avoid using. At the level of enframement, images structure argument and debate. The level of persuasion is where an image makes a view more convincing through the way it engages the attention of and appeals to the reader. The images of analytic philosophy work on one or more of the levels of embeddedness simultaneously, and have a number of important functions. Images conceal tensions (sometimes in the form of contradictions), cover assumptions (some of which are untenable), distract attention, elicit agreement, and exclude certain experiences and alternative views. Although the images of analytic philosophy perform these functions in different ways, similar tensions emerge in relation to a range of images. Consequently, a web of links joins the disparate fields of analytic philosophy.

Michèle Le Dœuff's work on the philosophical imaginary, which I discussed in chapter 1, provides an important basis for understanding the analytic imaginary, although her analyses do not concentrate on analytic philosophy. The distinctiveness of the images of contemporary analytic philosophy has to be taken into account to comprehend the unique character of the analytic imaginary—its "affective resonance" or emotional coloring. All the images facilitate the continuation of a particular philosophic approach and set of questions. The analytic imaginary is characterized by the denial of difference and a fantasy about the imaginative capacity of each individual to fully understand the experience of others. Understanding the characteristic ways in which analytic philosophy's images work suggests possibilities for its enrichment.

In chapter 2, I demonstrated how Thomson's violinist analogy works on the level of persuasiveness, because it elicits agreement with the conclusion from readers who accept it as a genuine analogy. It also works on the level of enframement by giving substance to the view that abortion must be understood in terms of rights and the liberal self. This argument by analogy elicits agreement with Thomson's views, and liberal views in general, so that the issues center on competing rights of the woman and the fetus. The assumptions reinforced by the violinist analogy are: that fetal rights are analogous to adult rights, that the central question concerning abortion is what kind of killing it is, that our bodies are a kind of property, and that we can only understand abortion by applying a principle relevant to other moral problems. The analogy covers certain difficulties or aporias in the argument and distracts attention from them, including the issue of responsibility, the relation between the woman and the fetus, and the need to theorize the pregnant body.

At the same time, argument by analogy excludes an understanding of the context in which the actual decision about abortion is made: the emotions and experiences of women considering abortion; more positive arguments pertaining to abortion, based on autonomy as self-determination, and phenomenological accounts of pregnant embodiment. Analogies are particularly inappropriate in this case, because of the uniqueness of abortion. My detailed examination of the analogy highlights problems with conceptualizing the fetus as an adult stranger, as well as suggesting how the abortion debate can move forward.

In chapter 3, I discussed three thought experiments used in analytic debates about personal identity: brain swapping, tele-transportation, and fission. The use of thought experiments in personal identity is sometimes challenged, yet it is clear that analytic philosophers generally accept them as worthwhile. The thought experiments give a legitimacy to certain philosophical questions, partly because of their philosophical pedigree in the images Locke and Hobbes use to explore personal identity. Thought experiments are also an attempt to legitimate the enterprise as scientific, but in fact they are borrowing, often quite explicitly, from science fiction, the imaginary counterpart to science.

Thought experiments are powerful persuasive tools that are used to provide immediate evidence and support for a philosopher's conclusions, rather than to merely clarify intuitions, as is purported. Philosophers often decide how people *ought* to respond to a particular thought experiment and design the experiment to reinforce a certain conclusion. There is a tension between the claim that thought experiments are intended as genuine tests and the philosophers' attempts to justify their own position. These thought experiments clearly work on the level of persuasiveness. They also work on the level of enframement in dictating the terms of the debate, and even come close to the level of expressibility, since it is difficult to see how certain questions could arise at all without the thought experiments.

The assumptions cloaked by the use of thought experiments include two polarizations of positions. The first polarization involves claims that either psychological continuity or bodily continuity are necessary for personal identity, based on the idea that mind and body are easily split, actually and conceptually. The second polarization occurs in the methodology; it accepts that we must choose between thought experiments and common sense in answering questions about personal identity. The thought experiments force a choice between the two, making it difficult to conceptualize any alternative approaches.

Furthermore, these thought experiments are self-generating in two respects. First, they justify and reproduce the debate through an endless proliferation of thought experiments. Second, they create a fable of male self-reproduction, because they ignore and erase actual reproduction by presenting thought experiments involving such fantasies as fission and teletransportation.

The personal identity thought experiments exclude recent developments in our understanding of the nature of personhood and mind-body relations. They enable a forestalling of questions about sexual difference and the experience of identity. It is impossible to present a view of persons as sexed embodied beings or to introduce cultural or historical considerations within this framework.

The myths of the social contract and the original position in John Rawls's work in political philosophy were examined in chapter 4. These myths function on the levels of enframement and persuasiveness, giving substance to the particular views being presented and making them appear more convincing and plausible than they would if argued for in detail. The myth of the social contract is an extremely pervasive image that has gained wide currency in Western societies, as has Rawls's particular version, the original position. His revival of the contract myth works to exclude other contemporary political philosophies. Rawls's contract is in fact not a contract at all, because it is not based on agreement between different people but on the theorizing of one moral reasoner. Yet the myth of the original position, based as it is on highly abstract and limiting notions of the individual and moral reasoning, masks social inequalities and makes it impossible to articulate group oppression.

The myths of the "original position" and "veil of ignorance" contain both explicit and implicit assumptions about political organization, human nature, and moral reasoning. The original position and veil of ignorance enable assumptions behind the appeal to impartiality to be overlooked—assumptions such as the elevation of the views of one moral reasoner to universal status and the notion of the abstract individual. Sexual difference, family and group structures cannot be incorporated into the original position. Furthermore, the oppression of women and ethnic groups cannot be theorized through the original position, and feminists, such as Susan Moller Okin, who have used the original position, have reproduced the assumptions integral to the contract myth.

My discussion of visual and spatial metaphors in the epistemology of Thomas Nagel in chapter 5 demonstrated the specific features of such metaphors in analytic philosophy. Epistemological metaphors, which rely on the sense of sight and ordinary experience of space are ubiquitous in spite of the fact that it has never been made clear how bringing together perspectives from different locations can add up to a coherent picture. These metaphors work at the level of enframement. Nagel's metaphor of the view from nowhere embodies the presupposition that having a particular perspective leads to errors. However, this ahistorical and disembodied view from nowhere turns out to be an impossible and undesirable goal in Nagel's own terms, because in order to be conscious the "I" needs to be located in a historical person to be conscious.

There are a number of tensions in Nagel's visual and spatial metaphors. Nagel's photographic metaphor and the metaphor of concentric spheres incorporate a confusion between two senses of objectification, which Jonathan Dancy identifies as Hegelian and absolute objectification. These tensions are more serious than the tension between subjectivity and objectivity that Nagel acknowledges, because they undermine the coherence of the entire project. The visual and spatial metaphors that Nagel uses reinforce splits between the physical and the mental, the senses and reason, the knower and the known, and mask differences between knowers. The metaphors are an attempt to advance the ideal of an individual and ahistorical view of knowing: that one God-like individual can understand all perspectives.

I compared Nagel's use of metaphors to certain metaphors employed within feminist epistemology, and I argued that a dialectical swap of metaphor and concept is at work here. Ideals of objectivity and visual and spatial metaphors are interconnected and conceal the same assumptions concerning the importance of overcoming particular perspectives. In addition to working at the level of enframement concerning conceptions of knowledge, these metaphors also work at the level of expressibility. Thus, when feminist epistemologists such as Donna Haraway and Sandra Harding try to reclaim these ideals and metaphors, they cannot avoid the implication that individuals can always incorporate the perspectives of others into their own. These visual and spatial metaphors are particularly embedded in our ways of thinking about knowing. The use of these specific metaphors in epistemology is difficult though not impossible to avoid. Because of the problems they lead to, we need to use other metaphors as well, such as listening and hearing metaphors.

Kendall Walton's use of the make-believe model in analytic aesthetics relies on the popular notion that art must have something to do with play, in this case children's games. Models are used to show that complex phenomena can be explained in terms of a basic structure. The use of a model itself is another example of the desire to imitate scientific method in analytic philosophy, because models are so important in science.

The model works principally at the level of enframement, although it is also persuasive to the extent that it is engaging as an image, and it limits the terms within which art can be discussed. The children's games model helps to promote a number of controversial claims, the most important being Walton's central thesis that our experience of art can be understood as playing games of make-believe. Tied to this model is the notion that all imaginings involve self-imagining— that we can easily imagine ourselves being someone else, such as a fictional character. The idea of self-imagining makes explicit a presupposition of the other images I discuss: that when we imagine ourselves in someone else's shoes, we are able to fully take on their situation.

There are a number of tensions partly concealed by the model. For example, two very different types of children's games are combined in order to try to accommodate the various features of art. The tree stump-bear game, in which children choose what something will represent, is used to imply a kind of freedom in creating and interpreting art: the idea that *we* make up the rules. The type of game played with dolls, in which particular toys represent people or objects, is used to capture the opposing view that particular characteristics of the artwork must affect our response to it. These two forms of the model are in conflict with each other and when combined together do not make up a coherent theory of aesthetic experience. Another tension emerges in the attempt to use make-believe to cover various distinct senses of imagining. A third tension is that between the phenomenology of the children's games and the phenomenology of our experience of art. The children's games involve the use of a prop that stands in place of, or represents something else, whereas our experience of artworks does not characteristically involve two distinct experiences, one which relates to the artwork, and another that relates to what we take it to represent.

The use of a model is fundamentally related to the attempt to provide a foundational theory that provides one basic explanation of all experiences of all the arts. Such an attempt reduces, simplifies, and avoids recognition of the varieties of art and the variations in our experience of art. The use of a model reinforces the metaphysical preoccupations of analytic aesthetics, so that art becomes simply the instantiation of the model's structure. A foundational theory demands that everyone respond in terms of the same structure, thus denying the particularity of artworks themselves and the diversity of our emotional responses to them. Walton's model also promotes a denial of the *genuineness* of emotional responses to art, leading him to claim that we have only quasi-emotions when we respond to art, just as a child has only quasi-emotions while playing make-believe.

In order to show how the model limits our understanding of artworks, I concentrated on one particular artwork, Italo Calvino's *If on a Winter's Night a Traveler*. By comparing Walton's comments on the novel with those of alternative readings, I demonstrated that the model prevents a focus on those features of the novel that are most relevant to understanding it and our different responses to it. The children's game of make-believe is familiar and appealing to some philosophers, and the idea that art is like play has some currency. However, the model would be more convincing if it had greater explanatory power and had more resonance with everyday experience of art.

The Analytic Imaginary

Although there is not a universal structure to the analytic imaginary, it has a coherence that is revealed by these influential images. This coherence distinguishes it within the philosophical imaginary as such, because the images are used in particular ways and have common effects. This exploration of the analytic imaginary has added complexity to Le Dœuff's characterization of the philosophical imaginary as a scholarly imaginary of a learned minority. The analytic imaginary does share some of the secular and scholarly characteristics of the philosophical imaginary pointed out by Le Dœuff. For example, the view from nowhere metaphor can be understood as a secularized version of earlier desires to be (like) God. Although the central images of analytic philosophy are displayed rather than hidden by the analytic philosopher, the use of these images works to disarm objections and divert attention from the precise way in which the image is delineated. Thus the images of the analytic imaginary can have a similar effect on readers as the discreet images Le Dœuff uncovers, without being bypassed. The analytic imaginary is not completely separated from the historical tradition to which other contemporary philosophical imaginaries lay claim. This can be seen in the personal identity thought experiments' links with the stories of Locke and Hobbes, the utopian aspects and historical precedents of the contract myths and the view from nowhere, and the connection of art with children's play. Walton's treatment of aesthetic experience connects interestingly with Le Dœuff's comments about the way in which images are regarded as "the resurgence of a primitive soul,"[1] because he uses his model to argue that our engagement with art is simply a more sophisticated version of children's games of make-believe. The violinist analogy, as I have said, is striking in its novelty. However, like the other images that are up-dated, sometimes futuristic, and more technical versions of their predecessors, it connects with contemporary technological obsessions.

The analytic imaginary also has distinctiveness in its deference to science. For example, physics is given the ultimate place in Nagel's concentric spheres. Scientific method gains a place in Walton's choice of a model as the central image in aesthetics. As emerged most clearly in relation to the thought experiments, science in the analytic imaginary becomes a fantasy science, resembling science fiction. Science is not the only profession represented, perhaps a reflection of the prevailing professionalization in analytic philosophy. Medicine features in the violinist analogy, brain operations in personal identity, and the legal profession in the mythical contracts of political philosophy. These references acknowledge the expertise of these other professionals at the same time as signaling a philosophical method that dispenses with their services.

Rather than the all-encompassing totalizing reason of Kant, Descartes, or Sartre exposed by Le Dœuff, reason in the analytic imaginary becomes a territorial, narrowing force. Just as analytic philosophy is difficult to define, yet instantly recognizable, the analytic imaginary evades precise definition, yet is strikingly familiar and distinct from other philosophical imaginaries. Instead of fostering an atmosphere of interdisciplinary excitement(the "open-ended" philosophy envisaged by Le Dœuff), the analytic imaginary reflects "closed-off" philosophy, a narrowing within the discipline of philosophy itself.

---

1. Michèle Le Dœuff, *The Philosophical Imaginary*, trans. Colin Gordon (London: Athlone Press, 1989), p. 6.

Rather than attempting to show through images that a complex meta-physical system is able to incorporate any experience a doubter might care to mention, the images of the analytic imaginary force out realms of experience as irrelevant. Nevertheless, one of the most obvious features of the images constituting the analytic imaginary is their function as "badges of the corporation" which both enable entry to analytic philosophy and validate the enterprise itself.

Sexism does not appear in remarks designed to paper over cracks in the system— as Le Dœuff demonstrates in her discussion of Sartre's sexism— but in a remarkable silence on the subject of women. Philosophical arrogance does not necessarily materialize in obvious ethnocentrism, but in avoidance of all questions of ethnicity. Yet it is this very avoidance that makes claims to the universal applicability of particular philosophical "results" seem more plausible.

Denial of Difference

There are a number of links between various images in analytic philosophy that draw together various strands of the analytic imaginary, and that allow for the description of pervasive features of that imaginary. In different ways these images are characterized by an avoidance and denial of one kind or another: avoidance of women's experiences, sexual difference, the body, emotions, and the variety of aesthetic experiences. The images are also used to suggest neutrality and objectivity.

The violinist analogy shows this in a direct appeal to the reader in order to establish a principle that will apply to abortion and to establish its similarity to cases of self-defense. These inferences erased the experiential differences between men and women in relation to abortion, the different circumstances in which women may consider abortion, and the differences between abortion and other moral issues.

In the thought experiments, the reader is supposed to imagine a character, or the philosopher writing, having their brains or minds swapped with another, being cloned, or dividing by fission. Differences between ethnic groups and the sexes, for example, were denied by privileging the figure of the philosopher and by using relatively similar persons in the thought experiments (such as two men, like Brown and Robinson), hence excluding ethnic and sexual differences as irrelevant or inessential. The entire question of bodily difference is overlooked partly through focus on psychological characteristics alone, and partly through ignoring real sexual reproduction and replacing it with reproduction fantasies taken from science fiction.

The contract myth works by extracting so-called essential features of persons or essential features of moral reasoning, and claiming that all would reason similarly if involved in the contract. Instead of different individuals or different groups being represented, the contract myth involves heads of families which on closer examination really implies the representation of just one moral reasoner. This moral reasoner is said to be fair and disinterested, but in reality is based on a specific type of reasoning, a specific theory of human nature, and political theory that ignores the oppression of a number of groups.

The view from nowhere metaphor involves the aim of removing differences by incorporating different perspectives into one perspective and by abstracting from particularities. By making such a goal appear desirable and even possible, however difficult, the metaphor suggests that differences will disappear through the overlap of agreement. In this way, conflicts can be ignored, and it can be claimed that the viewer from nowhere has taken the differences into account.

The children's games model works by positing an essential structure to the experience of art and trying to force all different experience into that mould. The model suggests that everyone should experience art similarly, provided they play authorized games of make-believe. It does not allow that there may be quite different ways of experiencing and interpreting art, which are not idiosyncratic irrelevancies to be dismissed.

In each case, the raising of the question of difference and the insertion of differences threatens the use of the image. The imaginary of analytic philosophy is in part characterized by an overwhelming desire to make the indeterminate determinate, the different the same, and to subsume disparate experiences under one principle. There is a marked denial of difference. Reinsertion of difference into the images and arguments reveals the tensions and exclusions at work.

Structuring Debates

Images are not primarily pedagogic, if that implies that they are easily understood. As Le Dœuff argues, they need to be explained and taught, just as concepts do. On the other hand, images work as a kind of induction: the reader or student introduced to the topic via its images accepts fundamental assumptions, possibilities, and implications before thinking about the broader issues involved. By tracing an image through the work of a number of philosophers, I have shown how images constrain debates in spite of the apparently disparate nature of the views represented within them. In this way the philosophical community involved is able to repel innovation and maintain its borders. Images affect philosophers' views, even when they are trying to argue against prevailing positions. For example, feminists who try to use the original position in political philosophy, or visual metaphors in epistemology, or to argue for abortion choice using analogies of self-defense, are constrained in what they are able convincingly to assert. At the same time, other philosophers working on the topics concerned find their work is not recognized or debated as such because they do not use the images which structure those debates. Thus, the philosophers who use these images rarely discuss the work of those who do not use them or respond directly to them. This is another way to repel or deny difference.

Universalism and Imaginative Self-Projection

A hypothesis or dogma which both underlies and is reinforced by the analytic imaginary is a belief in the power of the imagination, of the ability of each individual to think their way into the lives of others. The idea of the imagination as capable of making the experience of different people not just intelligible, but so clear as to justify judgments made on their behalf, underlies the move to universal, abstract reasoning based on male, white, Anglo, and heterosexual characteristics and ways of thinking. As such, it is imperialistic. The self appears as an omniscient creature, able to decide for others. These two mutually supportive attributes: a faith in the power of imaginative self-projection and a tendency towards abstraction and universalization, characterize and pervade the analytic imaginary.

Both aspects are clearly evident in Thomson's treatment of abortion by way of the violinist analogy. Thomson presents abortion as something which could happen to anyone, so anyone, through imaginative self-projection, could come to a universally valid judgment on the issue. Both aspects are also very obvious in the personal identity debate. Readers are asked to judge how they would regard themselves, if, for example, they were able to spontaneously reproduce themselves. The universal character of personal identity is also sought through abstraction from the particular aspects of identity. In the context of contractarian myths in analytic political philosophy, the notion of the impartial reasoner embodied by the original position and the veil of ignorance relies on the idea that one reasoner can envision the principles of a just society. The image of the view from nowhere itself conveys a thesis of universalism: that there can be one and only one way of understanding all perspectives. Finally, in analytic aesthetics, Walton explicitly articulates and relies upon the claim that one can imagine oneself in another's place. The preoccupation with universalization is also evident in the claim that there is one characteristic form of response to art. The idea that the imagination is capable of thinking itself into the shoes of others means that a view can be justified without really listening to the concerns of others, while at the same time claiming to incorporate them. So, what is presented as a neutral and objective approach to philosophical issues is often a projection of a very particular kind of experience.

Future Directions

In relation to all of these stock images of analytic philosophy, we saw how alternative approaches fared. Those who tried to use the images to their own advantage tended to underestimate the power of the images and failed to break out of their grip. This problem is evident in the case of Okin's use of the myth of the original position, and in Harding's and Haraway's use of visual metaphors. The other possibility, using different images and approaches, often leads to the marginalization of a philosopher's work within the community of analytic philosophers or the exclusion from that community. The work is seen as not contributing to the debate, as changing the topic, or as not doing philosophy at all. That is why this close reading of these central images of analytic philosophy was necessary, to understand the pervasive features of the analytic imaginary and to explore fresh means of philosophizing. While much work is under way, the problems identified here open up fruitful ways of proceeding and ways to ask new questions. I have shown how we need to be sensitive to the implications of the images we use, and how we may be able to include and advance reconceptions by expanding debates and rethinking our use of images. Reflecting on the role of images can also begin debate between disparate approaches to philosophy.

Images are necessary to philosophy, and we should not try to eliminate them. However, if they are problematic and they reveal serious tensions and untenable assumptions, we need to think carefully about them and the concepts related to them. It is not just the work images do for philosophers, but also the work that they exclude, which is important. We may need to experiment with different images, or to rethink the entire line of a thought or project. In any case, sensitivity to the nature of imagery in philosophy and the characteristics of particular imaginaries, like the analytic imaginary, can lead us to a more complex understanding of the assumptions, the projects, and the blind spots in all philosophical activity. Such sensitivity can also teach us to philosophize in a way that connects us with others, help make philosophy more open to the world, and hence ultimately more philosophical.

Bibliography

Ackerman, Bruce. "Political Liberalisms." *Journal of Philosophy* 91, no. 7 (1994): 364–386.

Ammerman, Robert R., ed. *Classics of Analytic Philosophy*. Indianapolis: Hackett, 1990.

Antony, Louise, and Charlotte Witt, eds. *A Mind of One's Own: Feminist Essays on Reason and Objectivity*. Boulder: Westview Press, 1993.

Aristotle. *The Complete Works of Aristotle*. Edited by Jonathan Barnes. 2 vols. Princeton: Princeton University Press, 1984.

Audi, Robert, ed. *The Cambridge Dictionary of Philosophy*. Cambridge: Cambridge University Press, 1995.

Bacon, Francis. *The Philosophical Works of Francis Bacon*. Edited by John Robertson. London: Routledge, 1905.

Ball, Terence. *Reappraising Political Theory: Revisionist Studies in the History of Political Thought*. Oxford: Clarendon Press, 1995.

Beauvoir, Simone de. *The Second Sex*. Translated by H. M. Parshley. Harmondsworth: Penguin, 1983.

Berghoffen, Debra B. *The Philosophy of Simone de Beauvoir: Gendered Phenomenologies, Erotic Generosities*. Albany: State University of New York Press, 1997.

Black, Max. *Models and Metaphors*. Ithaca: Cornell University Press, 1962.

——. *Perplexities*. Ithaca: Cornell University Press, 1990.

Bordo, Susan. "Feminism, Postmodernism, and Gender-Scepticism." In *Feminism/Postmodernism*, edited by Linda J. Nicholson, pp. 133–156. New York: Routledge, 1990.

Brennan, Teresa, and Martin Jay, eds. *Vision in Context: Historical and Contemporary Perspectives on Sight*. London: Routledge, 1996.

Brody, Baruch. "Thomson on Abortion." *Philosophy and Public Affairs* 1, no. 3 (1972): 335–340.

Brown, Alan. *Modern Political Philosophy*. London: Penguin, 1986.

Budd, Malcolm. Review of *Mimesis as Make-Believe* by Kendall Walton. *Mind* 101, no. 401 (1992): 195–198.

Calvino, Italo. *If on a Winter's Night a Traveler*. London: Minerva, 1992.

183

Chalmers, David. *The Conscious Mind.* Cambridge: MIT Press, 1997.

Charlton, William. Review of *Mimesis as Make-Believe,* by Kendall Walton. *British Journal of Aesthetics* 31, no. 4 (1991): 369–370.

Chodorow, Nancy. *The Reproduction of Mothering.* Berkeley: University of California Press, 1978.

Code, Lorraine. *What Can She Know? Feminist Theory and the Construction of Knowledge.* Ithaca: Cornell University Press, 1991.

Collingwood, R. G. *Principles of Art.* Oxford: Oxford University Press, 1938.

Corbett, Edward P. J. *Classical Rhetoric for the Modern Student.* Oxford: Oxford University Press, 1971.

Cornell, Drucilla. *The Imaginary Domain: Abortion, Pornography, and Sexual Harassment.* New York: Routledge, 1995.

Currie, Gregory. *The Nature of Fiction.* Cambridge: Cambridge University Press, 1990.

Dancy, Jonathan. "Contemplating One's Nagel." *Philosophical Books* 29, no. 1 (1988): 1–16.

Daniels, Norman, ed. *Reading Rawls: Critical Studies of "A Theory of Justice."* Oxford: Basil Blackwell, 1975.

David, Anthony. "Le Dœuff and Irigaray on Descartes." *Philosophy Today* 41 (1997): 367–382.

Davidson, Donald. "What Metaphors Mean." *Critical Inquiry* 5, no. 1 (1978): 31–47.

——. "Knowing One's Own Mind." *Proceedings and Addresses of the American Philosophy Association* 60, no. 3(1987): 441–458.

Davis, Nancy. "Abortion and Self-Defense." *Philosophy and Public Affairs* 13, no. 3 (1984): 173–207.

Dennett, Daniel. *Consciousness Explained.* Boston: Little, Brown and Company, 1991.

Derrida, Jacques. "White Mythology: Metaphor in the Text of Philosophy." In *Margins of Philosophy,* translated by Alan Bass, 207–271. Chicago: University of Chicago Press, 1982.

Descartes, René. *The Philosophical Writings of Descartes.* Translated by John Cottingham, Robert Stoothoff, and Dugald Murdoch. 3 vols. Cambridge: Cambridge University Press, 1984.

Feinberg, Joel. "The Nature and Value of Rights." In *Ethical Theory: Classical and Contemporary Readings,* edited by Louis P. Pojman, pp. 602–611. Belmont: Wadsworth, 1989.

Finn, Geraldine. "On the Oppression of Women in Philosophy—Or, Whatever Happened to Objectivity?" In *Feminism in Canada: From Pressure to Politics,* pp. 145–173. Montreal: Black Rose Books, 1982.

Finnis, John. "The Rights and Wrongs of Abortion: A Reply to Judith Thomson." *Philosophy and Public Affairs* 2, no. 2 (1973): 117–145.

Fiumara, Gemma Corradi. *The Other Side of Language: A Philosophy of Listening.* London: Routledge, 1990.

Fraser, Nancy. "Debate: Recognition or Redistribution? A Critical Reading of Iris Marion Young's *Justice and the Politics of Difference.*" *Journal of Political Philosophy* 3, no. 2 (1995): 166–180.

Fricker, Miranda. "Reason and Emotion." *Radical Philosophy* 57 (Spring 1991): 14–19.

Garry, Ann. "A Minimally Decent Philosophical Method? Analytic Philosophy and Feminism." *Hypatia* 10, no. 3 (1995): 7–30.

Gaut, Berys. Review of *Mimesis as Make-Believe*, by Kendall Walton. *Journal of Value Inquiry* 26, no. 2 (1992): 297–300.

Gilligan, Carol. *In a Different Voice*. Cambridge: Harvard University Press, 1982.

Glover, Jonathan. *I: The Philosophy and Psychology of Personal Identity*. London: Allen Lane, 1988.

Goldman, Alan. "Representation and Make-Believe." *Inquiry* 36, no. 3 (1993): 335–350.

Goodman, Nelson. *Languages of Art: An Approach to a Theory of Symbols*. Indianapolis: Hackett, 1976.

Griffiths, Morwenna, and Margaret Whitford, eds. *Feminist Perspectives in Philosophy*. Bloomington: Indiana University Press, 1988.

Grimshaw, Jean. *Feminist Philosophers*. Brighton: Wheatsheaf Books, 1986.

Grosz, Elizabeth. *Sexual Subversions: Three French Feminists*. Sydney: Allen and Unwin, 1989.

——. *Volatile Bodies: Toward a Corporeal Feminism*. Sydney: Allen and Unwin, 1994.

Group μ. *A General Rhetoric*. Translated by Paul B. Burrell and Edgar M. Slotkin. Baltimore: Johns Hopkins University Press, 1981.

Haraway, Donna. "Situated Knowledges: The Science Question in Feminism and the Privilege of Partial Perspective." *Feminist Studies* 14, no. 3 (1988): 575–599.

Harding, Sandra. *Whose Science? Whose Knowledge? Thinking from Women's Lives*. Ithaca: Cornell University Press, 1991.

——. "Rethinking Standpoint Epistemology: What Is 'Strong Objectivity'?" In *Feminist Epistemologies*, edited by Linda Alcoff and Elizabeth Potter, pp. 49–82. New York: Routledge, 1993.

Hare, R. M. "Abortion and the Golden Rule." *Philosophy and Public Affairs* 4, no. 3 (1975): 201–222.

Hartsock, Nancy. "The Feminist Standpoint: Developing the Ground for a Specifically Feminist Historical Materialism." In *Feminism and Methodology: Social Science Issues*, edited by Sandra Harding, pp. 157–180. Bloomington: Indiana University Press, 1987.

Hegel, G. W. F. *The Philosophy of Right*. Translated by T. M. Knox. Oxford: Oxford University Press, 1952.

Henle, Paul. "Metaphor." In *Language, Thought, and Culture*, edited by Paul Henle, pp. 173–195. Ann Arbor: University of Michigan Press, 1958.

Hobbes, Thomas. *Leviathan*. London: Aldine Press, 1953.

——. *The Metaphysical System of Hobbes*. Edited by Mary Whiton Calkins. Chicago: Open Court, 1910.

Honderich, Ted, ed. *The Oxford Companion to Philosophy*. Oxford: Oxford University Press, 1995.

Hopkins, Rob. Review of *Mimesis as Make-Believe*, by Kendall Walton. *Philosophical Books* 33, no. 2 (1992): 126–128.

Hume, David. *A Treatise of Human Nature*. Edited by L. A. Selby-Bigge. Oxford: Clarendon, 1978.

Hursthouse, Rosalind. "Virtue Theory and Abortion." *Philosophy and Public Affairs* 20, no. 3 (1991): 223–246.

Irigaray, Luce. *This Sex Which Is Not One*. Translated by Catherine Porter with Carolyn Burke. Ithaca : Cornell University Press, 1985.

Jackson, Frank. "Epiphenomenal Qualia." *Philosophical Quarterly* 32 (1982): 127–136.

Jaggar, Alison. "Love and Knowledge: Emotion in Feminist Epistemology." *Inquiry* 32 (1989): 151–176.

James, Susan. "Feminism in Philosophy of Mind: The Question of Personal Identity." In *The Cambridge Companion to Feminism in Philosophy*, edited by Miranda Fricker and Jennifer Hornsby, pp. 29–48. Cambridge: Cambridge University Press, 2000.

Jay, Martin. *Downcast Eyes: The Denigration of Vision in Twentieth Century French Thought.* Berkeley: University of California Press, 1993.

Johnson, Mark, ed. *Philosophical Perspectives on Metaphor.* Minneapolis: University of Minnesota Press, 1981.

Johnston, Mark. "Human Beings." *Journal of Philosophy* 84, no. 2 (1987): 59–83.

Kamm, F. M. *Creation and Abortion: A Study in Moral and Legal Philosophy.* Oxford: Oxford University Press, 1992.

Kant, Immanuel. *The Critique of Pure Reason.* Translated by Norman Kemp Smith. London: Macmillan, 1958.

——. *Perpetual Peace and Other Essays.* Translated by Ted Humphrey. Indianapolis: Hackett, 1983.

Keller, Evelyn Fox. *Reflections on Gender and Science.* New Haven: Yale University Press, 1991.

Keller, Evelyn Fox, and Christine R. Grontkowski. "The Mind's Eye." In *Discovering Reality: Feminist Perspectives on Epistemology, Metaphysics, Methodology, and Philosophy of Science*, edited by Sandra Harding and Merrill B. Hintikka, pp. 207–224. Dordrecht: D. Reidel, 1983.

Kelly, George Armstrong. "Veils: The Poetics of John Rawls." *Journal of the History of Ideas* 57, no. 2 (1996): 343–364.

Kolak, Daniel. "The Metaphysics and Metapsychology of Personal Identity: Why Thought Experiments Matter in Deciding Who We Are." *American Philosophical Quarterly* 30, no. 1 (1993): 39–50.

Kymlicka, Will. *Liberalism, Community, and Culture.* Oxford: Clarendon Press, 1991.

——. "The Social Contract Tradition." In *A Companion to Ethics*, edited by Peter Singer, pp. 186–196. Oxford: Blackwell, 1991.

Lacan, Jacques. *Écrits: A Selection.* Translated by Alan Sheridan. New York: Norton, 1977.

La Caze, Marguerite. "Simone de Beauvoir and Female Bodies." *Australian Feminist Studies*, no. 20 (1994): 91–106.

Lacey, A. R., ed. *A Dictionary of Philosophy*, 3d ed. London: Routledge, 1996.

Lakoff, George, and Mark Johnson. *Metaphors We Live By.* Chicago: University of Chicago Press, 1980.

——. *Philosophy in the Flesh: The Embodied Mind and Its Challenge to Western Thought.* New York: Basic Books, 1999.

Lamarque, Peter. "How Can We Fear and Pity Fictions?" *British Journal of Aesthetics* 21 (1981): 291–304.

Lauretis, Teresa de. "Calvino and the Amazons: Reading the (Post) Modern Text." In *Technologies of Gender: Essays on Theory, Film, and Fiction*, pp. 70–83. Bloomington: Indiana University Press, 1987.

Le Dœuff, Michèle. "Simone de Beauvoir and Existentialism." *Feminist Studies* 6, no. 20 (1980): 277–289.

——. "Utopias: Scholarly." *Social Research* 49, no. 2 (1984): 441–466.

——. "Women and Philosophy." In *French Feminist Thought: A Reader*, edited by Toril Moi, pp. 181–209. Cambridge: Blackwell, 1987.

——. "Ants and Women, or Philosophy without Borders." In *Contemporary French Thought*, edited by A. Phillips Griffiths, pp. 41–54. New York: Cambridge University Press, 1987.

——. *The Philosophical Imaginary*, translated by Colin Gordon. London: Athlone Press, 1989.

———. *Hipparchia's Choice: An Essay Concerning Women, Philosophy, etc.* Translated by Trista Selous. Oxford: Blackwell, 1989.

———. "Women, Reason, etc." *differences: A Journal of Feminist Cultural Studies* 2.3 (1990): 1–13.

———. "Modern Life." *New Left Review,* no. 199 (1993): 127–139.

———. "On Some Philosophical Pacts." *Journal of the Institute of Romance Studies* 2 (1993): 395–40

Lévinas, Emmanuel. *The Lévinas Reader.* Edited by Seán Hand. Oxford: Blackwell, 1989.

Lloyd, Genevieve. *Being in Time: Selves and Narrators in Philosophy and Literature.* London: Routledge, 1993.

———. "Maleness, Metaphor and the 'Crisis' of Reason." In *A Mind of One's Own: Feminist Essays on Reason and Objectivity,* edited by Louise M. Antony and Charlotte Witt, pp. 69–83. Boulder: Westview Press, 1993.

———. *The Man of Reason: "Male" and "Female" in Western Philosophy.* London: Methuen, 1984.

Locke, John. *An Essay Concerning Human Understanding.* Oxford: Oxford University Press, 1979.

———. *Two Treatises of Government.* New York: Hafner Publishing Company, 1956.

Lyas, Colin. Review of *Mimesis as Make-Believe* by Kendall Walton. *Philosophy* 66, no. 258 (1991): 527–529.

Mackenzie, Catriona. "Abortion and Embodiment." *Australasian Journal of Philosophy* 70, no. 2 (1992): 136–155.

Malcolm, Norman. "Subjectivity." *Philosophy* 63, no. 244 (1988): 147–160.

Mason, Jeff. *Philosophical Rhetoric: The Function of Indirection in Philosophical Writing.* London: Routledge, 1989.

Mautner, Thomas. *A Dictionary of Philosophy.* Oxford: Blackwell, 1996.
6, no. 382 (1987): 263–272.

Merchant, Carolyn. *The Death of Nature: Women, Ecology, and the Scientific Revolution.* San Francisco: Harper, 1980.

Merleau-Ponty, Maurice. *Phenomenology of Perception.* Translated by Colin Smith. London: Routledge and Kegan Paul, 1962.

Meyers, Diana Tietjens. *Subjection and Subjectivity: Psychoanalytic Feminism and Moral Philosophy.* New York: Routledge, 1994.

Moi, Toril. *Simone de Beauvoir: The Making of an Intellectual Woman.* Oxford, Blackwell, 1994.

Morgan, Vance G. *Foundations of Cartesian Ethics.* Atlantic Highlands: Humanities Press, 1994.

Morris, Meaghan. *The Pirate's Fiancée.* London: Verso, 1988.

Mortley, Raoul. *French Philosophers in Conversation: Lévinas, Schneider, Serres, Irigaray, Le Dœuff, Derrida.* London: Routledge, 1991.

Moulton, Janice. "A Paradigm of Philosophy: The Adversary Method." In *Discovering Reality: Feminist Perspectives on Epistemology, Metaphysics, Methodology, and Philosophy of Science,* edited by Sandra Harding and Merrill B. Hintikka, pp. 149–164. Dordrecht: D. Reidel, 1983.

Nagel, Thomas. "What Is It Like to Be a Bat?." *Philosophical Review* 73, no. 1 (1974): 435–450.

———. *The View from Nowhere.* Oxford: Oxford University Press, 1986.

———. *Equality and Partiality*. Oxford: Oxford University Press, 1991.

Narayan, Uma. "The Project of Feminist Epistemology: Perspectives from a Nonwestern Feminist." In *Gender/Body/Knowledge: Feminist Reconstructions of Being and Knowing*, edited by Alison Jaggar and Susan Bordo, pp. 256–269. New Brunswick: Rutgers University Press, 1989.

Neurath, Otto. "Protocol Sentences." In *Logical Positivism*, edited by A. J. Ayer, pp. 199–208. New York: Macmillan, 1959.

Nietzsche, Friedrich. *Early Greek Philosophy and Other Essays*, translated by Maximilian A. Mügge. New York: Russell and Russell, 1964.

Nochlin, Linda. *The Politics of Vision: Essays on Nineteenth-Century Art and Society*. New York: Harper and Row, 1989.

Novitz, David. Critical discussion of *Mimesis as Make-Believe* by Kendall Walton. *Philosophy and Literature* 15, no. 1 (1991): 118–128.

Nozick, Robert. *Anarchy, State, and Utopia*. Oxford: Blackwell, 1974.

Nye, Andrea. *Feminist Theory and the Philosophies of Man*. London: Croon Helm, 1988.

Okeley, Judith. *Simone de Beauvoir: A Re-reading*. London: Virago, 1986.

Okin, Susan Moller. *Justice, Gender, and the Family*. New York: Basic Books, 1989.

———. "John Rawls: Justice as Fairness—For Whom?" In *Feminist Interpretations and Political Theory*, edited by Mary Lyndon Shanley and Carole Pateman, pp. 181–198. Cambridge: Polity Press, 1991.

Parfit, Derek. *Reasons and Persons*. Oxford: Oxford University Press, 1986.

Pateman, Carole. *The Sexual Contract*. Stanford: Stanford University Press, 1988.

Perelman, Chaim. *The Realm of Rhetoric*. Translated by William Kluback. Notre Dame: University of Notre Dame Press, 1982.

Pettersson, Anders. "On Walton's and Currie's Analyses of Literary Fiction." *Philosophy and Literature* 17, no. 1 (1993): 84–97.

Plato. *The Collected Dialogues*. Edited by Edith Hamilton and Huntington Cairns. Princeton: Bollingen, 1999.

Poole, Ross. "On Being a Person." *Australasian Journal of Philosophy* 74, no. 1 (1996): 38–56.

Porter, Elizabeth J. *Women and Moral Identity*. Sydney: Allen and Unwin, 1991.

Pugmire, David. "Bat or Batman?" *Philosophy* 64, no. 248 (1989): 207–217.

Putnam, Hilary. *Mind, Language, and Reality: Philosophical Papers*. 2 vols. Cambridge: Cambridge University Press, 1975.

———. *Representation and Reality*. Cambridge: MIT Press, 1988.

Quine, W. V. O. *From a Logical Point of View: Logico-Philosophical Essays*. Cambridge: Harvard University Press, 1953.

———. Review of *Identity and Individuation* edited by Milton K. Munitz. *Journal of Philosophy* 69, no. 16 (1972): 488–497.

Quine, W. V. O., and J. S. Ullian. *The Web of Belief*. New York: Random House, 1970.

Quinn, Warren. "Abortion: Identity and Loss." *Philosophy and Public Affairs* 13, no. 1 (1984): 24–54.

Radford, Colin. "How Can We Be Moved by the Fate of Anna Karenina?" *Proceedings of the Aristotelian Society*, 49 (supp.) 1975: 67–80.

Rawls, John. *A Theory of Justice*. Cambridge: Harvard University Press, 1971.

———. "The Basic Structure as Subject." *The American Philosophical Quarterly* 14, no. 2 (1977): 159–165.

———. *Political Liberalism*. New York: Columbia University Press, 1993.

Reese, William L. *Dictionary of Philosophy and Religion: Eastern and Western Thought.* Atlantic Highlands: Humanities Press, 1980.

Regan, Tom, ed. *Matters of Life and Death.* New York: Random House, 1980.

Richards, I. A. *Philosophy and Rhetoric.* Oxford: Oxford University Press, 1936.

Richards, Janet Radcliffe. *The Sceptical Feminist.* Harmondsworth: Penguin, 1982.

Ricoeur, Paul. *Oneself as Another.* Translated by Kathleen Blamey. Chicago: University of Chicago Press, 1992.

——. *The Rule of Metaphor: Multidisciplinary Studies of the Creation of Meaning in Language.* Translated by Robert Czerny. Toronto: University of Toronto Press, 1977.

Robinson, Gillian, and John Rundell, eds. *Rethinking Imagination: Culture and Creativity.* London: Routledge, 1994.

Rorty, Amélie Oksenberg, ed. *The Identities of Persons.* Berkeley: University of California Press, 1976.

Ross, Steven L. "Abortion and the Death of the Fetus." *Philosophy and Public Affairs* 11, no. 3 (1982): 232–245.

Sartre, Jean-Paul. *Being and Nothingness.* Translated by Hazel E. Barnes. New York: Pocket Books, 1956.

Searle, John. *Minds, Brains, and Science.* London: Penguin, 1984.

Seigfried, Charlene Haddock. "Gender-Specific Values." *Philosophical Forum,* no. 15 (1984): 425–442.

Sherwin, Susan. "Philosophical Methodology and Feminist Methodology: Are They Compatible?" In *Feminist Perspectives: Philosophical Essays on Method and Morals,* edited by Lorraine Code et al., pp. 13–28. Toronto: University of Toronto Press, 1988.

——. "Abortion through a Feminist Ethics Lens." In *Living with Contradictions: Controversies in Feminist Social Ethics,* edited by Alison M. Jaggar, pp. 314–324. Boulder: Westview Press, 1994.

Shoemaker, Sydney. *Self-Knowledge and Self-Identity.* Ithaca: Cornell University Press, 1963.

Simons, Margaret A. *Beauvoir and "The Second Sex": Feminism, Race, and the Origins of Existentialism.* Lanham: Rowman and Littlefield, 1999.

Smith, Janet Farrell. "Rights-Conflict, Pregnancy, and Abortion." In *Beyond Domination: New Perspectives on Women and Philosophy,* edited by Carole C. Gould, pp. 265–273. Totowa: Rowman and Allanheld, 1983.

Smith, P. Christopher. *The Hermeneutics of Original Argument: Demonstration, Dialectic, Rhetoric.* Evanston: Northwestern University Press, 1998.

Solomon, Robert. *The Passions: Emotions and the Meaning of Life.* Indianapolis: Hackett, 1993.

Sorapure, Madeleine. "Being in the Midst: Italo Calvino's *If on a Winter's Night a Traveler.*" *Modern Fiction Studies* 31, no. 4 (1985): 702–709.

Sorell, Tom. *Scientism: Philosophy and the Infatuation with Science.* London: Routledge, 1991.

Tallis, Raymond. "Tye on 'The Subjective Qualities of Experience': A Critique." *Philosophical Investigations* 12, no. 3 (1989): 217–222.

Tapper, Marion. "Can a Feminist Be a Liberal?" *Australasian Journal of Philosophy* 64 (supp.) 1986: 37–47.

Thomson, Judith Jarvis. "A Defense of Abortion." *Philosophy and Public Affairs* 1, no. 1 (1971): 47–66.

Tirrell, Lynne. "Reductive and Nonreductive Simile Theories of Metaphor." *Journal of Philosophy* 88, no. 7 (1991): 337–358.

Tooley, Michael. *Abortion and Infanticide*. Oxford: Clarendon Press, 1983.

Toulmin, Stephen. *The Uses of Argument*. Cambridge: Cambridge University Press, 1958.

Vintges, Karen. *Philosophy as Passion: The Thinking of Simone de Beauvoir*. Bloomington: Indiana University Press, 1996.

Vogler, Candice. "Philosophical Feminism, Feminist Philosophy." *Philosophical Topics* 23, no. 2 (1995): 295–319.

Walton, Kendall. *Mimesis as Make-Believe: On the Foundations of the Representational Arts*. Cambridge: Harvard University Press, 1990.

Warner, Martin. "Rhetoric and Philosophy." *Philosophy and Literature* 19 (1995): 106–115.

Warren, Mary Anne. "On the Moral and Legal Status of Abortion." *The Monist* 57 (1973): 43–61.

Watts, Melissa. "Reinscribing a Dead Author in *If on a Winter's Night a Traveler*." *Modern Fiction Studies* 37, no. 4 (1991): 705–716.

Whitbeck, Caroline. "Women as People: Pregnancy and Personhood." In *Abortion and the Status of the Fetus*, edited by William B. Bondeson et al., pp. 247–272. Dordrecht: D. Reidel, 1983.

White, Roger. *The Structure of Metaphor: The Way the Language of Metaphor Works (Philosophical Theory)*. Oxford: Blackwell, 1996.

Wider, Kathleen. "Overtones of Solipsism in Thomas Nagel's 'What Is It Like to Be a Bat?' and *The View from Nowhere*." *Philosophy and Phenomenological Research* 50, no. 3 (1990): 481–499.

——. "The Desire to Be God: Subjective and Objective in Nagel's *The View from Nowhere* and Sartre's *Being and Nothingness*." *Journal of Philosophical Research* 17 (1992): 443–463.

Wilkes, Kathleen V. *Real People: Personal Identity without Thought Experiments*. Oxford: Clarendon Press, 1988.

Williams, Bernard. *Problems of the Self: Philosophical Papers, 1956–72*. Cambridge: Cambridge University Press, 1973.

Williams, Bernard, and J. J. C. Smart. *Utilitarianism: For and Against*. Cambridge: Cambridge University Press, 1973.

Wittgenstein, Ludwig. *Philosophical Investigations*. Translated by G. E. M. Anscombe. Oxford: Blackwell, 1983.

Wollheim, Richard. *On Art and the Mind*. Cambridge: Harvard University Press, 1974.

——. "A Note on *Mimesis as Make-Believe*." *Philosophy and Phenomenological Research* 51, no. 2 (1991): 401–406.

Young, Iris Marion. *Justice and the Politics of Difference*. Princeton: Princeton University Press, 1990.

——. "Pregnant Embodiment: Subjectivity and Alienation." In *Throwing Like a Girl and Other Essays in Feminist Philosophy and Social Theory*, pp. 160–174. Bloomington: Indiana University Press, 1990.

Index